Deborah Prothrow-Stith

Howard R. Spivak

Murder Is No Accident

Understanding and Preventing Youth Violence in America

JOSSEY-BASS
A Wiley Imprint
www.josseybass.com

Published by Jossey-Bass
A Wiley Imprint
989 Market Street, San Francisco, CA 94103-1741   www.josseybass.com

Jossey-Bass books and products are available through most bookstores. To contact Jossey-Bass
directly call our Customer Care Department within the U.S. at 800-956-7739, outside the
U.S. at 317-572-3986, or fax 317-572-4002.

Jossey-Bass also publishes its books in a variety of electronic formats. Some content that
appears in print may not be available in electronic books.

"Star Wrestler Subpoenaed by Attorney for Boy Charged in Playmate's Death" reprinted by
permission of the Associated Press.

Library of Congress Cataloging-in-Publication Data

Prothrow-Stith, Deborah, date.
  Murder is no accident : understanding and preventing youth violence in America / Deborah
Prothrow-Stith, Howard R. Spivak.— 1st ed.
    p. cm.
Includes bibliographical references and index.
  ISBN 0-7879-6980-X (alk. paper)
  1. Violence in adolescence—United States. 2. Violence in
children—United States. 3. Violence in adolescence—United
States—Prevention. 4. Violence in children—United States—Prevention.
5. Violence in adolescence—Massachusetts—Boston—Prevention. 6.
Violence in children—Massachusetts—Boston—Prevention. 7. Youth and
violence—United States. I. Spivak, Howard R., date. II. Title.
  HQ799.2.V56P76 2003
  303.6'083'0973—dc21

                                                        2003010509

Printed in the United States of America
FIRST EDITION
HB Printing   10 9 8 7 6 5 4 3 2 1

Contents

For the multitudes committed to the violence prevention movement who give us inspiration, and

To my family with love
—DP-S

Janet, Zoë, and Lee with love
—HRS

Introduction

The city of Boston has been showcased by many politicians, criminal justice professionals, the media, and others, as the premier example of success in youth violence prevention. Compared to much of the rest of the country, Boston has experienced a dramatic reduction in juvenile murder rates. The city went for almost three years during the mid- to late 1990s without a juvenile homicide, whereas in previous years it experienced almost one juvenile murder per month. Since then the rates have remained quite low.

We take credit for this, as do many others. President Clinton claimed credit, as did Attorney General Janet Reno. Boston police commissioner William Bratton did too. So did the U.S. federal prosecutor located in Boston, the Boston Police Department, a number of academicians and criminologists, religious leaders, the Ten Point Coalition of Boston, the last three mayors of Boston, and a number of superintendents of the Boston Public Schools. And this is just the short list. In fact all of these individuals and groups, as well as many, many others, do deserve the credit.

Our Reasons for Writing This Book

We go into detail later about our personal stories and our motivations for writing this book, but in brief, both of us are physicians and public health practitioners who came to the issue of youth violence through personal and professional experiences. We were struck and appalled by the toll that violence was taking on the children and youth of this nation and on the nation as a whole. We had learned in our professional training that many health problems were preventable and yet in all of our training had heard nothing about violence, its consequences, or approaches to address it. Many of our colleagues challenged our efforts to focus on this issue in our careers and tried to discourage us from doing so. But violence was one of the leading causes of death and disability for American youth, and we could not ignore it.

Our work together started in Boston. We were among the first in the health field to apply public health perspectives and strategies to the issue of violence at the community level. Consequently we had little background information and few to consult and to guide us. We learned by trial and error and experienced a range of successes and failures. We at times made false starts and at times took huge jumps forward. We wrote this book to share our experience in the hope that it would provide guidance or even a road map for others. We also hope that our story and the stories of others that we share in this book contribute to the advancement of the violence prevention movement in this country and around the world. It helps to know that you are not going into uncharted territory. Most of all, it helps to know that you are not alone in taking on such a huge and complex problem.

We strongly believe that violence is preventable. There is much evidence to support that belief. We share our experiences to help others understand this and use this information to contribute to the prevention effort.

The Boston Model

So, what did happen in Boston? Can you simply follow the "Boston Model" to reduce violence in your community? Many funders, public health officials, government representatives, and legal and criminal justice professionals believe that you can. We want to tell you that there is no single model to replicate. What happened in Boston is a broad community process that led to changes in attitudes and beliefs and to the development of a wide spectrum of programs throughout the city. We believe it is this process that is responsible for Boston's success. You can use this process to change your community. In fact we're sure that you already have some of the programs in place, but you may need the connections, synergy, the professional-community partnerships and information dissemination to pull it all together—the *process*.

The secret behind the Boston story is very simple: straightforward strategies and hard work. In 1982 we started the Boston Violence Prevention Program. The program provided a wealth of information—research, stories, cases, examples—to as many people as possible, who then used that information to organize their communities and create the programs that would work in their neighborhoods. Program staff provided the data on violence in Boston's neighborhoods, the city, and the nation (especially compared to other countries) in such a way that others could use them. This was information that challenged a fundamental assumption in U.S. society—in its justice system, school system, health care system. That assumption is that violence is inevitable.

If you assume that violence is inevitable then rather than try to prevent it you are left only with the option of trying to respond aggressively when it occurs, as many U.S. institutions do. The aggressive response is usually some form of severe punishment. Actual prevention isn't a priority unless you believe violence is preventable. Our information shows that violence is (1) not inevitable and (2) eminently preventable.

Challenging the Status Quo

In this book we provide you with the same information so that you too can go out and build the connections and create the process that will work in your community. We stress connections and process because a single program will not turn violence around. A few programs won't turn violence around. You need a critical mass of people and programs. In Boston that critical mass consisted of several thousand individuals and scores of community-based programs that developed and evolved over a ten-year period. How do you create this critical mass? You need to provide information to as many people as possible in as many venues as possible and galvanize those people so that they go out and pass the information on and create solutions. This is what happened in Boston. The Boston Violence Prevention Program provided a simple, but profound message, "violence is preventable," and the evidence to support the message.

Although we used Deborah's school-based violence prevention curriculum (as a starting point) to create the Boston Violence Prevention Program and to illustrate possible responses, we did not expect people to exactly replicate the curriculum in their programs and settings. We told them to use the curriculum as an example of what could be done and to adapt it, change it, add to it, and leave out parts as they saw fit. We asked them to not use it if they had another approach that excited them. We are not against replicating successful programs. But we are against a cookie-cutter, franchisee kind of approach that ignores the process and the need for a movement.

In this book we challenge the following common assumptions about the best way to approach a problem like violence:

- *Communities need prescriptive solutions to their problems.* On the contrary, we believe that communities need information from which they can create the approaches that fit into their community context. The talent and skills to solve problems exist in most communities once the information for understanding those problems becomes available. Often the prescriptive approach dampens the motivation and energy of a community effort.
- *Limited time and resources are best used replicating a single program or "best practices," rather than developing an understanding of the problem and devising strategies that reflect the community culture and available resources.* The program examples we offer here are not intended to tell you what to do but to give you a sense of what can and has been tried in other

places. Some of these may fit your community and contribute to the larger success. Some may need to be modified, and some may not be appropriate. Furthermore, you may come up with new ideas that others have not attempted and thus create an opportunity for others to learn from you.

- *Problems that evolve over a long period of time can be solved in three to five years (that is, within the typical time frame of a public sector or private foundation grant).* In fact almost all success stories in public health (reducing tobacco use, improving automobile safety, and preventing childhood poisoning, among others) have required decades and multiple strategies.
- *Complex problems can be solved with a single program.* For example, a single Boston program, the Cease Fire Program, has been touted and replicated as such an intervention. Some have even subtitled it the "Boston Strategy." Yet this program began after the start of the decline in juvenile murder rates in the city, and it is hard to believe that any program could show even modest effects that quickly. Complex problems require multifaceted approaches that grow out of an understanding of the various components of the problem.
- *Mean-spirited and punitive after-the-fact strategies, such as "zero tolerance" policies, are effective prevention approaches.* There is no evidence that this is the case. We know that it is often hurt children who hurt other children. Knee-jerk punishing of hurt and traumatized children may make things worse. Also, by definition, prevention means proactive not reactive efforts.

We believe that these and similar assumptions must be challenged, because if communities do the same things the same old way, they will get the same old nonresults. The status quo makes no sense and can no longer be tolerated when children's lives are at stake.

We want you to do more than merely start or replicate a program. We want you to join and contribute to a movement. To do this you need good information, opportunities for collaboration with others, and a larger vision for your work. We want you to do more than replicate a program others created. We want you to create the process that will achieve real sustained success.

Acknowledgments

We have many people to thank for inspiring the content of this book and for assistance with its completion.

First and foremost we want to acknowledge and thank the army of violence prevention workers across the nation who on a daily basis talk the talk and walk the walk of the violence prevention movement. They are all heroes and sheroes who are consistently both swimming upstream and maintaining and building the energy level necessary to keep communities moving forward. Coming from all walks of life, they are professionals, community activists, politicians, academicians, youth, parents, survivors, and representatives of communities of all types. They are the heart and soul of the movement, and this book is in good part their story. We want to give a special thanks to survivors of violence, because they struggle daily to turn pain into prevention power and have inspired us both.

We certainly want to thank our families, who have put up with both the time it has taken to get this book done and the mood swings brought on by the process. They have been there for us throughout the two decades we have been involved in violence prevention, as cheerleaders, advisers, friends, and nurturers. We have also had the support of staff in preparing the manuscript and in organizing our lives to get this writing completed—specifically our administrative assistants, CatAshleigh Jackson-Mead and Micki Diegel. Cat also made many changes to the manuscript to reflect our revisions and edits along the way and assisted with the initial editing. In this list also belong Kristen Wainwright, our agent and a friend and cheerleader supreme, and Alan Rinzler, our editor at Jossey-Bass, who recognized the importance of telling this story and understood the need to share it.

Finally, we are grateful to the many people and groups whose stories we tell in this book. Their contributions to the process of preventing violence have enriched our lives and taught us important lessons. We encourage you to read on and discover these contributions and lessons for yourself.

Deborah Prothrow-Stith
Howard R. Spivak
Boston, Massachusetts

Part One

The Problem

Chapter One

A Shocked America

The Epidemic Spreads

Tanya, almost seventeen, had attended more funerals than dances. Sixteen that she could recall. All were for children: family members, friends, classmates, and neighbors. She made this nearly unbelievable observation while being interviewed by a local television producer whom we were helping in the making of a documentary on youth violence. Tanya (not her real name) was in training to be a peer counselor for a youth outreach program. She had agreed to share her story as a way of letting the world know about life in the inner city. The year was 1989. The city was Boston.

Her first funeral was for her brother. She was eight at the time; he was fifteen. He was shot during an argument with another teenager. Tanya didn't even know what the argument was about. All she knew was that her brother was not coming back. The brother who had teased her, protected her, and taken care of her was gone. The funeral was a haze in her mind, with lots of people crying. The only thing she could remember about it was staying in the corner trying to figure out what was going on.

The second funeral, less than a year later, was for her cousin. He had been stabbed to death during an argument at a barbershop over who was next in line. She knew this cousin only from occasional family gatherings but was still very much affected by his death. Once again she found herself in the corner watching what was happening and wondering what it all meant.

Over the next three years she found herself at a funeral about once a year, first for the child of a neighbor, then for the friend of her older sister, then for a classmate of one of her brothers. After that things really got bad.

It was as though the world had gone mad. Tanya was attending funerals at a record pace. Kids in her neighborhood were literally disappearing. An eleven-year-old girl was shot in the cross fire between two rival youth gangs while sitting on a mailbox in front of her house talking to some friends. Two young boys were shot as they rode their bicycles down a street, possibly the motive was robbery. Another boy, a friend of Tanya's, was shot at a party, as a result of an argument earlier in the day. One of her classmates was stabbed in a fight over a pair of sneakers. Another of her cousins was killed in a fight trying to protect one of his friends. Her sister's boyfriend was shot by a rival for her sister's attention. And so it went, on and on. The number of deaths this child experienced during her childhood is startling to begin with, but the fact that her story is far from unique is the real tragedy.

At the time Tanya shared her personal experiences with us, we were going regularly into high schools in urban communities across America and finding many similar stories. When we asked a classroom filled with teenagers if they knew someone who had been murdered, every hand would go up. When we asked who had lost a family member by homicide, two-thirds or more of the hands would remain in the air. Murder and violent death were becoming a familiar part of the lives of these children. The first wave of the epidemic of youth violence in this country was in full swing in our urban communities. And it was not to stop there.

We Are All Vulnerable

For years in our speeches we have proclaimed to our audiences that despite the traditional "bad guy" stereotypes, everyone is vulnerable to violence. For far too long that message went unheeded. Glassy-eyed audiences easily shrugged off the information. That risk factors (family violence, child abuse, weapon carrying, "kick-butt" attitudes) cut across race and class and geography in America was not an easily accepted concept. As long as youth homicide was primarily a problem affecting urban black, Hispanic, and poor white communities, as long as there was a place (somewhere else) where the problem was "really" bad, then our audiences nodded politely. It was someone else's problem, not theirs. They might have been horrified, saddened, and moved to sympathy by the violence we discussed, but it was far enough away from them. They felt safe. Too safe.

Things have changed! The recent rash of youth violence in schools, and perhaps particularly the horror of Columbine, has shocked America to its senses (we hope). These tragic episodes of violence involving schools and children, teenagers, and young adults have upset America to the point of universal recognition of the problem. Even this partial list is startling:

2/19/97, Bethel, Alaska. A sixteen-year-old killed two and wounded two. Gun: 12 gauge Mossberg pump shotgun.

10/1/97, Pearl, Mississippi. A sixteen-year-old stabbed his mother to death and then opened fire at Pearl High School, killing two students (one was his ex-girlfriend) and wounding seven others. Gun: .30 caliber hunting rifle.

12/1/97, West Paducah, Kentucky. A fourteen-year-old son of a lawyer opened fire on a prayer group at Heath High School, killing three students and wounding five. Gun: .22 caliber Ruger pistol.

3/24/98, Jonesboro, Arkansas. A thirteen-year-old and an eleven-year-old killed a teacher and four students, and wounded ten others at Westside Middle School, after pulling a school fire alarm. Guns: Remington .30-06 caliber rifle, .44 caliber Ruger, Smith and Wesson .38 caliber revolver, Remington 742, Universal .30 caliber rifle.

4/24/98, Edenboro, Pennsylvania. A fourteen-year-old shot and killed one and wounded two at James Parker Middle School during a school dance. Gun: .25 caliber Raven pistol.

5/19/98, Fayetteville, Tennessee. An eighteen-year-old killed one at Lincoln County High School. Gun: .22 caliber Marlin bolt-action rifle.

5/21/98, Springfield, Oregon. A fifteen-year-old killed two Thurston High School students and shot twenty-two others, after killing his parents the day before. Gun: .22 caliber Ruger semiautomatic rifle, Glock 9mm pistol.

6/15/98, Richmond, Virginia. A fourteen-year-old wounded two at Armstrong High School. Gun: .32 caliber semiautomatic pistol.

4/20/99, Littleton, Colorado. A seventeen-year-old and an eighteen-year-old killed twelve students and a teacher and wounded twenty-three others before shooting themselves at Columbine High School. Guns: TEC-DC9 handgun, sawed-off double-barreled shotgun, pump-action shotgun, 9mm semiautomatic rifle.

5/20/99, Conyers, Georgia. A fifteen-year-old entered Heritage High School and opened fire, wounding six students then threatening to shoot himself. Gun: .22 caliber rifle, .357 magnum revolver.

11/19/99, Deming, New Mexico. A thirteen-year-old killed one at Deming Middle School. Gun: .22 caliber handgun.

12/6/99, Fort Gibson, Oklahoma. A thirteen-year-old wounded five at Fort Gibson Middle School. Gun: 9mm automatic handgun.

2/14/00, Littleton, Colorado, again. Two Columbine High School students murdered in a sandwich shop near the school. Gun: unknown.

2/29/00, Mt. Morris Township, Michigan. A six-year-old pulled a gun and shot and killed a six-year-old classmate, in the classroom, after uttering the words, "I don't like you." Gun: .32 caliber semiautomatic.

9/26/00, New Orleans, Louisiana. Two teenaged boys at a middle school shot and wounded each other during a fight. The gun had been slipped through the schoolyard fence to one of the two by a third thirteen-year-old student, who had been expelled. Gun: .38 caliber revolver.

1/10/01, Oxnard, California. A seventeen-year-old fired shots at Hueneme High School and took a student hostage before being killed by the Oxnard Police SWAT team. Gun: unknown.

3/5/01, Santee, California. A fifteen-year-old killed two and wounded thirteen after firing from a high school bathroom. Gun: unknown.

3/7/01, Williamsport, Pennsylvania. A fourteen-year-old, who said she was depressed and frequently teased, wounded another student with a gun in a high school cafeteria. Gun: unknown.

11/12/01, Caro, Michigan. A seventeen-year-old student wielding two guns took a teacher and a classmate hostage for three hours before freeing his captives and killing himself. Guns: .22 caliber rifle, 20 gauge shotgun.

The first few school killings did not make significant news stories. In fact, in the early 1990s, the stabbing death of a girl in a North Carolina suburban middle school received little attention. But by the time the shootings in Littleton, Colorado, occurred, the country was on edge and aware. Everyone, from the president to news reporters to the general public, showed increased concern, asked more thoughtful questions focused on prevention, and dropped the tough-guy, zero tolerance, "lock them up and throw away the key" rhetoric. The whole country began to experience what children like Tanya had lived through for over a decade. Tragedy after tragedy. Funeral after funeral. Always asking, "What can be done? How can we stop this?"

Our Mission

We wrote this book because we want to make something positive come of these tragedies and to give meaning to all of these children who have lost their lives. We have spent the majority of our professional careers, almost twenty years each, dealing with this nation's epidemic of youth violence. For the last five years, we have both traveled to an average of two cities a month to give speeches as part of our effort to help build a national movement to prevent violence. In these speeches we share with our audiences a prevention perspective—a public health perspective.

We wrote this book because America is at last more interested in prevention, mental health, and addressing the problems children face. Numbers of children are expected to "fit in" at school each day despite witnessing daily family violence or being regularly victimized at home or being afraid to come to school because they are bullied or embarrassed there.

These children face problems most people can't even imagine. Some will act out or demonstrate aggressive behavior resulting from their pain, fear, anger, and grief. As youth violence tragedies increasingly take place in middle-class America, victims and perpetrators are less and less likely to be portrayed as demonized superpredators of the big cities; they are "nice looking" kids, from "nice looking" families, living in "nice" communities. America has been forced to stop labeling children as demons and superpredators and start the introspection, reflection, and examination necessary for prevention.

The shift in labeling from *superpredators* to *troubled kids* signals an opportunity to further the cause of prevention. It also tells of a long affront to those who have lived and worked for years with America's youth violence epidemic, which initially traumatized urban communities. The research and money wasted on labeling and blaming the "bad seed," the bad parent, the subculture of violence, anything and everything but the larger society, is insulting. The insult is in the failure to meet the needs of children's mental health and social needs. The insult is that until middle-class kids were killed, people were satisfied with labeling and punishing and tougher laws.

We wrote this book to take advantage of the current opportunity to shift from mean-spirited solutions to proactive strategies that grow out of data, prevention, and basic understanding of child development. We are tired of the ineffective get-tough strategies. This is an opportunity to stop implementing simple solutions to a very complex problem. This is an opportunity to stop demonizing children and start looking at them as fragile, essential, and in need.

The Epidemic of Youth Violence

The recent school shootings in suburban, small-town, and middle-class America are not isolated incidents of violence involving seriously "mentally ill" children, just as the first few scattered incidents of homicide involving urban children in the early 1980s were not isolated episodes precipitated by "criminally ill" children. In 1988, when an eleven-year-old girl, Tiffany Moore, was shot and killed while sitting on a mailbox outside her apartment in Boston, it appeared to be an isolated horror. In retrospect her murder and a few other seemingly isolated child murders were the scattered beginnings of a child homicide epidemic in Boston that paralleled America's national epidemic of youth violence.

At its height, between 1989 and 1991, there was almost one homicide a month in Boston involving a child aged sixteen or younger and a gun. Boston learned the hard way, with the rest of urban America, that the early horrors were not isolated events reflecting individual pathology but were the outcomes of the impact of social and cultural forces on the most vulnerable children. More was to come, an unimaginable, tragic torrent of murders of children in urban America, now followed by horror in suburban and rural America.

In the last several years there has been considerable attention to and much celebration of the decline in youth violent crime in the United States. The national rates are down primarily because the youth violence rates in urban America are down. However, the arrest rates among girls for violent crime have actually risen, as have the rates for very young teens and for many small towns, rural communities, and suburbs. Despite the reduced national rates of youth violence over the last five years, America's epidemic of youth violence is not over.

The Three Waves of the Epidemic

Often, epidemics come in waves; they affect the most vulnerable populations first, spreading to less and less vulnerable groups in subsequent waves. The first wave of America's youth violence epidemic hit primarily poor communities in cities of more than five hundred thousand. It hit America's most vulnerable children. A second wave of this epidemic, affecting small towns, rural, and suburban communities, has emerged as school violence.

Some experts, who were quite vocal after the first few suburban school shootings, called the events isolated, anomalies, and not reflective of a larger problem. They urged all of us not to get too worried because there was no larger problem. Others suggested that this was just copycat behavior and, again, not indicative of any larger problem. Mistaking the upsurge in school homicide for a series of isolated events, and not recognizing the full potential of this second wave, only added to the tragedy.

The similarities between the urban and nonurban waves of the youth violence epidemic are striking. In both settings the same basic equation is at work:

TROUBLED KIDS + GLAMORIZATION OF EXPLOSIVE
    VIOLENT SOLUTIONS + GUNS + A PRECIPITATING
    EVENT (hearsay, boyfriend or girlfriend tangles, breakups,
    and putdowns) = DEADLY CONSEQUENCES.

Although it may seem odd to boil this down to mathematics, this is America's deadly equation.

Another important similarity between the first two waves of youth violence is the presence of clues and hints that foreshadow the violent tragedies. In some cases children actually told others that something bad or horrible was going to happen. In other instances students, family members, and even teachers or administrators knew a conflict was escalating. In the past, when suicidal individuals' offered clues about their intentions, these clues too were often overlooked, until mental health professionals learned the hard way not to ignore a person's comments about suicide. Professional protocols then changed to require the asking of questions designed to seek out such information and respond appropriately. No doubt, schools will now take threats of violence seriously. Yet protocols must be developed that recognize the seriousness of a threat and respond appropriately. At the present such protocols are not well developed and not enough training has been done.

The differences between the first and second waves of the youth violence epidemic are also striking. School-based killings with multiple victims, involving large and automatic weaponry, and ending in a suicide characterize the second wave. These characteristics are distinct from those of the urban epidemic, where out-of-school killings and single victims were the rule. Furthermore, in urban violence, a suicide following the episodes of violence was unusual. The precipitating events in many urban episodes were, and often still are, boyfriend-girlfriend, territorial, or he-said–she-said dramas. Nonurban violence seems to involve an "outcast" or group of outcasts, individuals who have withdrawn or have been shut out of mainstream student life, or it involves bullying.

There is the potential for a third wave in America's youth violence epidemic, a wave involving girls. Girls now make up 25 percent of the adolescents arrested for violent crime. In the past it was uncommon or even rare to have a girl arrested for violent crime. Although homicides are not a significant part of the picture with girls at this point, it doesn't require much speculation to anticipate a wave of homicide among girls.

This potential third wave follows a decade and a half of media portrayals of female superheroes beating people up and getting beaten up just as male superheroes do—the feminization of the superhero. The other risk factors for violence—poverty, witnessing violence, victimization, alcohol and other drug use, and availability of guns—have not changed differentially for boys and girls. So the rise in girls using violence to respond to situations forces an appreciation of the role of environment and culture. America's toxic environment for children has been well described by James Garbarino, in *Lost Boys*,[1] Sissela Bok, in *Mayhem: Violence as Public Entertainment*,[2] and many others. In the past, traumatized girls would resort to self-destructive behaviors, running away, drug abuse, prostitution, and so forth. The prevalence of violence in entertainment media appears to have expanded these options to include acts of violence against others. What other explanation is there?

The toxic environment sets the stage for episodes of violence and perpetuates the cycle of violence, fear, isolation, meanness, and ultimately more violence, more fear, more isolation, and even greater meanness. Breaking the cycle for vulnerable children is difficult but possible. The longer the cycle is in place, the more difficult and expensive it is to break.

Bad Seed Versus Toxic Environment

Instead of trying to change our toxic environment, professional practices and policies have focused on identifying, isolating, punishing, or treating the "bad seed." These efforts and the general discussions of nature versus nurture have constantly caused us some consternation. The canary used in the coal mines to signal when the air was too dangerous for the miners to breathe is seen by those in public health as analogous to society's most vulnerable, who likewise signal a toxic environment. Extending this symbolic analogy, we find the strategies to identify, study, change, or incarcerate the bad seed analogous to efforts to understand and save one canary at a time. Such strategies lack a prevention focus and ignore the impact of the environment and of the social context on behavior. This is narrow-minded and unforgivable in the case of teenagers, who are particularly responsive to social norms within their peer group. Adolescents, particularly those living in poverty or experiencing racism, are our modern-day canaries. Society must heed their warning signs.

The nature, bad seed, and genetic explanations for violence are unable to account for patterns of violence in America and, in particular, the recent youth violence epidemic. Also these explanations fall apart completely when the recent rise in arrests of girls for violence is considered—unless one is postulating a recent change in the genetic makeup of girls in America.

America responded to the first wave of violence by labeling the youth involved as demons and funding criminal justice interventions. The second wave has generated more empathy for perpetrators, with calls for mental health intervention for troubled children. Although a mental health focus is more therapeutic, both responses focus on individuals and not on cultural influences—the toxic environment.

It is true that those urban children who committed horrific violent acts are criminals, as are the perpetrators in the second wave. And it is true that the perpetrators in middle-class nonurban America responsible for the second wave show signs of mental health problems (as do the young perpetrators in urban America). Yet a sole focus on individual vulnerabilities—with budgetary priorities given first to criminal justice interventions (with urban children) and now mental health early interventions (with nonurban children)—represents a limited, reactive agenda. Complex problems require complex solutions. No one action or professional sector can in any way take this on alone.

All children, regardless of where they live, are vulnerable if they have witnessed a lot of violence or have been victims of violence. Family violence is often a precursor to peer violence, gang violence, and school violence. Children who have been hurt are more likely to hurt other children. Often, hurt or troubled children exhibit early warning signs before a crisis or a horrible violent tragedy. Professionals who serve children have done a poor job of responding to these early warning signs. Practices and protocols tend to ignore small problems and minimize resources until some awful tragedy occurs. School psychologists are made available after a tragedy in the same settings where they are virtually unavailable before.

Few Resources for Prevention

Budgetary constraints are rarely discussed in a crisis, yet they are often the fatal limitation when prevention efforts are considered. Politicians, youth-serving professionals, and school administrators would be viewed as callous, out-of-touch, and lacking in judgment if they suggested that because of budgetary constraints a thorough investigation into the shootings at Columbine High School could not be done or the necessary counseling and intervention could not be given to the students at that school. Yet, across America, principals annually make budget requests for more school psychologists and counselors, art and recreation programs, extended day programs, smaller classrooms, peer mediation programs, conflict resolution programs, after-school programs, and other prevention programs—budget requests that are rarely granted, that are thought to be extravagant. It is quite possible that the principal of Columbine High School has made such fruitless requests prior to the massacre. He will have little trouble getting such requests met now. Should other principals have to wait for tragedy to strike?

There is hardly a professional in America who wouldn't respond positively to a call to help at Columbine High School. Yet most are too busy to provide ordinary pretragedy assistance to local principals. It is difficult to get media coverage for the good news happening in public schools across the country. Yet keeping media away from Columbine is impossible. Time, attention, and money seem to flow without question into a well-publicized crisis. But when enough people have the proper information and understanding and when enough people have the motivation to address the issue of violence when there is no crisis, together they can prevent such tragedies and reduce the violence in children's lives.

During the height of the urban wave of violence, money flowed to the police departments. Now, after Columbine, it seems to be flowing in the direction of mental health services, a necessary part of the response. Yet criminal justice and mental health are crisis oriented and at the reactive end of the service spectrum. Prevention has been slow to move to the top of America's agenda and still seems to be secondary to the crisis response agenda. However, former President Clinton's gun control initiative and challenge to the entertainment media are welcomed additions to the prevention efforts. Sooner would have been better, but such a bold use of his bully pulpit nevertheless opens a significant opportunity that must be used. After a tragedy like the Columbine High School massacre, it would be a failure not to bring all of the outstanding prevention programs to every public school in the country.

The Process in Boston

Yes, things have changed! The challenge before this nation is unlike any other we have witnessed in our many years of working on this problem. This is clearly everyone's problem, and there isn't an American who can safely say, "it isn't my problem." The problem is complicated, and there are no magic quick-fix solutions, but there are notable prevention successes that have resulted from many grassroots and community-based efforts to address the first wave. Boston is a place noted for its successful reduction in youth violence. There, having thousands of people working over the last fifteen years has paid off. The city went two and a half years without a juvenile homicide due to the hard work and persistence of those thousands of people.

As you will see in Part Three of this book, which tells the whole story of what happened in Boston, there is no single cause for the epidemic of adolescent violence that affected Boston in the 1980s, and no single effort or discipline created the dramatic decline. Like it or not, there is no single or simple solution. The nation can learn from the Boston's experience only if the full story is told. Often the so-called Boston Model is misrepresented as a single strategy of improved policing with particular emphasis on the relationship between the police and the urban neighborhoods. This misrepresentation tends to reinforce stereotypes about violence (that it occurs only in urban, minority areas) and the popular tendency to look for the magical silver bullet (irony intended). Its danger lies in promulgating to others the message that "you too can solve your problem if you use the Boston Police Model." It also discourages the thousands of people whom it fails to credit for their significant contribution.

The penchant among policy analysts, journalists, and funders for the latest quick fixes is frustrating for those of us who work directly with youth. In 1982, Boston City Hospital was the first hospital in the country to begin a comprehensive violence prevention program based on public health strategies. Because public health is a multidisciplinary arena focused on prevention, labeling violence as a public health problem created a commitment to prevention. This challenged youth-serving professionals to complement the intervention role of police. Responding to episodes of violence became only a fraction of the job.

Building a Critical Mass

Everyone was involved. A critical mass of people was recruited, and programs began to evolve and spring up around the city. Violence prevention became a movement in Boston. Educators, youth outreach workers, peer educators, police, lawyers, community agency staff, clergy, probation officers, activists, nurses, doctors, and emergency response teams were all trained and challenged to begin programs. They integrated violence prevention strategies into their existing work and created new violence prevention programs, many of which are described in this book. The Boston Public School system deserves particular recognition as the site for the development of the country's first violence prevention curriculum intended to address peer fighting in high schools. It was also one of the first public school systems to begin in-service training in violence prevention for teachers.

Over the last two decades, America has lined up the risk factors for youth violence like a sequence of slot machine windows that work in concert to yield a result. In this case, that result was not a jackpot but a pile of tragedies—an epidemic of youth violence such as no other industrialized country has experienced.

The work we did in Boston, a model for a national movement to prevent violence, was based on several premises that reflect our fundamental philosophies as physicians, violence prevention experts, community activists, and parents.

First, we believe that youth violence is preventable and that the U.S. can achieve the low rates of other industrialized nations. Second, arresting perpetrators after a violent incident is not prevention; it is a necessary reaction but is not to be confused with prevention. Third, everyone, especially young people and survivors, has a contribution to make. Fourth, professionals cannot be the leaders of this movement; they must support the leadership of community activists, especially survivors. Fifth, youth-serving professionals across disciplines are currently a part of the problem in their tolerance for ineffective, biased, and crisis-oriented protocols. No longer can we continue to stitch kids up and send them out of emergency rooms. No longer can the police responding to domestic violence calls ignore children who witnessed their mother or father beaten.

We have learned much over the years. We came to our work from different perspectives and have been driven by a love of children and of country. We want the nation to learn from Boston's experience. This book is our manifesto on youth violence prevention for America because we want to stop the injury and deaths from violence. We want a peaceful society. We believe, in fact we know, it is possible.

Chapter Two

Who Are We?

We began our work together almost two decades ago. The early seeds of the violence prevention movement were planted. We started with passion, optimism, commitment, concern, and naiveté. Good thing, because with passion came energy; with optimism, hopefulness; with commitment, sincerity; with concern, motivation; and with naiveté, protection from the overwhelming demands of the task and the skepticism that surrounded us. We were inadequately trained to take on the job of preventing violence. In fact, as physicians we had not been trained to think of violence as a health problem. "Stitch them up and send them out" was the rule. We had been trained in a *don't ask* policy, because addressing the underlying issues leading to a violent injury was not considered part of our job. Our personal backgrounds, however, set a different stage, and public health offered a different professional opportunity. Fueled by our personal agenda and grounded in public health perspectives, we were off.

We are an unlikely pair. One of us is an African American woman, born and raised in the South in a warm and nurturing family, the daughter of an insurance executive and schoolteacher, the wife of a Methodist minister, trained as an internist. The other is a Jewish man, grandson of a poor Russian immigrant tailor, born in the Bronx and raised in the suburbs of New York City in a dysfunctional and violent family, married to a nutritionist, trained as a pediatrician. Both of us are parents, currently of teenagers, grappling with all the issues that teenagers bring into a family. In 1981, we met while working at Boston City Hospital in a situation where we had been set up by our boss to be competitors and rivals. Yet we got past our dramatically different backgrounds and not only overcame a factious professional environment but established an enduring friendship and a professional collaboration that has been both personally rewarding and extremely productive.

We are offering a description of who we are because response to violence is such a personal issue. Knowing our stories may help others grappling with this issue to look within themselves for the needed strength and guidance. Others who are intent on turning the tide of the epidemic of youth violence inundating this nation may find motivation directly in our experiences.

We didn't come to this issue by chance. Personal and professional experiences drew us to it. When we first got involved, we had to challenge and support each other because we felt very much alone. At that time little to no attention was paid to violence prevention, and the health care community was treating only the physical injuries once violence had happened. America approached violence as an inevitable and hopeless aspect of society, confined to "bad" neighborhoods, with the response left to the police and occasionally to psychiatrists. We hope this book and the sharing of our experiences and thoughts will help others get involved.

Deborah's Story

I was raised in the segregated South in a family and community of people trying to do the right thing. I was raised to try to make the world better. I knew some of the pain and violence of racism and segregation; my parents knew it better. They were determined to change America and were active participants in the civil rights and voting rights movements. My sister and I were expected to make a contribution, and these expectations were regularly reinforced not just by words but by my parents' actions and examples as well. At Spelman College (a historically black woman's college in Atlanta) these expectations were further reinforced, and I internalized them.

They became the expectations I had for myself. Therefore I arrived at Harvard Medical School, aged twenty-one, with a deep desire to become a physician dedicated to serving urban adolescents. In 1978, during my third year of med school, I was quite disturbed to learn, from an *Ebony* magazine article, that homicide was the leading cause of death for young black men and to realize that in all my training at one of America's most prestigious institutions no one had raised this issue. The toll taken by violence on the lives and health of the population I wanted to serve had not even been raised in my training!

Also during my third year of medical school, during my rotation in the emergency room, I was assigned to take care of a young man who needed stitches. It was three o'clock in the morning and the young man had been cut in a fight. His words to me after I finished putting in the stitches and as he prepared to leave rang in my mind again and again. He told me not to go to bed because the person who cut him was going to be in the emergency room in about an hour needing many stitches. He smiled and assured me I would get much more practice suturing up wounds. His intended victim didn't arrive on my shift that morning—maybe this planned act of revenge was prevented. I don't know. What I do know is that, despite his humor and bravado, my patient had told me of a significant risk to his health and life—and I had no response. I had not been trained in a violence prevention protocol. In fact, violence as a health risk had not even been mentioned. I didn't know what to say or do. As it turned out this was a common situation for physicians, making our lack of a response even more distasteful. "Stitch them up and send them out" was the protocol. There were no prevention obligations like those for suicide attempts or heart disease or lead poisoning. We had prevention protocols—whether behavioral, political, economic, or policy oriented—for so many other things. I was taught that you call the psychiatric nurse for all suicide attempts, and you specifically ask about the patient's intentions. I was taught that every opportunity to discuss exercise, diet, and smoking with a patient with heart disease was to be exploited.

I was taught that you don't send a child who has suffered lead poisoning home until you are sure the house has been deleaded.

Prevention was a part of my training, except when it came to violence against others. I knew that the medical system's tolerance of interpersonal violence, a problem affecting urban poor communities and young black men in particular, stank of racism, institutional racism, systemic racism. Physicians did not know what to do and had not even started asking questions. Violence was accepted as a norm for "some" people. It was treated as inevitable and not deserving of much attention. The rule was stitch them up and send them out with no questions asked. Our lack of attention to or concerns for future risk of injury, our not even asking what had happened, was a clear unspoken message that violent injury was inevitable in their lives. Failing to offer prevention strategies repeatedly indicated to provider and patient alike that violence could not be prevented.

Questioning the Inevitability of Violence

I grew up in a nonviolent family. I wasn't even spanked, and my parents went to the basement to argue so as not to upset my sister and me. Not only was my father nonviolent but I also knew many black men who were not violent, my husband, my cousins, my friends' fathers. My personal experience caused me to question the inevitability of violence and the neglect of a major health problem for young black men. I started questioning the lack of prevention protocols. I wrote a health curriculum for high schools on suicide and homicide prevention. I became attracted to public health, where the focus is on prevention and on whole communities. I started down the uncharted path of fashioning a career in violence prevention.

Not everybody thought I was talking nonsense. Some of my colleagues were receptive and helpful and became partners. I received help from the experts at the Education Development Center, in Newton, Massachusetts, and was able to turn my work into the Violence Prevention Curriculum for Adolescents, a curriculum based on sound social theory and teaching practices.[1] David Nee, then executive director of the Burden Foundation, became interested in funding the work after hearing me speak at the Surgeon General's Conference on Violence as a Public Health Problem, in 1985, during C. Everett Koop's tenure as surgeon general. Fortunately, at this same time Mark Rosenberg was heading the new Violence Epidemiology Branch at the Centers for Disease Control, and he had begun collecting homicide and suicide data and working to convince the public health community to start addressing the problem.

One of the most important fortunate events in my work to create a violence prevention movement was that I met Howard—a colleague who shared my commitment to making the world better, who shared my abhorrence of violence, and who was struggling to fashion his career but willing to take the risk to follow an uncharted path with me.

In my years of working to prevent violence another important milestone came in 1996 when I hosted a national meeting of survivors—parents whose children had been murdered. Although it was painful, I found renewed motivation in this meeting and in the stories of these families who were committed to prevention. The power of the forgiveness I heard expressed by many survivors was amazing. I learned an important lesson—we are all survivors; they are all our children.

Working to prevent violence has been a rewarding professional and personal journey. Things have changed and the progress is measurable. In 1982, I wished to focus my senior resident talk at Boston City Hospital on violence and was told that it was not an appropriate topic. Today, I am invited to do grand rounds on violence all over the country, recognition that is both affirming and gratifying. The personal gain has also been noteworthy. I am better at handling my anger and responding to conflict. I am more creative in my ability to anticipate and prevent conflict. I believe that I am a better parent and wife because of efforts to value nonviolence and continually grow in my conflict resolution skills. My prayers are that I have been and will be able to make a contribution to making the world better (it is the way I was raised). However I am judged in the professional arena, this work has made me a more capable person, and for that alone the work has been worth it.

Howard's Story

When I first got involved with the issue of youth violence and the violence prevention movement almost twenty years ago, I learned and observed many new things that were out of my realm of experience. One of the most striking things was that violence was a very personal and intimate issue for most people. Almost everyone I talked with had been touched by violence, either directly or indirectly through a friend or family member. I don't think I had previously thought about or realized the ways in which this issue affected so many people and how many people had fears and concerns about it.

It isn't that I went looking for this; it just kept coming up. For example, a nurse practitioner, Ann Bishop, was presenting at a meeting early on in Deborah's and my efforts to establish a role for the schools in violence prevention. Ann had been working with us in the development of violence prevention education in schools. She was discussing the experiences she was having teaching violence prevention to students in the school where she worked. In the middle of her presentation, almost out of the blue, she began to talk about her own fears for her son who was in middle school and was being bullied daily. She became choked up and tearful while talking about this and ended up giving one of the most powerful and insightful moments of the entire meeting. In fact this is the only part of the conference I remember in any detail.

This was not just an isolated incident. I have rarely been to a meeting or conference on this subject where something similar hasn't happened. Sometimes the stories are small and just mentioned in passing. But at other times, such as at conferences involving survivors of violence or those who have lost a child, sibling, or parent to violence, the stories are extremely moving and powerful. Furthermore, when friends and acquaintances heard that I was working on this issue, they began to share their experiences, and I discovered that many people I knew outside my professional context had their own stories to tell. Over the years, I have continued to get phone calls from professional colleagues, family members, and personal friends who were seeking advice or just wanted to share their concerns about how to deal with situations where violence occurred or was threatened. It appears that this issue has touched so many, and yet we have taken so long to address it. We have actually just been sweeping it under the rug.

These various incidents have taught me several things. One is how powerful and important it is for people to share their own fears about and personal experiences with violence. This is a way to engage others in the issue and makes it possible for others to realize that they can no longer say, "this isn't my problem." It is common for many to point their fingers at inner-city communities and say, "it is their problem, not mine." Everyone needs to identify with violence as a problem that all have faced directly or indirectly. Exposing the more personal and intimate level is an important strategy for getting people on board.

In addition, recognizing and coming to grips with your own issues with violence provides a valuable opportunity to better understand the issue itself. Looking at how violence touches you and affects your life experience provides insights into what can be done and how violence may be affecting others. It brings you closer to the problem and helps you motivate others into action.

Experiencing Family Violence Firsthand

The most important lesson I learned in discovering the violence that has affected many others is a very personal one. I grew up in a very violent family, believing that I was alone in this experience. In my household the victims were my siblings and myself. This was at a time when child abuse was barely on the radar screen for the health care community and the first articles in the medical literature on this subject were just being published. It was still commonly believed that parents would never hurt their children unless they somehow deserved punishment. It was a private matter.

The incidents of violence toward myself, my older brother, and my two younger sisters were frequent and sometimes quite frightening. Although I long ago acknowledged them and came to peace with them, some of the memories remain extremely clear, almost like movies playing in my head. One such incident occurred when I was eight or nine years old. I was discovered playing with my father's shaving cream in the bathroom and found myself wedged in the corner between the wall and the toilet, being struck over and over and over again on whatever body part was exposed. I remember looking up at my mother's face and seeing such out-of-control rage that I thought she was going to kill me. She certainly appeared capable of it.

What I don't remember is any physical pain, probably because I was having something like an out-of-body experience where I became a third person in the room, watching what was going on rather than being a part of it. This went on until my mother's hand started to hurt from hitting me. I know this because when she stopped, she looked at and shook her hand, which was beet red; said, "See what you made me do"; and stormed out of the room. I just lay there, still crammed between the toilet and the wall, full of anger, scared, and feeling very small, knowing this would not be the last time, wondering if, when, or how it would ever end.

My childhood was filled with such events. If they weren't happening to me, then I was witnessing or hearing them happen to one of my siblings (and being grateful it wasn't me this time). When events weren't physical, they were violently verbal, occurring in unpredictable ways. Very minor things (like spilled milk or a broken glass) would set my mother off; major things (like drinking alcohol or not doing homework) would go unnoticed. In addition to hands, paddles, belts, and other objects were used. My father was often around while this was going on and knew what was happening but never intervened. He was generally lying on the couch reading a book, even when the incident was happening right in the same room. He was probably thinking that he was glad the violence wasn't also being directed at him. Going home after school was not something I ever looked forward to. Having friends over was too risky. This happened in a solidly middle-class, white, Jewish ("it never happens in Jewish families") home, in a solidly white, middle-class community. No one seemed to notice or, if they did, to react in any way. That goes for other family members, neighbors, and anyone else.

All four of us siblings are scarred in various ways from this. I spent much of my childhood depressed and fearful. It affected my peer relationships in many ways, from making me excessively self-conscious to making me withdrawn to making me afraid to have anyone over to my house. Over the years I have dealt with this. My anger has evolved into understanding and forgiveness. My self-consciousness has changed to pride in my accomplishments in spite of my unsettling start. My pain has been turned into energy and commitment to changing the factors that bring violence into so many lives.

What I learned from hearing other people's stories was just how profound my own experiences were in shaping my life. I certainly knew that these experiences had affected my behavior and self-perception. I spent many years dealing with that and building myself back up to become a successful, confident professional with a family of my own. I still deal with it when I find myself feeling angry and being drawn to behaviors that I experienced as a child. It continues to be work to use healthy responses to anger because I learned all the wrong, unhealthy ways. I do hope I am doing a better job with my own children. If I am, I have my wife to thank for much of that.

But until I connected with others around the issue of violence, I had never thought about how these early childhood experiences had so totally shaped who I had become. These experiences probably played a role in my decision to become a doctor. They most likely led me to choose pediatrics as my field of concentration.

Most certainly, they led to my being drawn to the field of violence prevention. Sharing this with others, particularly people I don't even know, is not very easy for me. I am a very private person; trust is still something I am working on. Like most people who have experienced violence, I felt isolated and alone for a good part of my early years.

My childhood experiences with violence influenced my life in almost every way. However, I hope my story illustrates that such exposures do not condemn a person to a life of violence and dysfunction, even though they definitely increase the likelihood of those outcomes. There are other options. Pain and anger can be turned around and used in prosocial and constructive ways. That is the core of violence prevention. That is what turning the tide of the epidemic of violence is all about.

Together

We bring our personal and professional experiences to our work in violence prevention; there is really no other way to do this work. We started our professional collaboration and journey in 1981, using the science of public health, the context of clinical medicine at a city hospital, and the personal passion to make the world safe for children. We have been motivated and inspired, as well as challenged and discouraged along the way. When we are at our lowest we use the science to remind us that violence is a preventable problem, and we immerse ourselves in the power and pain of survivors to inspire us onward. We have been at it for almost two decades and plan to continue to stick with it for as long as it takes.

Part Two

Issues and Solutions

Chapter Three

What Do We Know and
How Do We Know It?

Understanding violence and its characteristics is critical to prevention work. Therefore this chapter provides some basic information and, most important, highlights sources of useful data. Practitioners and community activists must stay abreast of the problem as they develop appropriate responses to it.

The Escalation of Juvenile Homicide

America has not only one of the highest homicide rates among the industrialized countries of the world but also the highest rate by far among the twenty-six wealthiest nations.

- A study of twenty-six industrialized nations revealed that 73 percent of all child homicides occurred in the United States.[1]
- The homicide rate in the United States is ten times as high as that of Western Europe, seventy times as high as that of Japan, and five times as high as that of Canada, New Zealand, and Australia.[2]

If current trends continue, by the early years of the twenty-first century more children will be dying from handgun shootings than from automobile crashes.[3]

In 1987, endemic rates of homicide among young men (aged fifteen to twenty-four) were already five to seventy times higher than in other countries (with the United States experiencing 22 homicides per 100,000 population per year; Scotland, 4.2 per 100,000; and Japan, .03 per 100,000).[4] The rates in the other industrialized countries (countries to which the United States usually compares itself with respect to economics, health, and just about everything else) fell between the rates for Scotland and Japan. America already stood out like a sore thumb.

Then something happened in the late eighties and early nineties; America's endemic problem escalated, beginning the epidemic of youth homicide, with rates that were literally off the existing charts. By 1991, this country's already high annual rate for young men jumped to an enormous 37 homicides per 100,000.[5]

The epidemic initially affected urban poor America, cities with populations greater than 500,000. Despite declines in national homicide rates since 1995, suburbs and rural communities, younger and younger children, and girls are being affected in greater numbers. Although the homicide rates for young men have fallen in the last several years, they have not fallen within the range of other industrialized countries' rates.

Nonfatal Violence

Homicide is clearly the extreme tip of the iceberg of interpersonal violence. The broad base of this iceberg is nonfatal episodes of violence; although the exact rates of this violence are poorly documented. The Northeast Ohio Trauma Study, led by researcher J. Barancik, demonstrated the difficulty of measuring nonfatal assaults.[6] This study of the SMSAs (Standard Metropolitan Statistical Areas) in Northeast Ohio compared the number of assaults reported in emergency departments to those reported to police. For every one homicide during the period of study, twenty-five assaults were reported to the police and one hundred were reported to the emergency departments. Four times the number of nonfatal episodes showed up at the emergency department as were reported to police!

Some emergency departments are now systematically measuring the number and characteristics of reported assaults. In Massachusetts, for example, the Massachusetts Department of Public Health Weapons Related Injury Surveillance System (WRISS) is used for this purpose. This kind of surveillance system can be very helpful in the design of local programs for responding to violence. In Boston, when people such as the state governor and federal prosecutor and the city police chief were touting police firearm intervention as the sole reason for the decline in youth homicide, emergency department data showed otherwise. The decline in emergency room visits for assaults with weapons other than firearms, along with evidence from the annual National Crime Victimization Surveys (discussed later in this chapter), suggested that an accumulation of broad community-based programs (including but not exclusively composed of police efforts) was responsible.

Who's Killing Whom

Regardless of the type of violence, another feature of violence in America is that it often involves acquaintances and family. Contrary to media-induced beliefs about the risk from the proverbial stranger "bad guy," in 1998, 27 percent of homicides occurred among family members and an additional 48 percent occurred among friends, acquaintances, neighbors, and the like. Thus a total of 75 percent of homicides involved a victim and a perpetrator who knew each other. When women are killed, over 65 percent of the time the perpetrator is a boyfriend, ex-boyfriend, husband, or ex-husband. Nonfatal assaults and rape are violent crimes in which the acquaintance and family characteristic also holds. Consistently, in surveys of women who report having been raped, a large percentage identify the rapist as a person known to them.[7]

This violence occurs largely at parties or dances, in bars or bedrooms, and on playgrounds in the course of arguments that grow out of altercations between friends, acquaintances, or family members. Much less of this violence occurs in dark alleys or in the course of preplanned criminal acts such as robbery or drug deals. Victims and assailants most often know each other, are from the same neighborhood, and are of the same race. A psychologist colleague of ours once half-jokingly said that if you don't want to be murdered, never go home and don't have friends. This runs counter to the beliefs of many who get their impressions from the media and from press coverage of violent events. In the typical violent scenario, the learned behavior of using violence to deal with anger and conflict is applied with little thought of the potential consequences.

Guns are a significant part of the picture of homicide and violence in America. Seventy-five percent of the homicides in the United States are firearm related: 60 percent involve handguns, and another 15 percent long guns. The victims of homicide are overwhelmingly young: 75 percent are between the ages of fifteen and thirty-four. Homicide has been and remains a predominately male event: 70 percent of the victims and 86 percent of the perpetrators are boys or men.[8]

A Surprising History

Although the homicide rates for young black men in the United States are currently the highest rates, in the 160 per 100,000 range, that was not always the case. The history and trend of violence among white males must also be acknowledged. *New York Times* reporter Fox Butterfield documents homicide rates among rural, rich southern whites in the eighteenth and nineteenth centuries that rival the current high rates in urban America.[9] Dueling was a legitimate and expected method of defending one's honor among the elite in, for example, Edgefield County in rural South Carolina. Elected officials and other respectable men often had histories of murdering a man in defense of their family's honor. (It is an interesting side note that Edgefield County is the home of South Carolina senator Strom Thurmond. Senator Thurmond's father shot and killed a man in 1897 after the man insulted him. He claimed self-defense, in spite of the fact that several eyewitnesses claimed that the man was unarmed and had not physically threatened him. He was acquitted by a jury after slightly over half an hour of deliberation.[10])

Butterfield postulates that slaves learned this culture of using violence to defend honor from their white masters and, after emancipation, carried it with them as they migrated into urban centers. *Dissing*, as it's known among young urbanites (that is, *dis*respecting, putting down, or insulting a person), is a direct derivative of the dueling of old postulates, according to Butterfield.

What is important to learn from this shift in high homicide rates from the rural to the urban setting, a disproportionately poor and minority setting, is that social norms, culture, and the expectations of others do have a tremendous impact on behavior.[11] Doubtlessly, poverty is a factor, but by no means is it the sole or the paramount one. Researcher Brandon Centerwall, in a study done in both Atlanta and New Orleans,[12] found that overcrowding (number of people per square foot of housing) as a measure of poverty completely explained the overrepresentation of blacks among the victims of domestic homicide. In urban America the structural conditions of overcrowding and poverty are strongly associated with homicide. Yet this does not seem to be the case in other countries: those like Hong Kong, where overcrowding is the norm, and those where poverty is much more prevalent yet where homicide rates remain dramatically lower than U.S. rates.

Biological and Genetic Risk Factors

Research, public policy, and program priorities often focus on the factors that make an individual more susceptible to committing acts of violence. In addition to the obvious risks present in the family, the schools, and community life, this individual focus has also looked at biological and genetic risk factors. There are two common but incorrect perceptions about biological and genetic risk factors: (1) all biological risk factors are genetic, or predestined, and (2) at birth a child possesses a pure genetic or biological template and the environmental influences begin thereafter.

In fact, biological and genetic risk factors are distinct, although they are often mistakenly referenced as one and the same, especially in lay publications but occasionally even in scientific literature. To assume that they are the same implies inevitability. Prevention efforts are then thwarted by the belief or assumption that it is inevitable that some individuals will behave violently.

In *Violence and the Brain*, Vernon Mark and Frank Irvin,[13] illustrate the impact of the environment on the brain and the translation of that impact into anatomical and biological changes. One of the examples these authors give concerns kittens that were blindfolded at birth. The kittens that then have their blindfolds removed before one month of age developed the ability to see. Those that remained blindfolded past one month were never able to gain sight. The optic pathways in their brains had atrophied (disappeared or shrunk), and the neurochemical impulses needed for sight were not there. Mark and Irvin conclude that everything from malnutrition to witnessing violence can have a structural impact on the brain that can lower the threshold for violence, producing a biological problem that is not genetic.

At birth a baby is a product of biology and nine months of environmental influences at one of the most sensitive and reactive times in the life cycle. If a fetus can hear and can see light by mid-pregnancy,[14] it isn't at all unreasonable to assume that the external environment has an impact on the biological development of the fetus. It is therefore possible to deduce that the mother's environment, stress, and trauma, among other things, during pregnancy can have a direct impact on her baby's personality and temperament as measured at birth.

That chemicals have an impact on fetal development and future childhood behavior and problems is not debated. Fetal alcohol syndrome, a well-documented set of physical and developmental defects secondary to alcohol intake during pregnancy, is probably the clearest example of such a direct impact on fetal development. But to date the impact on the fetus of emotions such as anger or fear has not been generally accepted as a major determinant of childhood behavior or brain function. Yet such a consideration is reasonable given that every emotion translates into some neurochemical process. Something chemical in the body goes up or down when love is in the air, or even lust. Similarly, chemical reactions happen in the body when anger, fear, or violence occurs. These chemical reactions and changes have the potential to affect a fetus growing in the body of a pregnant woman.

Even after birth, events can influence body chemistry in ways that can influence risk for violence. The work of child psychiatrist Carl Bell and others illustrates such a case. Individuals who experience or sustain a significant head injury show a higher rate of predisposition to violent behavior.[15] This shows that a physical experience can translate into biological changes that affect behavior. There is clearly an interplay between biological and chemical factors and behavior, the exact nature of which is still far from fully understood. There is also a clear interplay between the environment and biological or chemical functions in the body, again with much yet to be learned about its nature.

The research into the biology of behavior, including violence, is extremely interesting and progressing rapidly because of new brain imaging and measurement techniques. One area of interest is the link between serotonin, a neurotransmitter (a chemical made and released in the brain and nervous system as a part of normal brain function), and levels of aggression. The general consensus in the psychiatric literature is that low levels of serotonin are associated with violent behavior. Specifically, the research has shown that 5-HIAA (a chemical—specifically, a metabolite—derived from serotonin), which is found in the fluid of the spine, is found in low levels in people who display impulsive, violent behavior.[16] However, a low serotonin level does not necessarily signal a genetic predisposition. Low serotonin levels may be caused by many different factors, including a reaction to environmental stimuli such as malnutrition, witnessing violence, or fear during gestation, childhood, or later.

Another area of interest is testosterone, a naturally occurring hormone produced by the testicles in males. It has been and continues to be investigated to determine whether high testosterone levels explain the dominance of men as perpetrators of violence across cultures, countries, classes, and races. This male dominance has, pretty much by default, been the greatest indicator to many people of a biological (or according to some, a genetic) predisposition to violence. Our discussion in Chapter Eight of the relatively recent increase in the number of girls arrested for violence in the United States illustrates the fault we find with this focus. Paying primary attention to individual biological factors such as testosterone levels ultimately results in lack of attention to the work necessary to clearly delineate the environmental influences, the "socially toxic environments," that appear to be far more prominent and powerful in influencing risks for violence.

Dan Olweus, a Swedish professor who is a leading researcher into the phenomenon of children bullying other children, has described higher levels of testosterone among preschool bullies.[17] To date others have not replicated this finding. Again, as with serotonin levels, higher testosterone levels may be explained by victimization, witnessing violence, fear, anger, or other environmental factors. It is known that environment influences biology and therefore could influence factors such as testosterone levels.

Felton Earls, a professor at Harvard Medical School, has recently completed a large study of human development and antisocial behavior in Chicago.[18] Early findings have uncovered the presence of neighborhood and community factors relevant to the risk of violence. Individual and biological factors are variables also being assessed in the study. It is hoped that this study will put some of these risk factors into perspective. That some individuals may be genetically or biologically vulnerable to violence we would not necessarily debate. The work on the relationship between head injuries and violent behavior clearly illustrates this. However, it appears that these biological factors represent a very small piece of the big picture. That environmental factors are dominant and even influence biological factors we would argue forcefully.

In sum, there is overwhelming evidence that though genetics plays a role in the way individuals act out aggression, it is by no means the dominant factor for acts of violence. Rather, it seems to be the environmental and social factors that influence people (physiologically and otherwise) to commit acts of violence.

How Do We Know What We Know?

In America there are several important sources of data on violence. Some are accessible to the public; others are available through community partnerships with academic institutions. The National Center for Education Statistics (NCES) and the Bureau of Justice Statistics (BJS) are the primary federal entities that collect, analyze, and report data related to education and crime, both in the United States and abroad. The Department of the Treasury, Bureau of Alcohol, Tobacco, and Firearms (ATF) publication *Commerce in Firearms in the United States* is an annual report of activities relating to the regulation of firearms. The Youth Crime Gun Interdiction Initiative (YCGII), an ATF program, brings together federal, state, and local law enforcement officials to improve information about the illegal sources of guns recovered from juveniles and adult criminals. The latest YCGII publication is the 1999 *Crime Gun Trace Analysis Reports: The Illegal Youth Firearms Market in 27 Communities*.

The Uniform Crime Reports (UCRs), published by the Federal Bureau of Investigation, are the most frequently cited source of national information on violent crime. These annual reports date back to 1930. Local police data are submitted to the FBI and aggregated into a single, national-level data source. Homicides are mandatorily reported in these data sets, but other crimes are reported voluntarily, and thus data about the latter lack the consistency of the homicide data. In general, homicide rates are measured fairly accurately, and nonfatal episodes of violence are poorly measured. The reports give cursory information on homicides and assaults, including victim and perpetrator relationship, weapons used, location of the violent episode, and race of victim and of perpetrator.

In a pivotal UCR from the early 1980s, the high rates of homicides involving family members, friends, or acquaintances were described. An accompanying editorial stated, "Homicide is a societal problem over which law enforcement has little or no control." Furthermore, the report substantiated the prevalence of handguns as the weapon of choice and documented the early trend toward younger and younger victims and perpetrators.[19]

Despite their status as the best sources of national data, UCRs have several limitations. First, there is a two-year delay in the publication of annual data (the 1998 report came out in 2000, for example). Second, police departments don't collect local data in uniform ways, resulting in missing or misleading national data. For example, when aggregated, data on race become meaningless because some police departments label Hispanic men as "white," some label them as "black," and some label them as "other." This underscores the importance of uniform data collection.

Also, as illustrated by the SMSA study[20] mentioned earlier, police arrests for assaults represent a fraction of the violence that occurs, with many more individuals with injuries from violence presenting in hospitals than in police stations. Police data must be supplemented with data from emergency rooms and victimization surveys (the latter are discussed later in this chapter). Emergency departments, which see the results of far more violence than is captured by police data, do not routinely collect assault information. Massachusetts was the first state to collect such data, through WRISS,[21] which is now almost a decade old. Recently, nine other states have begun to build on this work that started in Massachusetts. These states are collecting emergency department data in a routine and concerted way. We are hopeful that this will prove a precursor to a national injury surveillance system measuring emergency room encounters involving injuries from violence.

Victim Surveys

The most widely used survey of victims is the ongoing National Crime Victimization Survey (NCVS) conducted by the Department of Justice, in place since 1965. Samplings of U.S. households are enrolled in the study for three-year periods. During this period all household members aged twelve and older are questioned at six-month intervals regarding their experiences with crime, usually in a structured phone interview. In its early years the survey under-counted episodes occurring among friends and family because the questions were framed with a focus on "crime" and none of them addressed interpersonal violence. In 1993, revisions were made, and questions asking specifically about neighbors, relatives, coworkers, and friends were included.

Cycle of Violence

Episodes of violence, despite different categorical names (domestic violence, child abuse, gang violence, suicide, and so forth), are related. The most obvious relationship is that children who witness a lot of violence or are victims of violence in early childhood are at elevated risk for participation in future episodes as victims, perpetrators, or both. Additional risk factors for the different types of violence are alcohol and other drug use; social and cultural norms and expectations that glamorize or promote violence; the vulnerability of young people, particularly adolescents; and the confounding variable of poverty.[22]

Furthermore the reactive response of criminal justice to violence, which makes the threat of punishment the primary deterrent, is not preventive. Consider the typical homicide in the United States. It involves two people, at least one of whom is armed, who have been drinking and who get into an escalating argument. What is the likelihood of either participant's stopping to consider the consequences of his or her behavior and the possible punishment he or she may face? It's very low!

In fact the severity of the punishment has little if any effect on such behavior, and therefore the threat of punishment is an ineffective strategy for preventing violence. Between 1980 and 1990, this country doubled its population of people in jail, from a half a million to a million, and in spite of this, violent crime rose about 13 percent.[23] Between 1990 and 1995, this dramatic increase continued, tripling the number of people in jails and prisons compared to 1980.[24]

This is certainly not a sign that severe punishment is an effective deterrent to violence. It results from a system designed to assign blame and punish after the fact, and it demonstrates little or no preventive effect. Preventive action has to be directed to changing the environment, attitudes, and social norms, especially the accepted and learned use of violence to resolve conflict.

Health and human service professionals label types of violence (child abuse, rape, battering, youth violence, and so on) as distinctly different areas and inappropriately treat them as unrelated. Integrating the cycle of violence[25] and its larger impact beyond the direct victim is a critical component of program development. Clinical services too often miss the importance of the interplay among different forms of violence and forget about those affected by violence who may not have been the direct victims.

For example, violence against women is certainly more than men hitting or exercising power over women. Women are the mothers, sisters, daughters, cousins, and aunts of both victims and perpetrators. After talking with a mother who has had a child murdered, it becomes clear that no greater violence could have been committed against her. Parents will say over and over again, "I would give anything to have had the murderer kill me rather than my child." Our professional views have created distinct definitions and divisions between categories of violence. Yet people are affected by violence in ways that make professional distinctions artificial and counterproductive.

Because violence is a learned behavior and because people operate in a family and social context, all violence is related. There is a cycle of violence. Victims become perpetrators, a setup for repeat victimization. Blame is not helpful when prevention is the goal. Establishing blame becomes essential only when punishment is the goal.

Different Professions—Different Perspectives

As an examination of the perspectives, issues, and concerns raised by various disciplines reveals, the work to prevent violence against women has its foundation in the feminist movement, the work to prevent child abuse has its origins in the social work and medical professions, the work to prevent adolescent interpersonal violence stems from public health, and gang intervention work has its roots in criminal justice. These different disciplines have very different "working definitions," jargon, practices, protocols, and values. The challenge of their working together is more difficult than it appears on the surface.

The police are concerned about crime and the violence that is defined as criminal. They are not concerned about noncriminal episodes such as spanking a child or a scuffle among friends. Escalating arguments, threats, playground fights, and rival team challenges rarely come to the attention of the police. Violence prevention experts in public health are concerned about violence but not concerned about all crime. Vandalism, other property crimes, and car theft are examples of crimes that certainly violate others but do not fall into a public health framework. But each of these events represents a distinct opportunity for early intervention and prevention strategies. It is time for a new paradigm for public health and criminal justice.[26]

Whereas the criminal justice system responds to violence with blame and punishment, public health focuses on understanding risk factors and preventing violence. These two distinct perspectives are quite complementary, but it's the overlap that requires more exploration and attention, the need for prevention after a child is already at greater risk and known to the service systems as, for example, a status offender or a first offender. Another example of the relationships between types of violence is that victims and perpetrators are rarely confined to one of these two categories; they may fall into both at different times or exhibit different forms of violence in different circumstances.

Pulling the different disciplines together, providing and disseminating information to as many people (professional and community) as possible, integrating the various definitions of violence, and creating programs and prevention strategies that cross artificially created boundaries are all essential activities for effectively addressing all forms of violence.

Chapter Four

Understanding Risk and Resiliency

Manuel: I'm a former member of the Almighty Latin Kings and Queens Organization. How I started out was I came from a broken home. Really searching the streets for love and stuff. I grew to love the brothers on the street. It wasn't a gang thing in the beginning. Before I knew, I was caught up in a world of violence. I've seen and probably done everything you could imagine—broken every commandment in the Bible. I was unfortunate. I was not raised by my mom, so that really left me out in the open to do anything I wanted to do. So there was no one who had control over me or my destiny so I just basically did anything I wanted to. I guess I had nothing to do and nobody really to tell me what to do. I used my better judgement, thinking that maybe that was the best thing for me, but as I started growing and getting older I found out that it really wasn't so.[1]

We all are gambling with our children's lives. Every member of American society continues to participate in a high-risk game at the cost of our children's success or failure.

We are aware of the factors that put individuals and communities at risk for violence; poverty and adult role modeling are two examples. Yet we continue to choose prison over prevention strategies.

Manuel's personal narrative is only one of the many stories of the many children who make random choices in their lives. Without an adult role model to help him see beyond short-term fun to the outcomes of a life of crime and drug dealing, Manuel is left to make dangerous choices from a list that is full of self-destructive, illegal, and high-risk behaviors such as selling drugs and joining gangs. If a kid like Manuel is to choose a life of high school and college graduation leading to a successful career and avoiding incarceration, he will require a vivid imagination, realistic role models, and an extraordinary ability to make and stick with good choices. He will have to do this without the guarantee of rewards or success. He will literally have to go against all the odds.

There are factors that put individuals and communities at risk, and there are factors that are protective and promote resiliency. The balance between risk and resiliency tips the scales toward or away from the likelihood of involvement with violence. The metaphor of a slot machine illustrates the way America has lined up the risk factors, resulting in an epidemic of youth violence. Just as chance determines the way the windows line up on a slot machine, chance determines how risks and resiliencies line up in life for any given child. However, chance does not determine the possible options that might fill each window—public policy does. Through its public policy, a society determines the amounts of services, resources, and options available to children in troubled families, available to fill their windows. The interplay and relationships among risk factors and protective factors present many opportunities for society to help children early and prevent unnecessary tragedy.

In order for a player to hit the jackpot on a slot machine, windows containing cherries or oranges or some other correct combination must all line up. America's epidemic of youth violence is of course not a jackpot, but it is the result of two decades of lining up risk factors that yield rising rates of violent death and injury. There are many risk factors, and they often exacerbate each other's impact in any individual situation. The epidemic cannot be fully explained by any one risk factor, nor are most individual acts of violence explained by a single factor. But understanding the collective impact of the multiple risk factors on a population gives us important insights into America's epidemic of youth violence. We can indeed hit the jackpot of a nearly violence-free society if we choose to offer and promote many more protective factors and thereby reduce the chances that any one child will have only risk factors in his or her windows of life.

We all know that America doesn't have to have extremely high homicide rates, because other countries don't have these high rates. If violence were an inevitable part of human nature in industrialized societies, then homicide and violent injury rates would be consistent around the world. This is not the case. The dramatically lower rates of violent death in the rest of the industrialized world gives us hope that with the right changes we could experience something different. Violence is preventable.

Violence in this country did not appear overnight. The epidemic of youth violence evolved over decades. Simple solutions and quick fixes cannot turn such an epidemic around. Hard work, investment in prevention, political action, and a long-term strategy that addresses causes and risk factors can and will. However, despite the complexity of the problem and its interdependent risk factors, it often seems as though America's approach to finding a solution is, to use the metaphor in a new way, as simplistic as using a slot machine. Pulling the handle, letting go, and taking a wait-and-see attitude simply is not adequate.

We ourselves are often asked why the homicide rates in the United States are so much higher than rates in almost every other industrialized country in the world. A concise answer is that this culture offers too many risk factors that promote, encourage, and tolerate violence and too few protective factors. By identifying what is known about violence (both what creates risk and what promotes resiliency) and applying that knowledge to public policy and professional practices, America can learn to change the contents of the windows offered to its children.

Lining Up the Risk Factors

Many factors contribute to the risk that kids will get involved in violence.

Poverty

One major risk factor for involvement in violence is poverty, the first slot machine window.[2] Poverty clearly creates vulnerability to violence, as it does for many health problems. Urban poverty and its consequences likely explain why rates of violent deaths and injuries rose much faster and sooner in inner-city communities.

It is not clear what aspects of poverty translate into greater vulnerability to violence. There is the obvious anger and frustration that arises from going without in a society that has so much. Poor children watch more television than other children and therefore are more often exposed to media images of violence, which are typically unrealistic because they do not show the consequences of violent behavior. Poor children are more likely to grow up without consistent contact with fathers or father figures. According to William Julius Wilson, poor black children are more likely than poor white children to live in neighborhoods where a large majority of the people are poor—places without nice playgrounds, organized recreational activities, or many small businesses offering summer and after-school jobs.[3] The consequences of poverty confound its role in creating vulnerability to violence.

Interestingly, although the rates of violent injury and death are dramatically higher in the African American community compared to the rates for the white population, these disparities essentially disappear when the rates are adjusted for socioeconomic status. This was demonstrated in two studies by Brandon Centerwall, conducted in Atlanta and New Orleans, that used overcrowding as a proxy for socioeconomic status.[4] Military data provide an interesting insight as well, because black men in the military have very low homicide rates compared to the general population of black men in America. These findings strongly suggest that cultural, social, and socioeconomic status are the strong risk factors, not race. The disparity between black and white populations in the numbers of violent deaths is related to disparities in financial resources. African Americans are significantly overrepresented among those living in poverty.

Most young people living in poverty are not violent, and afflu-ent communities are not by any means protected from violence merely by their economic resources. Poverty may be a risk factor as affluence may be protective, but other considerations also need careful attention. Poverty alone is not an adequate explanation for what is going on in most communities. But the fact that poverty is at least part of the explanation, means that interventions involv-ing economic development must be on the list of strategies that will likely reduce the rates of violent injury in those communities. In Boston, certainly, the rise in home ownership rates in poor neighborhoods has been a part of the success in stemming violence.

Alcohol

The typical homicide in this country, as we pointed out in Chapter Three, occurs in the context of two people who know each other and who get into an argument, often under the influence of alco-hol. The argument escalates into a physical fight, a gun is used, and someone gets killed. The role of alcohol as a drug that alters behav-ior requires careful attention as one of the risk factors. Alcohol, the second slot machine window that lines up for American kids, is known to lower the threshold for violent behavior, more so than many other drugs.[5] And it is by far the most frequently used drug among youth, even though it rarely gets the attention that is given to other drugs. It is also the most accessible drug for teenagers. Alcohol use and abuse among teenagers requires the level of atten-tion and investment that has been directed toward illegal drugs.[6] Its toll on the health of our youth is significantly greater than the effects of all other drugs combined.

Guns

Window number three is the availability of guns, specifically hand-guns, and the prevailing attitudes toward gun ownership and car-rying.[7] A handgun that is available when an argument or conflict arises greatly increases the chances of a serious injury occurring if the argument becomes physical. The relatively easy access to hand-guns is part of the problem. But the attitudes that encourage and even promote handgun ownership and the false impression that guns are protective rather than dangerous are equally concerning. Kids and guns are a bad mix.

Like some of the other issues already mentioned, this risk factor requires and will receive longer discussion later on.

Media

This culture's admiration of violence, particularly violence in entertainment, is the fourth window.[8] Children learn to use violence from the media. Television is the most obvious conveyor of the value, success, and reward attributed to superheroic, violent responses to problems. Five decades of sound scientific research have documented this fact and demonstrate direct causality between the viewing of violence on TV and the displaying of violent behavior. Young children are particularly susceptible to these exposures, but older children and adolescents are vulnerable as well. This too will be discussed in considerable detail later on in this book because it is such a powerful influence on children.

Witnessing and Experiencing Violence

The fifth window on the slot machine is exposure to violence as a witness or victim during early childhood.

Violence in the Home. First and foremost, children learn from the violence in their homes. Those children who experience violence firsthand as victims of child abuse are extremely vulnerable to the lessons of violence. Many more children learn about and experience violence as witnesses, most commonly in the form of domestic abuse or battering. Those working in the field of domestic violence estimate that as many as a third or more of families experience some form of domestic violence. This means that a large number of children are witnessing violence at home.

Despite some parents' beliefs to the contrary, if violence is occurring in the family, children are aware of it, even those children who are very young. Exposure, either as witnesses or victims, has serious, long-term consequences for children, putting them at significant risk for future violence as both victims and assailants.

Furthermore, a number of scientific studies have identified certain practices of punishment as increasing a child's risk for later involvement with the criminal justice system and violent behavior. Corporal punishment (hitting or spanking), particularly on a regular basis, is one such practice.[9] When such methods are used regularly and repeatedly, children are learning to associate anger with violent behavior. If the parents acknowledge their violent explosions as wrong and unnecessary, the effect can be lessened, but as primary role models for children, parents should avoid these hitting episodes.

More important, studies of child behavior and development strongly support the fact that violent punishment is not the most effective method of changing child behavior. There are far more effective ways of disciplining children that do not involve hurtful and sometimes frightening interactions. A good rule to remember is that hurt children hurt other children and become hurtful adults. Nurtured children nurture other children and become nurturing adults. The early exposure of young children to violence in the family is one of the strongest predictive factors for risk of involvement with violence later in life as a teenager or young adult. This is central to exploring options and approaches to violence prevention.

Violence in the School. Children learn to use violence in school as witnesses, victims, and perpetrators. When we made this statement in our early speeches, it was often received with skepticism and annoyance. No longer! Although schools remain, for the most part, safer places for kids than the streets or their homes, school violence in America is all too real and must be addressed.

A growing number of students bring guns or knives to school.[10] As many as a quarter of high school students (about a third of boys and a fifth of girls) have reported bringing a knife or gun to school at least once. Most of these young people report carrying weapons for self-protection, an all too familiar refrain among adult gun owners as well. But it doesn't matter why a gun is being carried once it is pulled in anger or frustration. Most often when a weapon is carried, nothing happens. The weapon isn't even detected. Yet armed students are likely to react more assertively than unarmed students to situations perceived as in any way threatening and, in the name of self-defense, may actually provoke a violent episode.

When students are scared in school they can feel the need to arm themselves in order to be safe. What they don't know is that carrying a weapon may increase their risk of injury. Students report fear at school because they are aware of the weapon carrying behaviors of their peers, and large numbers of students (as high as 70 percent) report having been victimized at school at some point.[11]

Children also learn to use violence by witnessing inappropriate adult behavior in school. Adults in school are important role models and are not necessarily appropriately skilled at dealing with conflict themselves. The behaviors they exhibit are observed by students, and when poor conflict resolution skills and anger management are displayed, those students have yet another opportunity to learn the wrong way to deal with difficult situations. Kids are very observant and pick up behaviors from those who are in positions of authority in school as they do at home. Because school personnel have the status of role models, they must exhibit healthy, prosocial conflict resolution skills. Time spent at school may be the only opportunity students exposed to family violence have to observe adults getting along without violence and thus to learn the skills they may not be learning in other places.

Violence in the Community.   Learning about violence is not limited to the home and school settings. Children also learn about violence in their communities. They witness violent events to varying degrees outside their homes, and they witness society's often violent response to those who commit such violence. They learn many things from this exposure, including fear and the sense that they have little or no protection from violence outside the home. In some communities, particularly densely populated, poor inner cities, their exposure may be extensive, although the visibility of violence is beginning to increase in suburban and rural areas as well. Again, children learn from this exposure and can be deeply influenced and affected. Communities with a great deal of violence create serious risks for their children because these children become afraid and learn to use violence to attain utilitarian goals.

We consider the experiences of racism and poverty to be forms of violence. Although this is a huge subject that deserves a book of its own, those working to prevent violence must recognize the contribution these experiences make to the risk of violence because they lie over and exacerbate all the other risks we are discussing.

How much each of these exposures influences any individual child is hard to determine. One saying we like to apply here is "In an avalanche, not one snowflake feels responsible." Consider a child who witnesses or experiences violence in his or her home (particularly a young child), is exposed to violence in the community, experiences or fears violence in the school, and observes an extensive amount of violence on TV (and unavoidably, most children witness huge quantities of TV violence). This becomes an overwhelming set of exposures that even the most resilient child will have difficulty processing and putting into perspective.

Such children are learning that violence is an acceptable, valued, and "normal" behavior for dealing with anger and conflict. They learn to believe that violence is more than likely to be a choice that gets them what they want. It leads to success. They learn to have little empathy for the victims of violence who are bad guys, stupid, or meaningless characters, insignificant to the main story line. This is happening to many, far too many, children in this country.

Adolescent Vulnerability

The sixth, and last, window of risk that we will identify is the specific vulnerability adolescents have to involvement in violence. It is not in adolescence that children learn to use violence. Those lessons come much earlier. But adolescence is the time when specific vulnerabilities to involvement in violence come to the forefront. These vulnerabilities are a result of the normal developmental stages of adolescence.

Adolescents are separating from their families as part of their transition from dependency to independence. For children to become functional independent adults, they must develop an identity separate from parents and family. You cannot be a healthy adult and have the same relationship with your parents as you had as a child. This separation process involves a period of extreme narcissism and self-absorption. For example, many teenagers cannot pass a reflective surface without looking at themselves and are preoccupied with their appearance. Similarly, many have a great need to talk only about things affecting themselves and are disinterested in conversations about anything or anyone else. With this self-absorption also comes considerable fragility.

Adolescents are vulnerable to even the most minor insult or criticism. In fact, when teenagers report what they fight about, these three categories seem to affect them most: an insult to themselves or their mothers; the threatened loss of a possession, such as a cap or jacket or pair of sneakers; and an indirect insult in the form of a he-said–she-said incident. Teenagers are fighting and hurting or killing each other over relatively minor insults, the loss of a baseball hat, or nasty rumors they hear secondhand from a friend. These are things most adults would shrug their shoulders over or walk away from. But for adolescents in the prime of narcissism these events seem overridingly important, as though they could change the course of one's life, and they can lead to serious conflicts and consequences.

Teenagers are also solidifying their sexual identities, which often involves an overidentification with gender role models. What is the effect on young men in this country when almost every male role model or hero put in front of them, from media heroes to sport figures, uses violence to solve his problems, is most often successful when he chooses violence, and rarely, if at all, experiences negative consequences for this behavior? This equates violence with manliness and gives the impression that the use of violence is part of being a man.

Increasingly, this culture is doing the same to girls, and it should not be surprising that rates of involvement with violence and fighting are increasing among girls in this country as well. There are a growing number of violent women role models and heroines in the media, and violent female images are being used for marketing. A handgun ad, for example, shows a young mother looking at her infant in a crib, with a caption suggesting that she should have a handgun to protect that infant. Such images are very powerful, especially to teenage girls, and as a consequence, violence is a characteristic creeping into the image of femininity.

Teenagers are also risk takers. This is the way that they learn their boundaries and limits and test their moral sense of what is right and wrong. They do not accept such boundaries merely because they are told to do so. They need to learn through their own experiences. All of us did things as teenagers that were stupid, and we rarely admit to them as adults. Many of us repress these memories because they are embarrassing, but the reality is that we all went through this and, to some extent, had to as part of our maturation process. The problem arises when young people have fewer and fewer places and healthy parameters within which to experiment with risky behaviors. The healthy parameters are completely demolished when weapons are a part of adolescents' environment. Squabbles that used to end in a black eye now end with a fatality.

James Garbarino, author of *Lost Boys* and *Children in Danger*,[12] illustrates this point with a description of an encounter with teenage boys from the Amish culture. These boys described the really rebellious boys in their community as the ones who would sneak rides in cars or who would put brass rings or other decorative objects on the horse-drawn carriages. Every society has children who get into trouble. Whether they are taking deadly chances or not is in large part determined by the cultural parameters set through public policy. Those in a toxic environment may be armed and keeping lookout for the local drug dealer, and those in a less toxic environment may be putting brass rings on their buggies.

Developing a value system and moral code is also central to the developmental stage of adolescence. Barraging teenagers with confusing and negative values is a serious complication to this process. Weapon carrying, smoking, drinking, drug use, fighting, and abusive language and behavior are all being modeled and promoted to youth in the media and in the adult behaviors they are seeing in their homes, communities, and at the national level. We cannot be surprised when they mirror back to us these same behaviors and reflect the values that these behaviors imply.

For those teenagers growing up in poor communities, this process is further complicated by the lack of visible economic opportunity. When the future looks bleak and there are few role models for economic success except unrealistic media images, there is often little to motivate a young person to adopt the values necessary for success and nonviolence. This in part explains the vulnerability of youth in poor and inner-city communities and the fact that the epidemic of violence began and grew more rapidly in such areas.

Lastly, as part of the separation process, teenagers are more greatly influenced by their peer groups than by their families or other adults in their lives. This can be a healthy phenomenon when the values of the peer group are prosocial and safe. However, when a peer group expects that fighting is the appropriate, if not the only, way to resolve a conflict, that puts a teenager at great risk. This is a common expectation among many peer groups, not just gangs. Often an argument starts in homeroom, and the insults and rumors are passed back and forth throughout the schoolday. Eventually, someone names the place, "three o'clock on the corner," and the pressure to fight escalates. At this point avoiding the showdown is nearly impossible because of the peer pressure from the "good kids," the nonfighters.

When teenagers are asked what their options are when they are angry or in conflict, two answers stand out: fighting and walking away. The problem is that walking away is for the most part a theoretical option. If a peer group has the expectation that fighting is the way to respond and has gathered to egg the fight on, then there is little choice. Walking away means losing face, and for most teenagers is not a real option. Boston child psychiatrist Alvin Poussaint has characterized this situation as being a choice between losing face for a moment and being dead for the rest of your life.[13] Unfortunately, many teenagers are not able to envision the seriousness of this choice or fully understand the consequences. Peer pressure is a very powerful factor in the lives of teenagers; it has enormous potential for positive effects if properly directed and guided but can result in severe negative consequences when the values surrounding adolescents are as negative as they are in this country.

Confronting These Factors

We, as a society, need to recognize the vulnerability and fragility of children going through this most difficult developmental stage and create a protective and nurturing context in which all young people can grow and develop.

Understanding the risk factors (the windows that have lined up on the slot machine) suggests important prevention strategies, illustrates the complexity of the problem and the need for a multiplicity of strategies, and reduces helpless or hopeless feelings. It is equally important to recognize and understand the factors that promote resiliency and are protective of children exposed to the risk factors. As noted earlier, most children living in poverty are not violent. Many children exposed to violence in their homes do not commit violent acts. Television violence does not affect everyone in the same way. All adolescents have vulnerabilities brought on by developmental changes, but most do not resort to violence. Clearly, resiliency factors play an important part in this picture. Increasing the number of children with resilience can only help to lessen the level of violence among youth in this country.

Resiliency

Unfortunately, we know far less about resiliency than risk. It is easier to study situations that have gone awry than to study factors that led to nothing bad happening. We do, however, have some understanding of resilient kids from studies of youth and adults who have achieved success even when coming from difficult, high-risk backgrounds. This knowledge is as important in creating effective programs as understanding the factors that create risk. Toxic environments exacerbate risks and reduce resiliency. Effective prevention reduces risks and promotes resiliency by creating nurturing environments.

First and foremost among the protective factors is the presence of a stable, positive emotional relationship with an adult. Who this adult is—a parent, a relative, a neighbor, a teacher, an outreach worker, a church member, and so on—may not matter as much as the simple fact of this person's being there. The presence of a nurturing, caring adult appears to be of great significance to almost every child. The presence of such a relationship promotes resiliency; the absence leaves a child open and vulnerable to negative influences. An evaluation of Big Brothers Big Sisters, for example, demonstrated the efficacy of mentoring programs even in the short range. The evaluation was scientifically very strong and showed that within eighteen months of receiving a big brother or big sister, the children improved on several outcomes, including school attendance and onset of experimentation with sex and drugs.[14]

Building on Success

Above and beyond this crucial factor are several other characteristics of children that telegraph their likelihood for success. Children who experience success in their lives are likely to continue to be successful and overcome adversity. Although this sounds obvious, it requires that children be given opportunities to be and feel successful. This isn't always as simple as it seems. It requires that the adults around children understand their developmental capabilities and expose them to tasks they can master. It also requires that kids who have innate disabilities be given specific opportunities to experience success, which may be different from the opportunities other children may need.

Similarly, children with the skills to thoroughly analyze their environment are able to manage and master that environment more successfully. Society's investment in maximizing the cognitive or intellectual development of children is essential and has a huge return. Necessary actions include reducing exposures that impair intellectual ability (such as lead poisoning) and increasing exposures that enhance development (such as attending Head Start programs).

Children who have the skills to actively approach challenges do better than children who passively react to stress. Imparting skills to parents so they can teach their children active problem solving can promote resilience. Incorporating, into early intervention, preschool, and school programs, curricula that promote active and proactive behaviors for facing challenges will as well. We have to get past teaching just academic content and what is right and wrong to also teaching process. How children learn to approach problems and tasks is as important as learning to read and add.

A Nurturing Environment

Lastly, children do better when they exist in nurturing environments. Feeling safe, loved, and supported promotes healthy behaviors and constructive coping mechanisms. The manner in which children are treated in their homes, their schools, and their communities can greatly influence the kind of teenagers and adults they become. This requires a greater level of child focus in our communities and even in our schools and requires that we provide more substantive support to families so they can better nurture their children.

People are not innately or biologically programmed to use violence when angry or facing conflict; we learned to do so, and we teach our children to do the same. The fight or flight response, which is biological, is designed to protect us from danger. The fact that conflict, in a context of poor conflict resolution skills, generates escalating anger and ultimately danger, is cultural not biological. What we must be aware of, however, is the strong evidence that this learning process occurs in many areas of a child's life and at very early ages. For this reason, changing this learning process involves addressing the many situations within which learning violent behaviors occurs. It also requires a better understanding of the situations and experiences that are protective or that instill resiliency and enhance the opportunities for children to be exposed to positive learning.

Ultimately, it is a mix of risk and resiliency features that affects the outcomes for individual children as well as for communities. We don't want these factors to line up by chance as the windows in a slot machine do. We want to make a conscious effort to maximize the number of protective windows appearing and to minimize the risk windows.

No one program or discipline is going to make this happen. To imply, for example, that the police, or the entire criminal justice system for that matter, can fix the current conditions is foolhardy. Similarly, in the context of all the recent highly publicized school violence, expecting the school system to take on what is a societal and broad community problem would be setting that system up for failure.

We do not yet have all the answers, and some of the things that need to happen will require serious changes in long-standing public policies and cultural values that are controversial, to say the least. But knowing the underlying risk and resiliency factors is an important first step to discovering and implementing solutions. There is no need to feel helpless or hopeless about the violence sweeping the nation. There are identifiable contributing factors that can be changed if we face up to the public policy and professional practice choices before us.

Turning the tide of the epidemic of youth violence facing this country requires the commitment, effort, and participation of all sectors of this country. In an avalanche, all snowflakes are responsible.

Chapter Five

Guns

Escalating the Consequences

The *Los Angeles Times* published a report on the public costs stemming from the shooting of a teenager in South Central Los Angeles, who is now a paraplegic as the result of a gunshot wound. The costs of the initial response at the crime scene, which involved the fire department, paramedics, police officers, and a helicopter, were $7,624. The hospital charged $34,794 for the first stage of treatment. The *Times*'s estimated cost of additional police investigation and subsequent arrests was $5,999. The teenage paraplegic incurred additional medical charges of $126,603. The public paid $11,627 for the preliminary stages of criminal proceedings and $1,200 for a hospital social worker. The total cost of the trial, incarceration, and appeal was estimated to be $352,649. In addition, the lifetime cost of medical care, disability payments, and special counseling and education classes for the victim was estimated at $490,302, resulting in a total cost of $1,030,798.[1]

When either of us speaks around the country on the subject of youth violence and violence prevention, one topic always provokes a dramatic and complex response. That topic is guns. Only the issue of spanking children evokes reactions that rival those to the topic of guns. Depending on the location of our talk and the audience, reactions range from standing ovations to boisterous boos to deafening silences. This is clearly one of the most controversial issues facing our nation; one that has dramatically polarized the citizens of this country. Yet it is an issue central to the epidemic of violence and, in particular, to the severity of injuries resulting from that violence.

The Tragic Facts and Figures

Every day approximately ninety people die from gunshot wounds in the United States, including four to six juveniles. Thirty-three percent of all murdered juveniles are under age six, 30 percent are female, 47 percent are black, 56 percent are killed with a firearm, and 40 percent are killed by a family member. On the day fifteen children died in the Columbine High School massacre, another seventy-five people also died from gunshots.[2] In 1995, the Centers for Disease Control dedicated $2.6 million to conduct research on gun-related injuries (the peak year of such funding), compared to $800 million for research on automobile safety. Researchers know more about dog bite injuries than they do about gun injuries.

Juveniles, those five to fourteen years of age, are six times more likely to be murdered in the United States than are juveniles in the other twenty-five wealthiest nations in the world. They are seventeen times more likely to be murdered with a gun; two times more likely to be murdered by other means. Juveniles in this country are also two times more likely to commit suicide than are juveniles in the other twenty-five nations, and those who do commit suicide are ten times more likely to do so with guns. Furthermore, juveniles in this country are nine times more likely to die from unintentional (accidental) gun injuries than are juveniles in the other twenty-five countries.[3] Over 40 percent of the households in the United States have guns. About one-third of households with children have guns, and of these households, over 40 percent store their guns unsafely.[4]

Not Just Bloody Noses

It is extremely unlikely that the epidemic of youth violence would be viewed as a national issue, let alone a crisis, if it involved thousands of children and youth experiencing bloody noses and other forms of minor injuries as a result of fighting. We would not see the oversized headlines in newspapers, the dramatic magazine covers, the consistent lead stories on the television news, the abundance of task forces and commissions, and the millions of dollars in federal and foundation funding for programs addressing violence and violence prevention. Youth violence would be relegated to the long list of minor issues that get occasional attention and human interest stories. One of the major reasons, if not the major reason, for the high level of attention given to youth violence is the seriousness of the injuries resulting from this violence. The primary factor contributing to these severe consequences of violence is guns.

Without the extensive use of handguns, the number of violent deaths in general, and among youth in particular, would be substantially lower. The dramatic increase in violent deaths and severe injuries from violent altercations over the past several decades is almost entirely the result of the increased availability and use of handguns during arguments and fights among teenagers. Children, youth, and adults are afraid. These fears often lead to increased handgun purchasing and carrying.

An increase in the availability of guns greatly increases the likelihood of those guns being used in anger or for that matter in a variety of other situations involving revenge, depression, and substance use and abuse. Guns, used in homicides and suicides and unintentional deaths, have become second only to automobiles as the instruments involved in the deaths of children ages ten through nineteen.[5] If current trends continue, guns will surpass automobiles as the leading cause of death of children in this age group early in this new millennium.

The use of firearms in juvenile homicides was common in the 1990s for both black victims and white victims. Homicides of older juveniles (ages fifteen to seventeen) were more likely to involve a firearm than were homicides of adults. In addition, between 1980 and 1997, 77 percent of juveniles ages fifteen and older who were killed by another juvenile were killed with a firearm.[6]

Guns are involved in over three-quarters of the violent deaths of teenagers in this country. Furthermore, guns are increasingly responsible for a growing number of nonfatal severe injuries among youth. Some communities are reporting that they are seeing more spinal cord injuries from gunshot wounds than from any other cause, a phenomenon that was rare not so long ago. And although this nation has begun to see a decline in violent deaths, severe injuries, and possibly gun carrying behavior among its youth over the past several years, the numbers continue to be way too high and remain unacceptable, especially when compared to the figures for other industrialized countries.

The Prevalence of Handguns

From the start, we need to point out several key elements of our thinking on the issue of guns and violence among youth. When we discuss this issue, we are specifically addressing handguns, which are far and away the most problematic weapons involved in serious violent injuries. Other types of guns are also involved in violent deaths and injuries, but when one looks at youth homicides involving guns, handguns predominate. If the number of handguns in circulation was reduced and access to these specific guns was reduced, we strongly believe that the number of violent deaths in this country would fall substantially. Comparison studies that evaluate homicide rates and handgun availability across cities strongly support this conclusion.[7]

We also believe that the issue of handguns has two important components. One is the issue of access to and availability of handguns. The other is the attitude that exists among many people in all regions of this country toward handgun ownership, an attitude that reflects what seems to be a national love affair with gun ownership. Both of these components need to be considered and addressed because the price of gun violence is increasing. Dealing with one without the other will not resolve the contribution that guns make to the epidemic.

Neither of us has anything against guns for hunting or any other recreational uses. To be up front about it, neither of us is a fan of recreational gun use, but we also see nothing innately wrong with the ownership and use of guns for recreational purposes. What we do take serious issue with and have grave concerns about is the widespread ownership of guns for self-protection, which often leads to self-harm or even provocation of violence instead of self-defense when the intent is to use the gun to harm another person.

Guns Replacing Common Sense

Often, in support of gun ownership, friends and colleagues tell "self-defense" stories that raise serious concerns for us. A woman physician in a large southern city told us that she was driving her convertible, late model, very expensive sports car home at 2:00 A.M., and while she was stopped at a red light a group of young men attracted to the car started coming toward her. She said, "I didn't know what they wanted but I wasn't going to find out either, so I reached in the glove compartment and pulled out my gun. They were frightened and ran away." This story raises an important question: why didn't she just pull off? At 2:00 A.M. there doesn't seem to be any need to stay at a red light and have a confrontation when you are in a car and can leave. It seems that only a person with a gun would feel enough courage to stay and wait for a confrontation. This woman was lucky, because this episode could have ended differently. If she had felt she had to use the gun, she would have found that even if she wasn't harmed herself, her life would have been tremendously affected once she had injured or killed someone because she made an assumption that he intended to harm her.

Another such story was told to one of the authors by an executive of a gun-lobbying group with moderate views compared to the National Rifle Association (NRA). He was on an expressway in a Southern state that allows licensed carrying of guns when a truck tried to run him off the road. He and the truck driver both pulled over (it wasn't clear who pulled over first), and the truck driver got out and started coming toward him. He said, "All I had to do was wave my gun at him and he ran back to his truck and sped off." Here again it is clear that there were other options. The main one being to get away once the truck driver pulled off the road. Only a person with a gun would have the courage to wait for the confrontation. What if the other man had emerged from his truck shooting? We think that stories like these illustrate the way a gun can cause people to have a false sense of security and courage and fail to choose the safer and most obvious method of self-defense. When someone you don't know and probably will never see again is "after" you, get the heck out of danger ASAP.

The Problem

It is important to lay out the big picture with respect to gun ownership and availability in the United States. This country is the most "armed" nation in the world. Personal gun ownership is dramatically higher in this country than in almost any other. It is estimated that there are over two hundred million guns currently in circulation in the United States. Of these, about sixty to eighty million are handguns. Approximately one-third of these handguns are unregistered and therefore untraceable. That is a lot of guns.

Until recently there were more gun dealers in this nation than gas stations. The Brady Bill helped to change this by increasing the cost of registering as a gun dealer and by requiring a more rigorous review of dealership applications. Applying for a license (good for three years) for gun dealership currently involves filling out a relatively short questionnaire, sending it into the Federal Bureau of Alcohol, Tobacco, and Firearms (ATF) with a check for $300 (the fee was $10 before the passage of the Brady Bill in 1994), and awaiting a response. The ATF has approximately 400 employees to deal with alcohol, tobacco, and firearms issues. If the application is not reviewed within sixty working days, it is automatically approved.

Even with the increased rigor of licensing review, in any given year thousands of gun dealer license applications are submitted and only a relatively small number are disapproved. There are still a lot of gun dealers, approximately 90,000. The manufacture and sale of guns is very big business in this country. And the Brady Bill did nothing to stop, limit, or regulate private gun sales and sales at gun shows.

The regulation of gun sales in this country is split between the federal and state governments, and state gun sale regulations vary widely. Some states have fairly lax gun regulation statutes; others are stricter. Some states, such as Texas and Florida (with others considering similar laws), have passed laws that permit the carrying of concealed weapons; many other states have passed laws that specifically disallow concealed weapons. Most states do have laws forbidding minors to own, carry, or purchase guns. Although national law (the Brady Bill) requires background checks before gun sales, many loopholes exist, particularly with respect to private sales. Very few types of guns are actually banned from sales, and almost no bans exist for handguns. It is pretty much an open market, and almost anyone can buy a handgun if he or she desires to do so. This is not true in almost any other nation.

A Right to Carry Handguns? No, a Wrong

The Second Amendment states: "A well regulated Militia, being necessary to the security of a free State, the right of the people to keep and bear Arms, shall not be infringed." This amendment, which is always invoked when gun sale regulation is considered, speaks to the right of states to maintain armed militias. Most people seem not to know this, primarily as the result of the extensive and effective campaign of misinformation carried out for decades by gun lobbyists like the National Rifle Association. However, the belief in the individual's right to own guns is deeply embedded in U.S. national culture, irrespective of what was said or what was intended by the writers of the Bill of Rights.

[Timothy Joe] Emerson was indicted by a federal grand jury on December 8, 1998, on five counts of possessing numerous firearms in violation of federal law while subject to a divorce court's order restraining him from threatening his wife and daughter. Emerson was indicted for illegally possessing not only two 9mm pistols, but a military issue, semi-automatic M1 carbine, a semi-automatic SKS

assault rifle with a bayonet, and a semi-automatic M-14 assault rifle.
Mr. Emerson had brandished a weapon in front of his wife and child
and had confided to co-workers that he had an AK-47 at his office
and he just needed bullets. After he got the necessary ammunition,
he said he planned to visit the city where his estranged wife and her
boyfriend lived. Appealing his indictments, Mr. Emerson claimed
that the Second Amendment protected his right to own firearms
despite his violation of a 1994 statute barring persons subject to
domestic-violence restraining orders from possessing guns.

· ·

[In 1999, a district court in *U.S. v. Emerson*] dismissed Timo-
thy Joe Emerson's federal indictment for possessing a firearm while
under a domestic-violence restraining order as violating Mr. Emerson's alleged right to own firearms under the Second Amendment.
This decision [flew] in the face of long-standing Supreme Court
precedent holding that the Second Amendment protects only the
right to bear arms as part of an organized state militia. . . . Specifically, in *U.S. v. Miller*, 307 U.S. 174 (1939), the Supreme Court
said in a unanimous decision that the Amendment protects only
conduct bearing "some reasonable relationship to the preservation
or efficiency of a well-regulated militia." All other federal court
decisions since *Miller* have confirmed that view.

· ·

Other courts have similarly refused to adopt the *Emerson* court's
flawed reasoning. On March 30, 1999, a federal court in Kansas
declined to "apply the Second Amendment so as to guarantee [a]
right to keep an unregistered firearm which has not been shown to
have any connection to the militia." *U.S. v. Boyd*, 52 F. Supp.2nd
1233 (D. Kan. 1999). On June 14, 1999, a federal court in West Virginia rejected a defendant's claim that the *Emerson* decision man-
dated the reversal of his indictment under the same federal statute.
U.S. v. Henson, 55 F. Supp. 2d 528 (S.D.W.Va. 1999). Finding that
"defendant's reliance is misplaced," the court refused to apply the
Emerson decision because the Supreme Court "has held consistently

that the Second Amendment confers a collective, rather than an individual right to keep and bear arms."[8]

Handguns, specifically, have little recreational value. They can be used for target practice, which some consider fun. However, their main purpose, the reason for which they have been developed and designed, is to harm another person. They have no value as hunting weapons. Yet some of the ammunition that has been developed for handguns is more deadly and damaging to the body than ammunition that has been developed for military use. And the marketing of handguns is extensive, with some marketing campaigns now in place specifically "targeting" women as handgun consumers.

The Myth of Self-Protection

Handguns are marketed primarily as instruments for self-protection. This marketing creates the impression that owning a handgun greatly increases one's safety, particularly at home. The intended message is that having a handgun in your home will protect you and your family from outside invasion. A number of finely done scientific studies, such as the work of Arthur Kellerman at Emory University, refute this impression.[9] Such studies have found that having a handgun in your home is extremely dangerous. An available gun at home is far more likely to be used to kill you or a family member in the context of a suicide or homicide than to be used to protect family members from an intruder. Kellerman, for example, discovered a three times greater chance of a homicide and a four times greater chance of a suicide in U.S. homes with guns as compared to U.S. homes without guns. A gun is also more likely to be stolen than used for a protective purpose.

Furthermore, the message that owning a gun is protection from intrusion runs counter to messages promoting the safe storage of handguns in the home. Separating the gun from the ammunition, locking the gun and the ammunition up separately in storage boxes, and hiding them away in separate places defeats the purpose of self-defense. If one wants a gun for protection, the safe storage process doesn't make any sense. That gun needs to be readily available. It needs to be loaded and accessible. And that is exactly what happens far too often (in as many as 50 percent of households with guns). The loaded gun is kept in the bedroom night table drawer or other equally accessible places. The obvious problem is that keeping a loaded handgun so accessible also makes it available to be stolen, taken by a child or teenager, or used in anger or in extreme depression. That most likely wasn't the intent when the handgun was purchased, but intended or not, that is what happens. The result is a chronically dangerous situation.

Despite the toll that handguns are taking across this nation, the response in terms of gun regulation, or the lack thereof, has been most disturbing. Despite what have now become numerous, highly publicized, gun-related massacres in schools in every region of this country, gun regulation efforts have not been able to overcome the heavily financed and powerful gun lobbies. We do have the Brady Bill, which was an important first step in handgun regulation, and the withdrawal of a few state-level referendums that would have permitted the possession of concealed weapons. California recently banned "Saturday Night Specials" (so called because they are inexpensive to manufacture and therefore inexpensive to purchase), but most regulatory initiatives at the state and national level are stalled or regularly fail to gain passage.

> Mount Morris Township, Michigan—A 6-year-old girl was shot to death in her classroom Tuesday [February 29, 2000] by a first-grade classmate with a stolen handgun, authorities said.
>
> Kayla Rolland died at 10:29 A.M. of a single gunshot wound to the chest after being rushed to Hurley Medical Center by Emergency Medical Service workers, who said she was in cardiac arrest. The suspected shooter was a 6-year-old boy who pulled a handgun

from his pants pocket and fired one shot, Mount Morris Township
Police Chief Eric King said.[10]

Could there be a more compelling reason to restrict handgun sales
and ownership in this country?

The failure of the United States to deal effectively with the regulation of handguns is even more perplexing in light of international comparisons. For example, the United Kingdom, after a
single school shooting episode (in a school in Scotland), passed
one of the strictest gun regulation laws in the world. There you
cannot even transport a handgun from a gun club to your home.
The gun must remain locked up in the gun club. Yet in the United
States, repeated, unspeakably horrible events have aroused little
action to address handgun accessibility.

When we get calls from the foreign press for interviews after
each school shooting, the manner in which we are asked questions
about gun policy in this country is quite revealing. Commonly the
question is phrased something like this, "What is wrong with people in your country that they are unwilling to address gun control?"
This is far from an objective way to ask a question and an atypical
phrasing for most questions from most reporters in the United
States and in other countries. What this reflects is just how incred-
ulous people in other countries find this situation. People around
the world seem to be shaking their heads in disbelief.

The social and cultural messages that promote gun ownership,
carrying, and use in the United States are extensive. Guns are
increasingly being marketed as a primary form of self-protection
and an essential component of home and family protection. One
need only consider the advertisement for handguns that has been
displayed in a number of magazines, and that we mentioned earlier,
showing a young mother looking down at her infant lying in a crib
to understand the degree to which this has evolved. This advertisement also has a picture of a handgun and a caption that suggests
that owning a handgun is part of the way in which this mother can

protect her child. What an incredible message to convey in such a manipulative manner, not to mention the serious danger that may be at hand for those that buy the message and the handgun.

Heroes Carry Big Guns

Gun use is extensively promoted in the media as well. Heroes and villains all carry and regularly use guns. The heroes often choose gun violence as their primary option for resolving problems, are usually successful, and rarely experience any significant or painful consequences. The villains are often killed or hurt, again generally without pain, and there is little or no remorse for their unfortunate fates (on the contrary, there is often a sense of glee). Again, as with the handgun advertisements, the message is clear, forceful, and dangerous. Handgun ownership and use is acceptable, valued, and gets you what you want, and it also determines your freedom as sup- posedly prescribed by the founding fathers, according to the NRA.

It is foolish to think that children are not influenced by these messages and behave accordingly. It should also not be surprising to learn that children and teenagers show up in hospital emergency rooms with gun shot wounds and sometimes state that they weren't expecting so much pain. They have seen so many people shot on television, in cartoons, and in the movies without demonstrating pain. Children have the rather bizarre impression that there is lit- tle to no pain involved with such injuries.

The nature of the public debate on this issue doesn't help either. Episode after episode of highly publicized violence occurs, followed by debate and angst over the easy accessibility of guns in this country yet with little change in public policy. Gun control discussions and arguments are commonplace, with the primary message being that right of gun ownership supersedes almost every- thing else including safety. This situation is compounded by the growing number of public referenda and state laws allowing the car- rying of concealed weapons. Again, it is foolish to believe that this goes unnoticed by youth, and the result is even further legitimiza- tion of having and using a gun.

Many people still believe that guns are not an issue in their community and that the problem resides only in inner cities. Yet guns are endemic in almost every community in this country. Almost half of the households in the United States have a gun. An impressive number of teenagers have or believe they have access to guns if they want them. And many of the gun-owning households also have children. Surveys suggest that as many as one-quarter of high school students carry guns at least on occasion, and although boys are more prominent in this picture, girls report gun carrying in significant numbers as well. Add this information to the highly publicized school shootings that have occurred in communities previously considered unlikely to have such a problem, including Jonesboro, Arkansas; Springfield, Oregon; and Littleton, Colorado, among others, and it is obviously incorrect for anyone to believe that his or her community is immune to or insulated from the issue.

What This Nation and Its Communities Can Do

As stated earlier, dealing with the epidemic of gunshot injuries and deaths involves addressing three major factors: gun availability, safety features, and the attitudes and values that promote gun ownership. In order to effectively address the problem, concerned groups and individuals need to consider and address all aspects of this situation. Dealing with one and not the other is likely to be ineffective and may create the illusion that something is being done when it isn't. Even if a strict ban on handgun sales were implemented tomorrow, it would be a century or more before the handguns currently in circulation were eliminated. Therefore, while all of us work to reduce access, we must also change attitudes.

Safety Features

Gun safety measures are important but have significant limitations. Gunlocks, for example, are effective only when they are actually used. If a handgun is kept in the home for protection, then it needs to be readily available, and removing a gunlock takes time. It is likely that many people will not want to create this barrier to quick access and use of the gun if they believe they need rapid access to the gun. A gunlock will also not prevent a handgun owner from using the gun in anger, and anger is often a factor in shootings. Furthermore, a number of the gunlocks on the market are easily removed and therefore ineffective.

Similarly, the development of guns that can be used only by the owner will have limited effectiveness for the same reason. Such a gun cannot be used if it is stolen, and children and teenagers will not be able to take it and use it. However, it can still be used by the owner himself or herself during an argument or in the context of a suicide attempt. Safer guns are better than nothing but will have, at best, limited effects on the violence epidemic.

From the regulatory perspective, a number of options should be considered in the area of accessibility to handguns. First and foremost is handgun control. This can be accomplished through the legislative process at both the state and federal levels. Although efforts to date have been relatively discouraging, it is important not to feel either hopeless or helpless about this. It is clear that this is a long-term battle. It must be fought, and the pressure to move this agenda along needs to be applied continually and vigorously. The growing number of highly publicized personal tragedies emphasizes the need to do something serious about handgun access.

Background Checks

The Brady Bill, which requires a background check and waiting period for handgun purchasers, was an encouraging first step and over time can lead to increased regulation of handgun sales. We must keep in mind that the limitations of the Brady Bill are significant. Background checks alone will not address the problem of gun accessibility and use. A majority of the people involved in shootings do not have backgrounds that would restrict their ability to buy guns. Remember that much of the gun-related violence that occurs stems from arguments between family members, friends, and acquaintances—not from criminals hiding in bushes and back alleys.

Nor will background checks be effective against the use of handguns in suicides, a large part of gun violence. Furthermore, the Brady Bill has some serious loopholes in that individuals can still buy handguns at gun shows and privately without any background check. The fact that the tragedies involving shootings in schools around the nation did not lead to stronger legislation makes it clear that new laws will take time but in no way implies that nothing more can be done.

Regulation

It is extremely important that grassroots efforts continue to promote stronger regulation. A number of national and local groups and coalitions formed over the past decade provide avenues for individuals to sign on to these efforts. Two such organizations are the Center to Prevent Handgun Violence (CPHV), chaired by Sarah Brady, which was founded in 1983 to reduce gun violence through education, legal advocacy, research, and outreach to the entertainment community, and the HELP (Handgun Epidemic Lowering Plan) Network, a program to reduce the incidence of handgun injuries and deaths that is based at the Children's Memorial Medical Center in Chicago, Illinois.[11]

It is clear that public opinion is very much behind these regulatory strategies, although that alone has not yet effectively countered the strong and well-financed activities of the progun lobbies such as the National Rifle Association. Among other things, these lobby groups have contributed large sums of money to the political campaigns of many state and national officials. This is one of the major reasons it has been so difficult to get gun regulation legislation passed in either state legislatures or Congress.

We should not forget, however, that elected officials are very sensitive to issues that affect their ability to get votes. Keeping the issue of gun regulation prominent in political campaigns and maintaining a vigorous, vocal outcry supporting the regulation of handguns will, over time, begin to counter the effectiveness of the money that the progun lobby continues to put out. We must keep up the energy behind the outcry against the easy access to handguns. Everyone who cares about the health and safety of children can, should, and needs to become involved.

Along these lines it is also essential that prevention advocates keep the debate clearly focused on handguns and not allow others to imply that there is any effort to limit all guns (such as hunting rifles). It is important to direct our energies toward addressing the major component of the problem. It is handguns that are the primary concern. The diffuse quality of the current debate is one of the things that is undercutting the effectiveness of the effort. There is a great need to help the nation understand that recreational gun use is not the issue.

Lawsuits

A second strategy beginning to be used in the effort to increase regulation of handguns is to bring cases of product liability before the legal system. This strategy, which has the potential to complement current efforts, is a relatively recent one that has begun to learn from the experience of the antitobacco movement. As that movement has succeeding in having the tobacco industry held accountable and liable for the consequences of smoking, so can the violence prevention movement attempt to have the gun manufacturers held accountable for the consequences of gun violence.

> On November 30, 1999, Judge Jennifer Duncan-Brice of the Circuit Court of Cook County, Illinois, issued a decision giving an important legal victory to families of shooting victims suing the gun industry for creating a public nuisance by making thousands of handguns available to children in Chicago. *Ceriale v. Smith & Wesson Corp.*, No. 99L5628 (Cook County, Il. 1999). . . .

The case arises from three murders, each committed with a handgun by a person under 18 years of age. Andrew Young stopped his car at a traffic light and died because two gang members with a gun mistook him for a member of a rival gang. Salada Smith was several months pregnant when she became the innocent victim of a drive-by shooting. Chicago police officer Michael Ceriale died in the line of duty from a bullet fired by a 16-year-old gang member. . . .

Like the lawsuits against the gun industry brought by cities and counties, the case relies on the law of public nuisance, under which a defendant is liable for conduct that creates an unreasonable interference with the public's right to health, safety, peace, or comfort. The shooting victims' families allege . . . that the gun companies' marketing and distribution practices are designed to appeal to criminals and juveniles, that they have caused large numbers of guns to be funneled into an underground market where they become freely available to juveniles in criminal street gangs, and that the gun makers oversupply the areas surrounding Chicago in order to circumvent that city's strict gun ordinances, where handguns have been banned since 1982.[12]

Experience in this area to date is limited but encouraging. Several lawsuits have been filed and heard in court charging that gun manufacturers bear responsibility in gun-related injuries and deaths. One such case occurred in Brooklyn, New York, where a jury found in favor of several plaintiffs suing gun manufacturers in the deaths of individuals murdered with guns. At present over twenty municipalities (including Chicago, Boston, and New Orleans) have filed large suits seeking retribution for the toll that guns have taken on residents of their communities. More such efforts need to be considered. Amazingly, in Chicago, undercover police officers have gone into gun stores and have been able to buy guns with the creative assistance of a salesperson, despite not meeting legal requirements. Although Boston has dropped its lawsuit because of the expense, this strategy continues to offer promise.

Even though it is unclear what the overall outcome of such actions will be, this strategy has two important agendas. It will begin to give a strong message to gun manufacturers that the current situation will not continue to be passively permitted. It will also begin to place a financial burden on the industry from both legal expenses and liability awards. In addition, these actions help to educate the public about the risks of guns in homes and communities and provide another avenue through which people can voice their concern and anger. This can and will contribute to the sense of empowerment the general public needs to develop around the issue of violence committed with guns. And the gun manufacturers do not have the deep pockets to protect themselves that the tobacco companies have.

Legal Prosecution

Yet another strategy to address gun access is modeled by a program called the Youth Crime Gun Interdiction Initiative (YCGII), started in 1996 in Boston (and sixteen other cities) and based on the successful Boston Gun Project begun in 1994. The Boston Police Department and U.S. Attorney's Office initiated an effort to trace the origins of guns confiscated after being used in a crime. The activity proved successful in that a handful of sites of origin were identified that were responsible for a significant number of the guns used in criminal acts. Identification of these sites created an opportunity to reduce the flow into Boston of guns likely to be used for illegal activities. This was apparently a relatively easy program to implement, with concrete outcomes and collaboration from the Federal Bureau of Alcohol, Tobacco, and Firearms. The actual impact of the effort is hard to assess as it began after the decline in youth homicides had begun in the city, but this strategy is a part of the Boston success story.

Limiting the number of guns individuals can buy at one time or over a specific time period might also be helpful. This might limit the stockpiling of guns or curtail large gun purchases for distribution to groups. To date the progun lobby has thwarted such efforts.

Other Possibilities

A further strategy proposed to address access to guns is to increase the cost of ammunition through taxation. The assumption is that if ammunition is more expensive then fewer people will buy it. This, however, discounts the reality that gun violence is not limited to poor communities. Pretty much every school shooting in the past several years has occurred in an affluent neighborhood, where cost would be an unlikely modifier.

We must never forget that this issue is affecting every community in this nation and is in no way limited to poor inner cities. We also cannot discount the likelihood that more costly ammunition would lead to a black market for bullets that would at least partly counter the effectiveness of the strategy. However, raising the cost of cigarettes by raising taxes has been effective in reducing the number of smokers, as part of the broader, comprehensive anti-smoking effort.

Ultimately the most effective approach to limiting the availability of handguns will be strict regulation of handguns. We must remain focused and energetic. We must also remember that the debate around the regulation of handguns is directly linked to public attitudes about gun ownership and the strong belief that guns are effective instruments for self-protection.

Social Norms and Attitudes Must Change

Efforts to promote gun regulations are only half of the solution. With some sixty to eighty million handguns currently in circulation, even if strict regulation of handgun sales were implemented tomorrow, the problem would not go away. Furthermore, many handguns are well made and do not easily break. Therefore those handguns currently available will be around for a long time. We must begin to more actively address attitudes about gun ownership.

This is no minor undertaking. Gun ownership is deeply engrained in the culture of this nation. The perception that handguns are protective and frequently used to thwart threats to one's person is powerful even though it is a misperception. Strong and explicit public education about the risks of handgun ownership is essential. As noted earlier, having a handgun in your home substantially escalates your risk for homicide and suicide. Helping people to understand and accept this reality is the challenge. This is where the focus and opportunities lie at the local community level. The message needs to be that it is easier to childproof your gun, or better yet get rid of it, than to bulletproof your child.

Changes in public opinion and attitudes have generally been most effective when initiated at the community level. And there are many things that can be done. Local media, schools, public forums, and community leaders' involvement are key avenues for these activities. Community strategies have been used with great success around issues such as tobacco use, seat belt use, and other safety and health-related agendas, and can be similarly used around the issue of guns.

One interesting example of community activity has been the creation of gun buyback programs. Although not very effective in removing large numbers of handguns from circulation, these programs have been an effective symbolic activity. The work of developing such programs can be contributed by many sources, including the police as well as community residents. In Boston one of the first gun buyback programs, in the early 1990s, was started through the efforts of a young man living in one of the poorest communities in Boston, South Boston. Michael McDonald had lost several of his brothers to guns, by both suicide and homicide.[13] He went public with his antiviolence efforts and eventually, in collaboration with the Boston police, initiated a gun buyback program that received considerable public attention and advanced the violence prevention efforts in the city.

To put this in perspective, in 1992 an FBI representative attending a conference told the authors that more than three decades of gun buyback programs across the nation have, in total, removed from circulation fewer handguns than are sold in six months in the United States. But this is not just a numbers game.

What these programs have done is to highlight at the local level the concern about handgun availability. These efforts generally attract a great deal of local media attention and create an important platform for public discussion of guns. They also reduce at least slightly the number of handguns in individual communities, and this should not be dismissed. The bottom line is that any activity that keeps this issue in the arena of public discussion and gives it greater visibility is of value.

Professional Responsibility

The police probably know more about guns than anyone else in any given community. Increasingly, police have been speaking out on the issue of access to guns. They are more aware than anyone of the risk of guns. They certainly don't want guns in the hands of potential criminals, but they are also knowledgeable about the use of handguns by others in the context of arguments and violent altercations as well as suicides. Enlisting the police as allies in gun regulation efforts is crucial. Police are often involved in gun buy-back programs. They can also be enormously helpful in public and school-based educational efforts. By bringing their firsthand experience to the discussion, they supply a level of credibility that few others can.

Similarly, health care professionals bring important experience and credibility. Emergency room staff (physicians, nurses, social workers, and others) and trauma surgeons are particularly valuable. Their personal experiences with handgun injuries can make the issue of gun violence particularly real to others. Pediatricians, internists, family medicine physicians, obstetricians, and other frontline primary care providers have a unique opportunity to screen for the presence of handguns in homes and can play a role in educating families on the risks.

It is essential that the professional community play a role in efforts to educate the public on the risks of handgun ownership. Physicians, educators, human service and mental health providers, police and various criminal justice professionals, and others have the responsibility to identify and create opportunities to speak out on this issue. There are good data to draw from.

The research in this area is solid and convincing. If you have a gun in your home, its presence dramatically increases the risk of homicide and suicide. If that handgun is kept loaded and accessible (that is, unsafely stored), these risks are significantly greater. That is irrefutable. The frequency with which handguns are actually used for protection is extremely low, despite the claims of some rather poorly done studies. These are simple messages that can be regularly and consistently communicated by many members of the professional community.

Educational Strategies

Schools have been and continue to be key settings for educational interventions around safety. One of the best examples is that educating children about the importance of seat belt use has been an important factor in changing the behavior of entire families. In the past, educational strategies focused on gun safety have promoted safe storage and safe behavior around guns (one such curriculum is the National Rifle Association's Eddie Eagle GunSafe Program).[14]

However, this is a questionable approach at best. Children are not likely to influence adult gun storage behavior. Furthermore, children are generally curious beings who are greatly influenced by media messages promoting the use of guns. They are unlikely to respond to instructions to stay away from guns if guns are accessible in their environment. In fact, hidden camera observations of children have demonstrated that children know where guns are kept in their homes, touch the gun when they find it, and don't necessarily call an adult as they are instructed to do in the gun safety curriculum.[15]

Children, however, can be taught about the dangers of guns in their environment. Changing the attitudes of children toward gun ownership is an important part of influencing the broader attitudes of the general public. Identifying ways of effectively communicating this message to children is an important role and the responsibility of educators.

Alternatives to Zero Tolerance

"No tolerance" policies on gun carrying in schools are part of this agenda. These policies need to be nonnegotiable rules. However, the response when this behavior does occur is equally important. Expelling students who carry weapons is not the answer. Such behaviors are serious red flags that require interventions. Expulsion results in the loss of an important opportunity to help a child in need. Rather than being expelled, such students need to be provided with an appropriate evaluation and the subsequent services that address the underlying issues. Kicking students out of school doesn't make them go away. They are still in the community, often hanging out around the school. The danger is still there. Schools need to find more effective ways of ensuring safety and responding appropriately. Some possibilities include alternative school programs (which remove these students from a particular school but keep them in the system), counseling, in-school suspensions, and special education services when indicated.

An example of an alternative response, developed in the Boston Public School system, is the Baron Assessment Center. This referral center is for all students in the system found carrying any weapon, including a gun. At the center, students continue their academic work, receive a comprehensive multidisciplinary evaluation, and have a full follow-up and intervention plan developed for them. They then return to a school, not necessarily the one they came from, with services in place and a clear plan to assist the school personnel.

Everyone Has a Role

Local media have particularly powerful roles to play in educating the public about gun ownership risks. In general the media often sensationalize community violence, with murder stories frequently capturing lead story status in television news programs and grabbing newspaper headlines. Currently, local early evening news programs are like advertisements for gun ownership. Instead of educating people about the risks of guns, they scare people, giving them no solutions, no information, and no understanding of the problem.

Such news stories could be important opportunities for education on the role of guns in violent death and injury. It would require little effort on the part of print and electronic media to highlight the issue of gun accessibility and risk as part of these presentations. Furthermore, in the context of consumer affairs, which is a growing agenda for local media outlets, exposés on the risks of handguns in the home and stories on efforts to reduce gun availability in the community would be both educational and represent a valuable public service.

We know how powerful the media, and in particular television, are in influencing public attitudes and opinions. We should make good use of this power and maintain strong pressure on these community institutions to accept responsibility for such educational efforts.

Those working in youth programs have important access to a particularly vulnerable population. And they have the skills and experience to know how to package messages that are likely to be effective in communicating risks to young people. While they are dealing with drugs and alcohol, tobacco, and other risk issues, they need to incorporate the issue of guns as well. This is particularly important given the growing presence of guns in the lives of youth and the increasing risk that guns bring to the health and safety of teenagers.

Youth workers, coaches, recreation directors, and other individuals have this access and should identify opportunities to incorporate safety messages in their interactions with teenagers. Many such activities have been developed in Boston, using modified and adapted components of the Violence Prevention Curriculum for Adolescents (described in Chapter Two), developed under the

Boston Youth Program. There is no magic to this. It requires an understanding of the problem and the skills involved in working with youth.

This is not just the work of the professional community. Local community groups that often address issues of community safety and quality of life should place the issue of guns on their agendas. Traffic and street safety, community appearance, economic development, and quality of schools, among other things, are common issues for local clubs and organizations. Given the growing presence of violence and gun injuries in many communities, attitudes toward guns should be of great importance to such groups. Again, this involves an understanding that much of the violence in communities does not fit into the stereotype of armed criminals hiding in the bushes.

The efforts of one single program or group will not fix current attitudes toward guns or turn the epidemic of gun violence around. This requires the involvement of many. The strategies to be used include education, law enforcement, product liability cases in the courts, raising ammunition costs through taxation, and more rigorous gun registration, licensing, and regulation. It is the cumulative effect of all these efforts that will create change. The values and attitudes that support the extensive ownership of handguns and promote the dangerous misperception that handguns are tools of self-protection are deeply rooted in our culture. Changing them will take time, energy, persistence, and commitment.

Chapter Six

It's the Television, Stupid

Fort Lauderdale—The attorney for a 12-year-old boy accused of killing a 6-year-old playmate by slamming her onto a table and railing has subpoenaed a star professional wrestler to testify at the boy's upcoming trial.

Dwayne Johnson, the World Wrestling Federation's "People's Champion" known as "The Rock," was subpoenaed Friday by the attorney for Lionel Tate, who faces a first-degree murder charge for the July [1999] beating death of Tiffany Eunick.

Attorney Jim Lewis wants Johnson to show jurors how pro wrestlers pull punches, choreograph body slams, and synchronize their moves so they don't hurt each other while making the televised action appear authentic.

The boy was mimicking such moves, but didn't realize the injuries they could cause when he allegedly gave Tiffany a bear hug, dropped her onto a table and then swung her into the railing, Lewis said.

"I've got to be able to show the difference between what wrestlers appear to be doing and what they are actually doing, how it's designed to make people think it's real," Lewis said. "They're able to pull these punches; these guys just pummel each other and flip people over their heads and no one seems to get hurt."

. . . .

The [World Wrestling Federation] and its rival, World Championship Wrestling, have begun showing advertisements during their televised shows warning children not to imitate the wrestlers' moves.

Both said the ads are not directly related to Tiffany's death or any other incidents where children were injured mimicking wrestlers, including a Texas case where a 7-year-old boy accidentally killed his 3-year-old brother by hitting him with a forearm.

. . . .

"The problem is that kids and young adults can't differentiate between what they see on TV and reality," Lewis added. "They don't see any consequences attached to extreme violence."[1]

We find it hard to believe that the debate continues about whether or not television violence has a negative impact on children. One wonders if there isn't an industry-sponsored conspiracy to keep information away from the public, because the evidence for the impact is so extensive. The debate should have been over years ago, and corrective action should have been taken in full force. Violence on television and in the other entertainment media does have a significant impact, with long-term effects, on the attitudes, values, and behavior of children.

The scientific literature demonstrating this impact crosses a number of professional boundaries, is peer reviewed, and scientifically rigorous. It now contains thousands of reports, particularly on the impact of television, that validate what parents already learn the hard way via everyday experiences with their children's demands for brand-name products and their imitation of behaviors seen on TV. The effects are very very clear. Yet the debate rages on, and the popularity of violent movies, video games, and music appears to be increasing.

Ignoring the Facts

If, as we all have recently discovered, the tobacco industry conspired to keep the information on the addictive quality of nicotine and the links between cancer and smoking away from the public, then one can reasonably propose a media industry conspiracy to avoid airing the abundant information available in the social science literature on television's impact on children. Indeed, deliberate efforts appear to have been made to keep the debates roaring and fingers pointed at parents, at viewers—at anyone but the industry. This has kept the public confused and uninformed of the true scientific evidence.

At one time "researchers" for the industry even proposed a catharsis theory: that it is good for children to watch violent programming because it relieves them of their innate need to act violently. This was and is a preposterous idea that was never scientifically supported yet that surfaced and resurfaced to defend the industry for over a decade.

Today the television industry, the major conveyor of information to the American public, ignores the facts. Talk shows host programs on almost every other topic under the sun. Everything but the information regarding the impact of television on children is covered. If cigarettes and alcohol need warning labels, then the entertainment industry needs to promulgate the information known about the impact of its products on children. The recent agreement to voluntarily display ratings on the violent content of a program is not enough. Given the level of violence in programming specifically developed for and marketed to young children, much more needs to be done.

An argument often raised by members of the industry to justify using gratuitous violence is that people want it. Finger pointing at viewers, they suggest that humans are naturally attracted to violence. There is nothing that can be done about it, or so they argue. The industry claims its programs are merely reflecting life and giving the public what it wants. Its spokespeople refer to a "natural appetite" for violence. Actually, an appetite for violence is not natural but learned. It appears to be constantly reinforced by indulging in viewing violent entertainment. Some researchers have even suggested an addiction model to explain the appetite for violence.

Laugh tracks on cartoons teach children that violence is funny. Children also learn to laugh at violence from their peers. Together, these experiences teach children to perceive violence as entertaining. The more they watch, the more they learn this. This begins the development of a "taste" for violence, much as one develops a taste for certain foods and drinks. The industry lays a good foundation for a lifetime of violent entertainment without consequences, pain, death, or sorrow. This is the foundation for the so-called natural appetite for violence.[2]

As they learn to laugh at violence, over time children also become numb to their natural empathy for victims of violence. A documentary from the early 1990s illustrates such numbing by portraying a father taking his eight-year-old son hunting for the first time. The son is about to shoot a deer and starts to cry. The father puts his arm around the boy and reassures him, telling him to go ahead because though it's hard the first time, it gets easier each time after that. What is initially horrifying and frightening becomes enjoyable, exciting, and addicting. The appetite for violent programming is created by the violent programming and is constantly reinforced by the programming itself. Sounds like an addiction, doesn't it?[3]

As with many bad exposures, those least able to deal with them often get the biggest doses. Whether it's urban environmental exhausts and lead poisoning or alcohol advertisements and liquor stores concentrated in poor communities or children's exposure to violence, bad things happen with worse consequences to those already having a difficult time.

It is startling to ponder the class and race issues involved in the way the entertainment media handle the impact of violent programming, both in their reluctance to respond to the scientific evidence and in media portrayals of negative stereotypes of poor and racial minorities. Poor children watch more television and are more likely to have parents who are not reading the latest magazines and books on parenting. If television isn't a source of information on the negative impact of violent programming on children, then these parents will be the last to know.

The Double Standard for Children's TV: Violence Is OK, Sex Is Not

When violence was perceived as a problem only for urban poor, black, and Hispanic communities, the producers of violent entertainment took the position that if you can prove that this is bad, we'll consider changing what is produced. Interestingly, this position has not been taken with issues of sexuality. Although it is true that the images of sex and of women as objects in entertainment media are unhealthy, there has been general agreement that explicit sexual acts should not be shown to children.

The industry has not demanded studies in which children are shown explicit sex and then observed for negative impacts. The position has been "let's be safe and not sorry." Perhaps those who produce, write, or act for the industry perceive possible vulnerability or harm to their own children. And nothing is more personal to a parent than the vulnerability of his or her own child. Thus there is a heightened sensitivity among producers, explicit sex is labeled, parents are almost universally aware that children should not watch such programming, X-rated shows are not aired on prime time television, and there is no debate. Even what is shown on the general audience cable stations is shown very late at night when children are less likely to watch. The industry has, to some extent, policed itself. Not so with violence.

Until the recent school shootings, the risk that TV programs would foster violence was viewed as a threat only to those "others" who were poor or members of minorities or both. Most writers, producers, and advertisers did not think of this risk as important. Few had any personal reasons to be cautious (their children seemed safe); no forces countered the tremendous economic incentive to continue creating the formulaic and destructive violent programming. Demand for scientific proof of its damage countered the calls for change. Not so with sexuality.

Because of today's greater awareness of the vulnerability of all children to violence, we have an opportunity—a tragically late but nevertheless significant one—to have the industry place value on all children. We must now demand higher standards, accountability, and responsibility from the entertainment industry. Those in the media must acknowledge and promulgate the truth about children and violent television and reduce the number of violent images available to children. It is very sad that it took a string of horrible tragedies to get us to a point we should have recognized years ago.

Television Violence Is Bad for Children

Children in America watch a lot of television. Preschool children in the average American home watch television for 3 to 4 hours each day. Children between the ages of six and eleven watch about 23 hours per week, and adolescents twelve to eighteen years of age watch 22 hours per week. Unfortunately, the most vulnerable children, those between the ages of two and five years, watch more television than any other age group, about 25 hours of television each week. The average American two-year-old child spends an annual total of 1,440 hours, or sixty days, in front of the television. Between age two and the time that child finishes high school, he or she will have spent almost three years watching television. During this time that child is also watching an enormous quantity of violence.

Albert Bandura was one of the first to study the effects of TV on children. As early as 1963 he concluded that exposure to violent or aggressive action on film not only increases the viewer's aggressive behavior but also determines the type of aggression. The *aggressor effect*, sometimes called the *imitative effect* or *modeling response*, refers to the connection between viewing television violence and engaging in aggressive or violent behavior. It is one of the main concerns among experts on the subject. Just as some children who are witnesses to real-world violence come to view aggression and violence as normal and even expected, some children exposed to large amounts of violent entertainment increasingly tend to view violence as a solution to their problems or conflicts.[4]

Bandura's work has been followed by thousands of subsequent studies that have repeatedly confirmed this observation. Media violence is one of those windows in the slot machine, discussed in Chapter Four. The overwhelming weight of the evidence from scientific studies is consistent and has been over the years: viewing violent television or having a preference for such television is related to aggressive attitudes, values, and behaviors. This result was true for the studies conducted when television was new and the measures of children's aggression were teachers' ratings. It is still true for more recent studies (which number in the hundreds) with measures of aggressiveness that are substantially more sophisticated.[5]

There is even strong evidence that very young children (infants and toddlers) imitate behavior they see on television. One study found that 65 percent of children as young as fourteen months were able to imitate the actions of an adult in an instructional video and manipulate a novel toy whereas only 20 percent of those who didn't watch the video could do so.[6]

Violence Without Consequences

It does appear that the context in which the violence occurs, what happens to the shooter after he kills someone for example, significantly affects the impression that the violent act has on the viewer. Leonard Eron, one of the better-known researchers on this topic, has concluded that the contextual presentation in which the violence occurs influences the degree to which the viewer is adversely affected.[7] How much the viewer identifies with each character (aggressor or victim) and the viewer's perception of the realism of the violence or aggression determine the extent of adverse impact.

If the violence is successful and rewarded, then the viewer feels excited by and supportive of violence in general. If, however, the violent character shows some feelings of guilt, redemption, or suffering as a result of his action, the viewer begins to see the violence and its consequences in a broader, more realistic context. Showing realistic consequences of violence or alternatives to violent behavior teaches much more valuable lessons to the viewer than the sanitized, successful, and entertaining violence that is currently shown so often on television, in cartoons, and in films.

Greater perceived realism is attributed to television by those younger in age, those whose friends and families appear to judge television to be like real life, and those who view greater-than-average amounts of television. Young viewers are more likely to be frightened and influenced by violence that is forcefully presented, involves household instruments, threatens a familiar or empathetic character, or occurs in a familiar environment. Although young children may be initially frightened by television violence, they are particularly vulnerable to imitating and learning the behaviors they observe. They do not draw boundaries between fantasy and reality. They are not developmentally prepared to handle these messages.

Eron and others, in an observational study, followed a group of children from age eight to adulthood.[8] They found that the more television aggressive boys viewed during childhood, the more likely they were to have been arrested as adults. Aggressive boys who didn't watch a lot of television had fewer if any arrests. Increased violence viewing as a child was also correlated with an increased tendency, years later, to abuse one's spouse and to use physical punishment to discipline children.

Although children of all ages are widely and constantly exposed to the violence in standard television programming, it is particularly troubling that so-called children's programs often contain more violent acts than other television entertainment does. Some television monitoring studies have concluded that because of cartoon violence, children are exposed to more television violence than any other group. The average American child, for example, sees 12,000 violent acts each year on television.[9]

Boys have generally been thought to be more adversely affected by television violence because violent behavior is usually exhibited by male characters. Many researchers have concluded that the difference in effects according to gender justified giving more attention to boys in their research. However, recent studies show that girls are also adversely affected, although in different ways. A 1986 meta-analysis (an analysis of the results of multiple studies), suggests that the effect of aggressive role models and violence on television is significant for girls but must be measured differently because female characters on television have not been as aggressive as male characters. Even though girls who are heavy viewers of television violence may show a tendency toward aggressiveness, they do not display aggressive behaviors or attitudes in the same way as boys. They tend to show more subtle forms of antisocial behavior such as anxiety, irritability, and intolerance of delay.[10]

The Most Vulnerable Are Often the Most Exposed

To a large degree television defines reality for children. This is especially problematic for younger children (because they have greater difficulty distinguishing between reality and fantasy), children in disadvantaged socioeconomic circumstances (because they tend to watch greater amounts of television), and minority children (because people of color are generally underrepresented or inaccurately represented on TV). The entertainment media often feed on and perpetuate stereotypes and fears about others based on race, class, and ethnicity. The most ill-fated and least empathetic characters on television are likely to be poor, Latino, African American, or foreign born. They are also more likely to be male than female. In the world of television programming, a significantly disproportionate number of criminals, murderers, suspects, and perpetrators of violence come from these groups.[11] According to one study, both white and black children are affected by negative portrayals of African Americans.[12] In addition to adversely affecting the black child's sense of self, such negative characterizations also cause the white child to hold a lower estimation of the competence of African Americans.

Heavy viewers of television violence tend to have similar worldviews, including the tendency to perceive people around them as similar to television characters. Some call this acceptance of stereotypes the *mainstreaming* or *cultivation* effect. Heavy viewers of television violence often have especially distorted views of girls, women, and people of racial or ethnic minority groups. They are more likely to see the world as a mean place and are at risk for acting on these perceptions. George Gerbner is professor of telecommunications at Temple University and director of the Cultural Indicators Project, an annual monitoring and analysis of prime-time network television dramatic program content. He labels this phenomenon among viewers the *mean world syndrome.*[13] These individuals may overestimate the level of violence in their community, display irrational fears, be reluctant to leave home, accumulate weapons, and be socially isolated.

The evidence of television's role in America and in the problem of youth violence is overwhelming, and the task of changing the industry is huge. Concerned consumers who want different programming and better information for parents are up against many odds. The use of gratuitous violence is reinforced by economic incentives, the proven box office success of the formulaic violent storyline, and the international appeal of violence as entertainment.

What Can Be Done?

There are growing efforts to address the entertainment industry's typical portrayal of violence that have demonstrated some successes and should be applauded. Whether initiated by outraged parents, informed professionals, or concerned people in the industry, these efforts are coming together to change the industry. To date the numerous small impacts haven't added up to a significant change in the overall industry, but with time and continued effort things can and will change.

According to a survey by *U.S. News & World Report,* 63 percent of television executives say that violence is glorified in entertainment media, and they "feel a sense of responsibility about the influence violence in entertainment is having on American society."[14] Some top-level Hollywood figures attribute the industry's reliance on excessive violence merely to bad habits by those who conceive, write, produce, and air television programs.

Regulation

The 1999 acknowledgment and acceptance of self-regulation by the television industry represents the first time that this industry recognized and accepted responsibility for the link between television violence and aggression. This is major progress for opponents of violent programming, although it has done little to date to change the level of violence in children's programming. Because participation in this rating system is voluntary, compliance has been inconsistent and of varying quality.

The work of Action for Children's Television (ACT) was probably the earliest and most concerted effort to influence children's programming. ACT, now defunct, was a national grassroots organization founded by Peggy Charren and based in Newtonville, Massachusetts. ACT's goal was to ensure quality and diversity in television programming for children and adolescents and to eliminate commercial abuses directed at children. Charren played a major role in the passage of the Children's Television Act of 1990. This federal law, which was expanded slightly several years ago (1994), requires TV stations to offer educational programming for children for at least three hours per week. However, this law is not well enforced, and TV stations are taking a very generous cut at what they define as educational (including situation comedies and some cartoon shows). Although the impact of this law has been limited, the work of ACT was groundbreaking and opened opportunities for others to take up the torch.

Leadership in the Industry

Some individuals in the entertainment industry have also become involved in efforts to solve the problem of violent entertainment. At times this involvement has sprung from a personal tragedy.

One CBS executive's son was killed. The son was a school-teacher who had worked for many years in a public high school in the Bronx. Some young men from the neighborhood murdered him, and there was a subsequent outpouring of self-reflective writings by people in the media industry. The connections between television violence and the behavior of the young men were inevitable, and they were made. The irony of this was frequently the indirect subject of the news reports on the murder.

Bill Cosby, the well-known actor and comedian, had dedicated himself to working on this issue years before his son, Ennis, was murdered in 1997. Cosby teamed up with an informed professional from the Harvard Medical School and the Judge Baker Children's Center, nationally known child psychiatrist Alvin Poussaint, and intentionally used his weekly television show to promote prosocial attitudes and behaviors. Poussaint read each script for its impact on mental health. We think that some process like this should become a prerequisite for all scripts. The decision to air a program would remain up to the station, but only after those responsible for this decision fully understood the public health risks or benefits of the program. Perhaps a private agency could give the mental health version of the Good Housekeeping Seal of Approval.

Media Literacy

An important area of work until programming changes occur is helping children understand the existing programming and its impact. *Media literacy,* having the skills to deal with media messages, is a strategy to counter media violence. Media literacy programs can teach skills children can use to mitigate the television message that violence is glamorous. Effective media literacy programs help children and adults to

- Analyze and thus reduce the effect of violent programming.
- Reduce their media exposure.
- Question the solutions to conflict that characters demonstrate, and explore alternative solutions.

- Understand the economic and political forces behind violent programming.
- Debate and discuss the issue of media violence in communities.

Children and adults (especially parents) alike can benefit by learning how to lessen the impact of TV violence in their lives.

Radio talk shows for young adults are one of the most recent efforts to provide an outlet that functions as an alternative to violence. KMEL, a radio station in San Francisco, for example, sponsors *Street Soldiers*, a radio show that encourages youth to call in and talk about the realities of the inner city. It allows youth the chance to express their anger, fear, and frustration to someone who will listen. The program host gives advice, encouragement, and offers various alternatives to violence. The show also offers links to community programs, services, and resources. A number of similar shows are appearing around the country.

The Center for Health Communication at the Harvard School of Public Health researches and analyzes the contributions of mass communication to behavioral change and policy. Media campaigns on the issue of drunk driving (Designated Driver) and violence prevention (Squash It!), produced by Jay Winsten, director of the center, rely heavily on collaboration with the media and proven public health methods to change behavior. According to Winsten, the keys to developing successful health promotion campaigns are to design simple target messages and to repeat these messages. Collaboration with managers of local media outlets is also important to determine the most effective times for airing messages and integrating them into local programming. Winsten also acknowledges that such media campaigns alone cannot change behavior and that such efforts need to be linked to broader strategies.

Parent Education

The National Institute on Media and the Family (NIMF) is a national resource for teachers, parents, community leaders, and other caring adults who are interested in the influence of electronic media on early childhood education, child development, academic performance, culture, and violence. It was founded in 1996 by David Walsh, a nationally recognized authority on family life, parenting, and the impact of media on children, and the author of *Selling Out America's Children: How America Puts Profits Before Values and What Parents Can Do*. NIMF is a response to the public's growing concern about the effects of media violence on children. Walsh and his colleagues focus on helping parents make positive media choices by developing ways to provide them with more and better information about the media.

NIMF has developed what it calls *children's impact statements:* independent, content-based evaluations of television programs, movies, video games, and computer games that are marketed to children or that children are most likely to see. These media products are evaluated for their amount and portrayal of violence, sexual content, use of language, and amount of danger and fear.

The children's impact statements are like "nutritional labels for the mind." They provide information that parents and viewers can use to evaluate what they should encourage or discourage for their children. The ratings give parents age-based guides to their children's entertainment.

Ratings

The institutionalization of clear, consistent, and reliable ratings can be a central element of dealing with TV violence. The fact that the major TV networks are even willing to discuss a self-imposed ratings system is something that a few years ago would have been described as wishful but unrealistic thinking.

Mediascope, Inc., headed by Marcy Kelly, is a national, nonprofit research and policy organization that deals with issues of social relevance in the entertainment industry. In 1996, Mediascope published the *National Television Violence Study*, which contained an analysis of television violence and a study of television ratings, advisories, and antiviolence messages, conducted in conjunction with the Universities of California, North Carolina, Texas, and Wisconsin.[15] The results of publishing this study were instantaneous. Within twenty-four hours of the release of the study findings, the major TV networks were talking about voluntary ratings, something they had been totally unwilling to do on every prior occasion that the FTC or media advocacy groups had pushed for it.

What was so compelling about the findings was that they showed the relative difference in effect the circumstances surrounding the portrayal of violence have on the viewer. Rather than considering all acts of violence to be equal—counting them up and publishing another study that oversimplified things by concluding that violent scenes are bad—this carefully conducted, scientifically rigorous analysis provided valuable insight into what made one violent scene potentially more harmful than another. Mediascope has been able to use research, publications, and other resources to provide producers, screenwriters and others in the entertainment industry with objective, timely information, and thus has become a credible resource and an effective link among the fields of public health, politics, and entertainment.

Biased News

Of course the entertainment media are not the only purveyors of violent scenes. Noting that the biased portrayal of news stories contributes to the problem of violence, some are working to change that aspect of the industry as well. People who view television news may think they are getting the truth, an accurate portrayal of what is going on in their community and society. But according to Paul Klite of the Rocky Mountain Media Watch (RMMW), they are getting a slanted and jaded view. RMMW, a media watchdog group that focuses on television news programs, was founded by activists with media and research skills in 1994, in response to the distortions they saw occurring on local news reports.[16] RMMW's activities are directed toward challenging the media to inform, educate, and connect communities. The organization conducts and disseminates research to policymakers, educators, journalists, academics, and individuals. It conducts national trainings to help activist citizens improve media skills and increase coverage of their issues. Though the organization is relatively new, it has had some success. One major television station in Austin, Texas, KVUE, has publicly announced new guidelines for reporting crime and violence. It is to be hoped that others will follow.

Although we believe that television is a large causative factor in the epidemic of violence, it is also clear that it is part of the solution. Media literacy, advocacy, and intentional efforts to produce informed and activist consumers are necessary. Fortunately, many people and groups have begun to offer solutions. Addressing violence on television and in other media is clearly a large and complex task. Reducing the quantity of violence and improving quality programming for children are essential parts of the solution. Using the media to promote healthy, safe values and behaviors is another component. Developing skills to better process and deal with the exposures to violence is yet another.

Some of this agenda involves advocacy at the national level to encourage media regulation and monitoring and to increase accountability among those producing and sponsoring programming. But change will also require community-level efforts to reduce viewing time, influence local media outlets, improve media literacy skills, and increase prosocial, healthy programming.

We believe that the greatest impact ultimately can and must come from within the media industry itself. Creating financially successful and socially responsible programming is the answer. Outraged parents, informed professionals, and concerned people in the industry need to make this happen.

Chapter Seven

The Demonization of Youth

Miners used to bring canaries down into the mines to act as a warning alarm for an inadequate oxygen supply. If there were a serious problem with the air, the canaries would pass out or suffocate before the miners did, allowing the miners to get themselves out of danger.

The danger faced by America's children is likewise a bellwether, signaling the toxic environment that without our concerted effort will eventually endanger us all. However, we adults, instead of changing ourselves, our professional practices, and our public policies to make the environment healthier and safer, have so far mostly chosen to demonize a few kids, the "bad kids." It has been easier and more politically expedient to make them the problem than to acknowledge that we are the problem. America's public policies and professional practices deal with these children as harshly as possible, and efforts to change laws so that they can be dealt with even more harshly are under way. America appears to be stepping deeper into this ill-conceived path of harsh strategies, rather than owning up to the real issues and real solutions.

The problem is harsh strategies do not work. The "bad kids" keep coming. And they are looking more and more like everybody's kids, like our own kids, like our next door neighbor's kids, like the "good kids." Focusing on harsher and harsher punishments for the bad kids is a losing proposition. It's a bit like trying to blame and punish the canaries for getting sick rather than getting them and us away from the toxic fumes of the mine.

Canaries are beautiful, fragile animals. Nevertheless, they were chosen for this important but hazardous task because the miners decided that human beings were more important than canaries. Thus the protection of human workers justified the sacrifice of canaries. However, this rationale fails when we use our youth as the canaries. The problem we thus create compounds when we then start blaming our children rather than heeding their warning.

It seems that unconsciously or unintentionally we have chosen our children to be a warning sign for danger. Why this is happening and what it means are two important questions that we as a community must answer if we are going to change the situation. A warning is due to all adults. Impending dangers to our children raise serious questions about who we are and what we value.

The U.S. problem with youth violence is serious and at epidemic levels, as the previous chapters have already conveyed. The epidemic of youth violence must be understood as a sign of deeper ills rather than a problem of bad kids. These deeper ills are a society entertained by violence, a society teaching its children to admire and laugh at violence, a society without properly trained professionals who are able to overcome personal bias and who have a full repertoire of behavior modification strategies at their fingertips, a society that places too much emphasis on money and too little value on the lives of children, a society that allows children to have access to guns and fails to make adequate efforts to change gun control laws or enforce existing laws, a society spending more on prison than on education—the list continues. What is really disheartening is that many elected officials continue to offer public policy changes that would take us further in the wrong direction.

Instead of valuing children beyond their potential as consumers and ensuring that they have "a healthy start, a head start, a fair start, a safe start, a moral start" (as Marian Wright Edelman, founder and president of the Children's Defense Fund, so often challenges America to do),[1] our culture blames and demonizes young people. We use negative, scary images of youth to sell movies, newspapers, television shows, and magazines. We look at youth as if they are responsible for all our ills. We act as if all would be well if only they would behave. If only we could get rid of the worst one hundred, the "bad kids," then we would no longer need to be afraid.

Glamorizing a Demonic Image

We consistently portray the wrong images of children and to children. "Our models can beat up your models" read a 1999 billboard caption used to advertise Levi jeans. Above the caption stood a group of young men dressed and positioned to look tough, ready for a fight—a gang.

Lest you think girls are left out, there is an ad using them too: a Marilyn Monroe–like model in a tough challenging pose above the same caption on free postcards. Clearly the company wants to sell jeans by associating wearing them with being tough and strong. The primary audience for this campaign is children.

We were moved to write an op-éd piece for the *Boston Globe* after Levi Strauss came up with this campaign. It was a blatant use of violence and tough images of kids to sell a commodity, with little regard for its impact on adolescents' images of themselves or adults' images of adolescents. Unfortunately, using a tough, violent, and seedy image to sell clothing or other items is not uncommon. Similar images are used every day to attract children to buy clothing, toys, video games, food and snacks, colognes, and almost everything else manufactured for them.

Along with their products these manufacturers also sell a set of values. Children are not only buying pants, they are buying the image, a belief system, and a way of behaving that is putting their lives at risk. Not only do these portrayals of adolescents create the wrong images for youth to imitate but they may also diminish adult empathy and concern for adolescents' problems.

What concerned adults find extremely frustrating is that despite what is known about the impact of such images on children and the larger society, the adults who control marketing strategies have continued to produce increasingly provocative and inflammatory ads. If anything, these images have gotten worse despite the

American epidemic of youth violence. While children were being shot and killed in urban America, adults were creating these ads. While children are being shot and killed in schools in middle-class and small-town America, adults continue to create these ads. What will it take to cause us all to feel responsible and to change?

For several decades we all have seen children and youth in urban America fight and even kill each other over articles of clothing such as hats, sneakers, and other minor things. We have watched this epidemic grow and spread throughout every community in this nation. We are now watching younger and younger children and more and more girls behave in violent ways we would have never imagined. Children do imitate these role models, these glamorized and idealized tough violent images.

Parents Cannot Overcome This Alone

Many adults are content to have an unregulated society and leave the protection of children up to their parents. Parents are then expected to counter and mitigate the negative influences. It's clear that parents cannot do this alone, but they can be a catalyst for change. Those adults who influence marketing and advertising and who control media programming in general have important positions of responsibility. Whereas most of us are only in positions to influence a few children at a time, the advertisement and entertainment media have the power to influence millions of children. They must take this responsibility seriously. Society must hold them accountable for their decisions. Marketing products with violent images and messages cannot be accepted any longer. The consequences are too serious. Barraging our children with violent heroes and overwhelming amounts of gratuitous violence can no longer be permitted. Reasonable adults have to help parents, and parents have to push reasonable adults.

These violent images also affect adults. It's not only our children who admire the tough and violent images. Adults also have bought into these images, admire them, and often treat children as tough and violent rather than sacred and special. Adults, even those professionals charged with providing services to children, have become mean and callous toward children. In adopting such violent images of children, adults release themselves from the parental, communal, and professional responsibility for children that is essential to a safe and healthy society. Instead of debating ways to make the environment safer for children, American society is engaged in a public policy debate centered around getting tougher on children. Punishment rather than prevention is the focus.

A particularly offensive example of the harsh and mean portrayal of children was a *Newsweek* magazine cover story in 1996 entitled "Superpredators."[2] This article covered the lives of several young "hard-core criminals" convicted of horrible acts of violence. The article did very little to expand the American public's understanding of violence and the pain and hurt these children had experienced in their short lives. It did nothing to indicate the many prevention opportunities society missed despite extensive professional contact with these children in their younger years. These were real opportunities to respond to these children's hurt and prevent their acts of violence.

Instead, the article used the typical journalism scare tactics, giving the general impression that these "superpredators" were just born that way and that they were running rampant throughout urban America. It gave a sinister, scary, and extremely worrisome portrayal of these children as somehow nonhuman. A reader could easily conclude that society's only responsibility to these children was to identify them early and lock them up as early as possible. They were portrayed as monsters.

First Portray Them as Demons: Then Punish the Hell Out of Them

What is especially frightening about mean and callous portrayals of children is that they not only scare the average adult but also diminish the empathy of those professional adults charged with the care, education, and nurturing of children. When children are demonized, caregivers are left with the impression that an individual-oriented, single-focused, punitive strategy is the solution for youth violence. Rather than addressing the cultural issues in a toxic environment, they focus on better and more intense punishment.

There is meanness in our public policy toward children, evidenced in some of our most popular political rhetoric: "zero tolerance" and "three strikes and you're out" (in reference to the mandatory sentence of twenty-five years to life in prison after three felony convictions). The meanness is in the dismantling of the juvenile justice system as we try more and more and younger and younger juveniles as adults. The long-term investment in our children needed to prevent many of the problems and eliminate the toxic environment is a low priority. Selfishness and the almighty dollar rule, and community development efforts, programs for children and youth, and public education are relegated to the back burner. For the first time in the history of our country, we are spending more money on prisons than on education.[3] The meanness is pervasive and causing significant problems for our children.

Too many children in our country feel isolated and suffer from low self-esteem and even self-hate. We have an increasing population of depressed, hopeless young people who are perpetrating acts of violence against themselves and others. We have forgotten how to nurture and almost always resort to blame and punishment to change a child's behavior.

One of the most painful aspects of working in this area has been witnessing the vicious cycle of punishment and labeling that characterizes the standard professional response to "bad" children who are actually hurt children. Professionals often further injure these hurt children with punitive responses to misbehavior. Once the cycle starts, unless heroic efforts are made by a mentor, a resourceful parent, or a concerned professional, the downward spiral of demonization begins. It may end with death or a prison sentence.

Demonizing the child who is having trouble keeps the professional community from facing its failures and excuses its lack of effectiveness. Some children are constantly up against the prevailing notion of the inevitability of badness—the idea—that they are just "bad seeds," born that way. Therefore adults conclude that there is nothing professional contact or institutional intervention can or should be expected to do. Whether this demonization occurs in the school, church, or the courts, we allow failure after failure and excuse after excuse without demanding a change in professional protocols or strategies. Professionals who are charged to serve youth are escaping scrutiny and are not held accountable for the failures because the blame is on the children—the demons.

The Problem with Zero Tolerance

When schools started proclaiming a zero tolerance policy for violence and weapon carrying, many adults concerned about violence were pleased. It represented an effort to take seriously a problem that many schools had swept under the rug. Weapon carrying and fighting in school should not be tolerated. Yet over time it has become increasingly clear that zero tolerance is being taken to mean "zero adult and professional responsibility for children's behavior" and that it is yet another way to punish and label children who are already hurt.

When kids act out, they are sending up a red flag, a warning that they are in trouble. The key is not zero tolerance but early assistance and intervention, not early blaming and exclusion. Exclusion, through expulsion, often results in lost opportunities, particularly opportunities to do something constructive. Pushing kids out the door, blaming them, doesn't make them go away. They are still in the community but now lost to services and assistance.

Zero tolerance has become another way of disregarding professional failure to respond to hurt children; it allows people to pretend that these children's behavior is inevitable and to exonerate the adults from any responsibility. We have, with that one policy slogan, legitimized an absence of tolerance for the humanity of our children, for their imperfections and their mistakes. We now have zero tolerance for their anger and pain. As a result, some of our children can expect zero help, zero resources, zero forgiveness, and zero nurturing from our schools. We are exposing all children to harm and adding the insult of willful misunderstanding to the injury of hurt children.

It's Not Always What You Think

Despite the rhetoric about demons and superpredators, even those children who have committed the worst crimes and seem the hardest of the hard-core wrongdoers have sad tales to tell. Every time we ourselves have gotten close to a situation involving a "child-demon" or "young hard-core criminal," we have been overwhelmed by the child's pain.

For example, Tracy Litthcut, a former Boston youth outreach worker and now director of youth development for the city of Boston, tells this story of his visit to a sixteen-year-old boy accused of murder. When Litthcut arrived at the boy's apartment in one of Boston's public housing developments, the boy's mother and a man were smoking crack together in the front room. The mother looked up—making no attempt to hide what she was doing—and told Litthcut that the boy was in a back room. When Litthcut was done with the visit and walked back through the front room, the mother was performing a sexual favor for the man. Again, no attempt was made to hide what was happening. This boy was accused of killing a drug dealer. He was being blamed, held accountable, for responding to an intolerable situation. Hurt children become hurtful children.[4]

Children Fighting Back

Sarah Buel, an attorney who formerly worked in the Suffolk County District Attorney's office in Massachusetts and a national leader in the prevention of violence against women, has estimated that over 60 percent of young men under seventeen in prison for murder murdered their mother's batterer.[5] This estimate seems high but is nevertheless believable, because when the details of unfortunate situation after unfortunate situation are discovered, it is hard to ignore the pain of the child turned killer.

In his book *When a Child Kills*, Paul Mones provides another angle into the pain of children and the violence that results.[6] He details eight cases of children killing a parent. These heartbreaking stories of children abused and raped yet unable to find help among the youth-serving professionals they reached out to are difficult to handle. To learn in such clear detail that children seeking help at school or even in the courts not only didn't find help but often had their situations made worse is painful.

In one case a child told the school counselor of the beatings he received at home. The counselor called the father in, but the father said the child was lying, and the child was sent home. Needless to say he was beaten at home for telling and at the same time punished at school for lying.

Another account tells of a fourteen-year-old girl who was raped repeatedly by her mother's boyfriend. The girl ran away from home, was arrested, and then pressed rape charges against her mother's boyfriend. The court, however, swayed by the boyfriend's testimony that she seduced him, ruled that she had consented to sex. She lived in one of the few states that consider fourteen the age of ability to consent to sex.

These stories represent the experience of thousands of children, many of whom commit acts of violence and end up being blamed for their fate. They are labeled demons instead of severely traumatized children who demonstrate demonic behavior.

The Power of Demonizing

We ourselves know that most children, even the ones with the worst behaviors, are not what the media portray. We know this because we have come close enough to hear these children's stories over and over again. We have heard their stories and have cried. What sometimes surprises us, however, is that despite our knowing better, the myth of the demon child can sometimes prevail even for us. We approach the worst schools with fear and trepidation even though they are always full of good kids. We approach the worst kid with angst and distrust even though he is a traumatized child who is often full of humanity. Despite what we know, we still struggle to rid ourselves of the prevailing images—the demon images.

Those who have never set foot in the worst schools, who have never met a poor kid whose mother is addicted to crack, who don't see the beauty and humanity of these children on a day-to-day basis, can't begin to struggle against the stereotypes that are repeatedly portrayed. They have no counterexperiences. They have only the six o'clock news or the advertisements or the entertainment media. Because there are no counterforces except the ones generated by direct contact, we are afraid that America's public policy will continue to be mean as long as this society allows the demonization of children to continue.

Superdemonization of Young Men of Color

The contrasts between *Newsweek*'s 1996 cover story entitled "Superpredators" and the same magazine's 1999 twenty-nine-page cover story and special report entitled "America Under the Gun"[7] are striking. The first story profiled the young, hard-core criminals of urban America with very little attention to their humanity or their hard luck stories. The public was left to conclude that early detection of the demons is necessary and that society must lock them up and throw away the key. There was nothing sympathetic about these children as they were portrayed, so readers were unable to feel empathetic toward them or invest in understanding them.

After the series of school killings in white, middle-class America, the second *Newsweek* cover story could not have been more different. Rather than just striking an alarm, the second cover also reads, "what must be done—protecting your kids." The focus is on the gun and not on the "criminals" who pulled the trigger. The focus is on early screening for mental health problems among troubled youth as opposed to hard-core bad kids. In the series of articles that make up this report, there is even one sidebar titled "Mourn for the Killers, Too," discussing the humanity of the shooters and the community's effort to understand them as well.

Among the articles is an unprecedented *Newsweek* editorial on the rational regulation of guns, a stand not provoked earlier by the murder of urban minority children. But this time the cover story was not about inner-city poor children; it was about suburban and rural youth in trouble. For these children there was sympathy, empathy, and a search for answers. Yet are these children any different from those described in the earlier story?

Newsweek isn't the only place where the media changed their tune. Questions of why these school shootings happened and what could be done prevailed. The *New York Times* ran a front-page story with a full-page treatment of the family of one of the shooters, eleven-year-old Andrew Goldman of Jonesboro, Arkansas. The humanity of this family and of their eleven-year-old grandson was portrayed. The take-home message in the *New York Times* was that there is something wrong in a society where people like these have these problems, a message rarely if ever conveyed about young urban minority shooters.[8]

Different Treatment of Young Black Men and Young White Men

The portrayal of young men of color as demons is so prevalent that even black adults who are parents have internalized the fear, and black professionals have publicly voiced their fears. A March 2, 2000, commentary by Jim Vance, a local TV anchor for WRC, Channel 4, in Washington, D.C., revisited his 1988 commentary that lambasted D.C. cab drivers for not picking up Harvard Law School professor Derrick Bell because he is black. Vance concluded that in March 2000, things had actually changed for the worse.

He was particularly aggravated by the comments of D.C. taxi commissioner Sandra Seegar, an African American woman. She stated that cabbies should drive right on by dangerous-looking people and avoid dangerous neighborhoods. She described a dangerous-looking fare: "a young black male with his hat on backwards, shirttail hanging below his coat, baggy pants below his underwear and unlaced tennis shoes." Jim Vance's response was that this description fit his son, a successful student at Columbia Law School, and his running buddies, a writer, two filmmakers, investment counselors, and businessmen, who aren't dangerous at all. He reminded his listeners of the way their parents felt about the way they used to dress, and then called for Seegar's resignation. "My son is not the enemy," he exclaimed. White suburban kids now dress to emulate popular rap music artists and others in the urban culture. Yet we rarely hear complaints that these suburban youth are being systematically and automatically labeled dangerous or have a high likelihood of being ignored by cabbies or, worse, arrested.

Minority youth without mentors and role models are particularly vulnerable to stereotyping and labeling. The impact of the demonization of young men of color is measurable in their life experiences. Ron Ferguson studied a group of young black men who graduated from Harvard and compared them to a group of young black men who had dropped out of high school. He asked both groups to respond to this sentence, "When people see me on the streets, they grab their belongings and walk fast as if they are afraid," by checking "never," "sometimes," or "always." Participants in both groups answered "sometimes" or "always." Not one responded "never"![9] If you aren't aware of this phenomenon, ask any man of color about his experience; it is universal. Society demonizes youth in general and viciously portrays young men of color as the most scary of all.

Race-Based Differences in Professional Treatment

It is not just the public response to young black men that is prejudiced by the images of them portrayed in the media; the bias and discrimination in professional practice is even more alarming. Dorothy O. Lewis, a psychiatrist in upstate New York and an internationally recognized expert on violence, has studied violent adolescents brought to emergency rooms for treatment and dispensation in the state of Connecticut. White adolescents went from the ER to a mental health institution; black adolescents went to prison. Regardless of insurance status, severity of the violence, or the adolescent's history of violence, race was the factor most strongly predicting where the adolescent was sent.[10]

This country is seeing this same phenomenon at the national level now. When the shooters and those shot were mostly urban young men of color, the news media criminalized them—both the victims and perpetrators. Many parents of these murdered children angrily report that reporters labeled their murdered child a gang member and searched for records of deviant and delinquent behavior. The recent upsurge of young, white, middle-class shooters and victims has generated a totally different and far more sympathetic rhetoric from professionals, from reporters, and from the general public.

Breaking the Cycle: Toward Preventive, Not Punitive, Strategies

One way to break the punishment and labeling cycle that affects all children and is particularly vicious for children of color is to train competent professionals, ones who are aware of their individual biases and are expert in childhood behavior and behavior modification. These professionals must then operate in a context that offers back-up referral mechanisms and resources for prevention, not just crisis-oriented intervention. Training teachers, foster care parents, clergy, police, and pediatricians in basic child development and behavior modification strategies is fundamental; adding cultural competency training is essential.

Poor parents will go to the pediatrician for advice and get information that comes from the doctor's personal experience. In regard to disciplining a child, he might say, "I take away some activity my child wants to do, like his ski weekend or his ice hockey practice." If a parent doesn't have his or her child enrolled in such costly activities, then it's meaningless to advise taking them away. For poor parents who are on fixed and limited incomes or who are working at or just above the minimum wage, just treating their children to an ice-cream cone can be expensive and uncommon enough that taking it away seems excessively cruel.

When we were going into classrooms to teach violence prevention, a child psychologist gave us two strategies for controlling a classroom and maintaining a good rapport with the students, and we have used them over and over again in the years since then. The first strategy is used at the outset when you need to get a rowdy classroom's attention. You start out talking loudly, almost shouting, but then quickly lower your voice to a level that is just audible to those paying attention. The desire to hear what you are saying and basic curiosity get the best of the students and they quiet down.

The second strategy comes in handy when, in the middle of your presentation, a group of students starts getting loud. You walk over to the leader of the group and get his attention by looking him in the eye, without changing your voice or your content. It appears as if you are speaking directly to him, and the eye contact makes it extremely hard for the student to continue the disruptive behavior, particularly because all eyes in the classroom are now turned to him. He gets the attention he is seeking without your having to disrupt the class or the lecture. It has worked over and over again for us.

For example, one of us (Deborah) was in White Plains, New York, speaking at the local high school to several hundred students in the auditorium. High school students are the toughest audience, and an auditorium full of them can be daunting. This particular time, several students sitting in tenth row or so from the front of the auditorium were being disruptive. The leader clearly wanted attention. They all began to talk loudly and laugh during the presentation. However, the classroom strategy of catching the eye of the leader and talking directly to him worked in this setting as well. The students quieted down. After the assembly an amazed teacher asked about the strategy; he wanted to know how to use it. If anyone should know these and other effective strategies that alter behavior rather than punishing it, teachers should.

We know that parents are generally not taught basic child behavior and manipulation and modification strategies. But many child-serving professionals are unschooled as well. Even the basic knowledge used in the mental health profession is not channeled into public knowledge and professional cross-training rarely takes place. We propose that all professionals serving youth, including teachers, be trained in child development, behavior modification, and cultural competency. Providers have to be made aware of their individual biases and taught strategies to overcome them so that they can understand the experiences of all children regardless of race.

Furthermore, all of us need to recognize and address the images and stereotypes of youth that greatly influence how we perceive and respond to children and adolescents. Society has to recognize that these images affect not only all adults but youth as well, contributing to negative attitudes and behaviors. Young people need to be portrayed fairly and addressed in humane, respectful, sympathetic, and empathetic ways. Demonizing images of them lead to inappropriate and ineffective responses to their behavior and may eventually become self-fulfilling prophecies. Adult attitudes toward youth must change first if the tragedies of violence are to be reduced.

We have allowed our children to become the modern equivalent of the miner's canary. They are our warning. The environment is toxic and sustaining elements are running out or in short supply. At stake is our survival as well as theirs. At stake is our legacy as well as theirs. Adults are not more important than children—if anything, the contrary is true.

Chapter Eight

Girls and Violence

Rambettes

My name is Melodie. I have two kids. I am nineteen now. When I was thirteen, fourteen, just entering high school, I joined a gang. I wanted to be a follower and see what they were doing, see what it was about. The fellows was making a little money, selling drugs, doing this and that and going against the other men for their name. Their name was Disciples, Vice Lords. All they names mean something to them. And I was running up behind em, just to see what they was doin. Running up behind them—I wanted to be a leader, too, and do what they was doing. They was leading me around to do bad things. When I got up to that point, I got up to be a leader. Then I seen it wasn't nothin to it. It was nothin to it but to tell the girls what to do. I told them what to do, ruled them around and got my little money. There wasn't nothin to it. I had fun for a while.

Then I got pregnant. So after I got pregnant, I said, "What am I good for? What I'm out here for?" It all was stupid. Stupidity. I had my baby. I realized I didn't want my child to grow up doing what they was doin. I didn't want my child runnin around, busting car windows, and trying to steal radios and sellin drugs. Sellin drugs to the other men and all the brother men and doing what they don't s'pose to be doin. I wanted my kids to go to school, get an education. Something that I didn't do. I left the gang. I felt it alone. Cause there wasn't nothin left for me. It couldn't help take care of my kids.

I could have stayed there. Had them bringing me money like I wanted, too, to take care my kids but that ain't enough. I should have had someone there to teach me education, tell me about the importance of education in school, what the school could do for you. I didn't want to go to school. Cause I wanted to run behind my friends. Run behind the gang members. And I wanted to be a leader to see what they could do. I did all that stuff. But now I'm fightin to get back in school. I start school next month. I want to get my education so I can teach my kids to get theirs, cause without their education you can't do nothin for life but join a gang.[1]

In the 1997 movie, *The Long Kiss Goodnight*, Geena Davis plays a Dr. Jekyll and Mr. Hyde type of character. She is a beautiful, sweet, loving suburban housewife and mother with a high-risk past. That past includes time spent as a federal spy in intense international conflict. She returns to her spy character (through flashbacks and a current situation demanding her involvement) and participates in a full-action drama as a superheroine. She goes at it in a "Rambo" style, getting beaten up badly (more than once) and beating up, blowing up, and defeating several horrific bad guys before they have a chance to kill her and her daughter.

The juxtaposition of her two roles and the reconciliation at the end when she returns to her sweet homemaker half provides a powerful and complex—and wrong—message to girls about violence. Geena Davis's violent "kick-butt" character is portrayed as correct and admirable: she beats up and gets beaten up with the best of them. In this fantasy she can also be the sweet, innocent, loving mother—all wrapped up into one twisted role model. This is unfortunately no longer a unique example of our culture's feminization of the violent superhero.

Beautiful and Dangerous: Myth Becomes Reality

With the portrayal of girls and women using violence to successfully solve problems with big guns and bombs and without pain or remorse or serious injury, we are headed down a dangerous and familiar path. Do we really want this for the other half of our children? Do we want girls to begin to follow the path we've already laid out for boys and young men? Until recently, girls and women were typically portrayed as the victims of violence, which was bad enough. Now we are seeing them as perpetrators.

Not too long ago, when we ourselves were asked to address the subject of girls and violence, we were expected to discuss dating violence, mostly boyfriends hitting their girlfriends. Dating violence remains an important and insufficiently addressed subject, but now people are asking us to discuss girls as perpetrators, reflecting an increasingly more common phenomenon. Now we are regularly asked by reporters, professionals, and parents alike, "How could a girl do this?"

Girls Are Not That Different

Society's astonishment when girls engage in violence suggests expectations of some sort of genetic or biological protection within girls. As if the XX chromosomes would protect girls from the effects of a toxic environment—violent images, guns, abuse. Just as this nation once ignored the violence found in inner cities, on the assumption that this violence would never reach the suburbs or small-town America, it is ignoring the vulnerability of girls exposed to violent female superheroes and images and to the other risk factors for violence.

Most people have images of disputes on school grounds as *arguments* between girls and *fights* between boys. In the past, just as boys once fought but rarely if ever used weapons, girls rarely fought. And it was even rarer for a girl to be arrested for a violent offense. Now middle school principals are as concerned about girls fighting as they are about boys fighting, if not more so. They have said to us, for example, "I haven't had to ever call an ambulance to my school except for when two girls were fighting," and, "Girls are fighting more than the boys and they are more vicious; they don't have any rules for their fighting."

Although the arrest rates for overall crime and violent crime are significantly lower for young women than for young men, recent increases in girls' arrests have started narrowing the gap.

From 1981 to 1995, there was a 129 percent increase in the violent crime arrest rate for young women, compared to a 56 percent increase over the same time period for young men.[2] Now girls account for 25 percent of the juvenile arrests for violent crime, a number unheard of two decades ago. More girls are entering the juvenile justice system, and they are doing so at younger ages;[3] there has been a 10 percent increase in the numbers of thirteen- and fourteen-year-olds coming into juvenile court.[4]

It's Not Just More Arrests

Some experts, including Meda Chesney-Lind, professor of women's studies at the University of Hawaii and the author of many monographs about women and crime, believe that there really has not been a significant increase in the proportion of young women committing crimes. Rather, "we're criminalizing a lot of schoolyard scuffles where, in the past, we'd call it a cat fight, we'd giggle and keep walking. Now we're calling the cops."[5]

Chesney-Lind and others also point to changes and biases in the juvenile justice system that they believe explain the increased number of girls arrested. For example, girls are twice as likely as boys to be detained, with the detention period lasting five times longer for girls than for their male counterparts.[6] Girls are more likely than boys to be charged with status offenses, offenses that, if committed by an adult, would not be considered a crime (for example, running away from home, truancy, incorrigibility), and are more likely to be incarcerated for these offenses than males.

Chesney-Lind also argues that increased *bootstrapping* (adding a new charge to an existing charge—specifically, in this case, adding a delinquency charge to a status offense), is also a cause of the rise in rates. The delinquency charge is added when a juvenile violates a court order related to the original status charge. For example, if a young woman is charged with truancy, a status offense, and then fails to appear in court on the scheduled date, a delinquency charge may be added, drastically increasing the severity of punishment.

Bootstrapping has been shown to result in harsh and inequitable treatment of girls charged with status offenses.[7]

We beg to differ. The increase in girls' arrest rates combined with the anecdotal experience of educators and youth-serving professionals portends real trouble. Structural inequalities in the juvenile justice system certainly do not explain the entire increase of female perpetration. To halt America's third wave of youth violence, girls as perpetrators, at its beginning all of us concerned about this violence must understand the factors that place young women at risk. We need to take care and heed these early warning signs. We must not explain them away as we did with the early signs of the first two waves of this epidemic.

Understanding Girls' Risk Factors

There is no single factor that can be identified as the cause of female perpetration. Rather, a series of often interrelated factors magnifies the likelihood that a young woman will find herself involved in the juvenile justice system. The slot machine windows line up for girls just as they do for boys, and the risk factors in those windows are actually quite similar.

Traditionally girls and boys have responded differently to the trauma and hurts in their lives, with these differences attributable in large part to gender socialization. Until recently those girls victimized at home, witnessing violence at home, or growing up with few attractive educational or job opportunities would respond by hurting themselves. Now, violence is becoming a socially acceptable way for girls to right the wrongs against them, just as it has always been for boys. Girls still resort to suicide attempts, running away, substance use, sexual promiscuity, and prostitution to deal with their hurt and trauma. But now acting violently has been added to their list.

Substance Abuse

As it is for boys, substance abuse is a significant risk factor for girls. The American Correctional Association's study of the girls in state training schools for girls in the juvenile justice system found that 60 percent of them needed substance abuse treatment at intake. The study also determined that almost half of the girls took drugs or drank alcohol as a form of self-medication. Most of the girls who were substance dependent had first started using drugs or alcohol when they were between the ages of twelve and fifteen,[8] which closely parallels the ages at which girls who are victims of sexual abuse typically first experience that abuse. And as previously discussed, sexual abuse may also lead to running away.

Research studies and anecdotal information indicate that if a young woman runs away from home and lives on the street, she is more likely than other young women to become involved in drug use or trafficking. Many young women also report being intoxicated or under the influence of illegal substances when committing criminal acts.[9]

Dating Violence

Studies have suggested that between 28 to 41 percent of all individuals (males and females, teens and adults) will be involved in intimate partner violence at some point while dating[10] and that one out of ten dating teens has experienced some form of violence in a relationship.[11] A survey of three high schools, one each from inner city, suburban, and rural communities, showed that 18 percent of the responding students reported experiencing some form of physical or sexual violence in a dating relationship.[12] Although the percentage of young women reporting dating violence varies depending on the circumstances surrounding the survey and the form of the questions, what is clear is the reality American girls face. Dating violence is real and occurs across color, community, and class lines.

Because of their lack of experience in relationships and the normal developmental tasks they face, adolescent girls are at particular risk for not recognizing and naming the abuse that occurs in their relationships. Confusing love and concern with dangerous jealousy and control is easier to do when you have little experience, have no nurturing family context, or are developing an identity separate from your family's (a developmental task of adolescence). If a girl has experienced family violence or direct victimization within the family, she is even more vulnerable to misunderstanding a boyfriend's abusive behavior, especially because the relationship has probably started off wonderfully, with her as the center of his attention and valued in a special way. Too special for her family and friends, she then becomes isolated, and he becomes her dominant source of information and feedback.

Although adult intimate partner violence is predominantly men controlling, hitting, and exercising power over women, both adolescent females and adolescent males may engage in dating violence as the abuser. Recent surveys have shown that adolescent males and females equally report using violence in dating relationships (although these findings are highly debated).[13] The physical size and power difference between boys and girls is often less in the early phases of dating relationships than it is among older couples, which would make female violence more feasible. However, in these surveys girls may simply be more open than boys in reporting their use of physical aggression, rather than being equal to boys in violence. This explanation would certainly be compatible with the situation among adults, where men have consistently been shown to underreport and minimize the violence they inflict whereas women do not. Young women report engaging in acts of physical violence in a dating relationship because of uncontrolled anger, jealousy, self-defense, or retaliation, whereas young men report their motives as wanting to intimidate, scare, or force their female partner to give them something.[14]

Victimization

Among girls, as with boys, a history of victimization increases the risk for future participation in violence, either as a victim or a perpetrator. Girls are more likely than boys to be victimized in the home, by a parent, stepparent, or guardian or by a boyfriend or intimate partner. In 1993, 603 girls under age nineteen were reported to have been murdered by their partners.[15] One in four women in the United States has been raped or has been the victim of an attempted rape by age twenty-five, and 75 percent of those acts are committed by a friend or acquaintance. Adolescent females who commit homicide are far more likely than boys to kill a parent, stepparent, or other family member. Only 14 percent of the adolescent males arrested for murder or nonnegligent homicide have killed a parent, compared to 44 percent of the adolescent females arrested.[16]

Frequently, society's view of those who commit crimes is one-dimensional: they are simply perpetrators who hurt victims and their families. But the picture is infinitely more complex, especially for girls. Unfortunately, very little is known about the relationship between victimization and subsequent perpetration. It is clear, however, that the vast majority of female offenders are victims, often victims of sexual abuse. Girls are three times more likely than boys to have been sexually abused. Among female delinquents the statistics are even more frightening; approximately 70 percent have a history of sexual abuse,[17] and most of this abuse (90 percent) has occurred prior to the young woman's fifteenth birthday.[18] The age of victimization is critical.

Adolescence is a naturally turbulent time as individuals try to answer the question Who am I? while also trying to succeed in academics, peer relationships, and romantic relationships and to define family relationships. Sexual, physical, or emotional victimization during this critical developmental period often results in such problems as decreased self-esteem, an inability to trust, academic failure, eating disorders, and teen pregnancy. Young women charged with running away frequently have fled to escape abusive situations in the home.[19]

Rape and Sexual Abuse

Sexual victimization at an early age consistently appears in the histories of girls and women who have been involved in episodes of violence and also those arrested or incarcerated. Sexual victimization ranges from repetitious, unwanted sexual advances and coercion by an abuser to frank rape with penetration. Sexual abuse or victimization also includes *date rape*, a euphemism for nonconsensual sex between people who are on a date or considered to be in a dating relationship. A 1992 study, using explicit language and a clear definition of rape, estimated that 683,000 adult women are raped in the United States each year.[20]

Teen pregnancy is also a risk factor for perpetration. As we have seen, the risk factors for violence frequently overlap in individual children and adolescents, creating numerous obstacles for them to overcome. Young women who are experiencing sexual abuse at home are more likely to become sexually active early. Moreover, if a young woman is also using illegal substances, she may be less likely to use birth control, increasing her chances of becoming pregnant or being infected with a sexually transmitted disease. Forty percent of women in the general population, 60 percent of the women on welfare, and 80 percent of the women incarcerated have histories of sexual and physical violence, usually perpetrated by a male intimate partner, relative, or friend and usually reported before age fifteen.[21]

Learning Disabilities

Like boys, young women with learning disabilities are also disproportionally represented in the juvenile justice system: 26 percent of female offenders have learning disabilities. Research also reveals that 78 percent of female juvenile offenders have not completed high school or obtained a GED. In addition, young women are also seven times more likely than boys to drop out of school for family reasons. Twenty-seven percent of girl offenders dropped out of school because they were pregnant and 20 percent because they already were parents and needed to care for their children.[22] Academic failure is the most significant risk factor relating to early onset of delinquency, in part because it leads to underemployment, and underemployment leads to poverty.[23]

As is also the case with young men, young women of color are disproportionally represented in the juvenile justice system. Fifty percent of the young women in secure detention facilities are African American, and 13 percent are Hispanic. Seven of every ten cases involving Caucasian girls are dismissed; only three of every ten cases are dismissed for African American girls.[24] African American, Asian, and Latina girls who are poor and addicted are more likely to be incarcerated than poor and addicted Caucasian girls are; the latter are more likely to be referred to mental health facilities. Does this sound familiar? This is essentially a replication of what we have already described for young men of color.

In addition to facing inequalities in the justice system, young women of color often encounter institutional racism that impedes their efforts to obtain a quality education and employment. Repeated lack of opportunity can create frustration, which in turn increases the possibility that a young woman may engage in destructive activities toward herself and others as a way to vent her frustration. Sometimes, perceived economic necessity can lead girls to commit crimes. A 1990 report issued by the American Correctional Association indicated that 9 percent of the girls surveyed broke the law because of economic pressure.[25]

However, employment does not, by itself, alleviate delinquency. In fact some studies have indicated that employment does not decrease the likelihood of engaging in street crime and may actually facilitate offending by providing additional funds to purchase illegal substances. This is clearly a complex situation, and more research is needed to further understand the interplay of these factors. As you can see, we cannot always assume that what seems obvious is indeed true.

What Has Changed?

Many of the problems and risks outlined in this chapter have plagued girls and young women for decades. So, what has changed? What explains the increase in rates of violence for girls at the same time as boys' rates have declined?

Some point to the women's liberation movement as the culprit, stating that the challenging of sex-role stereotypes increased the acceptability of female perpetration of violence. However, studies of adult female perpetrators reveal that they tend to be fairly traditional in terms of gender orientation and are less likely than other women to agree with sex-role equality theories.[26]

Media, Media, and More Media

One factor that has changed is the media portrayal of women. More and more frequently women are depicted committing acts of violence that are shown as being admirable. In the 1991 film *Thelma and Louise*, Susan Sarandon and Geena Davis avenged their poor treatment at the hands of men by shooting men or setting them on fire. In the film *Set It Off*, four women dissatisfied with their lives, led by Queen Latifah, commit various violent and illegal acts and are portrayed as heroes. On TV we see *Xena: Warrior Princess*. In print ads we see women carrying handguns that are "sleek and beautiful" and "fit easily into your purse," and billboards show gorgeous young women and this one sentence, "Our models can beat up your models"—this in an attempt to sell blue jeans.

Perhaps more disturbing is the trend in children's programming. Cartoons, already the most violent genre on TV, have expanded their violence repertoire to include a small but growing number of violent female characters. The list includes the pink Power Ranger, using violence to bring about justice, and Angelica, the spoiled and short-tempered Rug Rat. More and more frequently we hear woman musicians glorifying and justifying violence. Hiphopper Eve sings about killing an abusive man, and Courtney Love's songs are filled with violent images. It is difficult to evaluate the impact of these media messages on young people. However, research by Albert Bandura clearly shows that children and adults alike learn through example. Thus, seeing violence glorified on TV as admirable and without consequences, particularly when the perpetrator is someone similar to oneself, increases the chances that the child viewer will see violence as acceptable.

The Power Rangers are the first example the authors can remember of girls (the ones in pink, yellow, and light blue suits) beating up and getting beaten up in the name of solving a problem, just like the boys. Fifteen years later this nation has an epidemic of girls as violent perpetrators. Obviously, we can't blame this solely on the Power Rangers, yet the only risk factor that seems to have changed for girls and not for boys over the last two decades is this feminization of the violent superhero. The Power Rangers may have been among the first, but they have been followed by an ever increasing number of violent female heroes.

A New Social Norm: Girls Fight Back Too

Why should girls tolerate real or perceived bad treatment any more than boys do? With guns as the great power equalizers, girls are able to defend themselves, seek revenge, and right wrongs just as boys are expected to do. Is this an unintended consequence of the women's liberation movement and the move to equalize the roles for men and women? Is the phenomenon of girls fighting back a bad thing or a good thing? We reserve judgment on this but do feel strongly that when a person decides to defend him- or herself in a society where violence is the admired, glamorized, and most frequently portrayed problem solver, then the result will be violence. All of us certainly want girls to feel and be empowered to defend themselves, seek equality, and achieve success equally with boys. But do we want them to fall into the same deep hole we have already dug for boys? On the contrary, we want their success to lead us down a different path while we try to fix the situation we have created for boys.

From Victim to Perpetrator

Although the link between victimization and further perpetration of violence is poorly explored in girls, the studies that have been conducted indicate a relationship similar to the one found with boys. Cathy Spatz Widom's work clearly demonstrates the higher risk abused and neglected children have for arrests for violence.[27] This effect is true for both boys and girls. The evidence that hurt children then hurt other children is strong and persistent. One study of female adolescents incarcerated in juvenile facilities showed that 62 percent had been physically abused, and 30 percent said that the abuse had begun when they were between the ages of five and nine.[28]

Girls' attitudes about violence and using violence have not been rigorously measured over time, but the recent snapshots are nevertheless revealing. The Center for Women Policy Studies found that girls who had been physically abused were twice as likely as girls who had not to view violence as "always okay when someone threatens you." The same survey not surprisingly indicated that 82 percent of the girls said they felt justified in being violent if someone tries to force them to have sex. Particularly striking were the 23 percent who said that violence is justified if someone starts a "bad rumor" about them.[29]

Prevention for Girls

Despite the successes and achievements of the youth violence prevention movement over the last two decades, the increasing number of girls involved in episodes of violence is disturbing. There is a serious dearth of both violence prevention programs for girls and research focusing on girls who are perpetrators. In 1991, the Center for the Study of Youth Policy wrote, "there are few, if any, meaningful community-based programs for girls and research focusing on girl perpetrators."[30] The Office of Juvenile Justice and Delinquency Prevention reports that 50 percent of all juvenile crimes occurs in the three hours after school,[31] yet girls are often discouraged from participating in after-school programs because of concern for their safety. There are also fewer resources allocated to programs that focus specifically on girls.

Even though the situation facing young women is complex and critical, communities and this nation as a whole can take steps to stem the flow of violence. Although the number of female perpetrators has been increasing, the number of services geared to meet girls' needs has not. A study of juvenile justice programs revealed that only 5.9 percent of these programs served primarily girls, whereas 42.4 percent served primarily boys.[32] A comprehensive study of individual programs for delinquent and nondelinquent youth revealed that less than 8 percent provided services to girls ages nine to fifteen.[33] This picture has improved somewhat as a result of the 1992 reauthorization of the Juvenile Justice and Delinquency Prevention Act of 1974, which funds block grants for states that provide programs in any of ten "challenge areas," of which girls and violence is one.

The girls and young women who are committing acts of violence have been left out of prevention efforts because, until recently, the "numbers" didn't support focusing on them. However, the data-driven decision to focus on boys may have also been a consequence of falling into traps created by misleading stereotypes. Girls, imagined to be resistant or resilient, were not expected to become involved in violence, and there has been a significant delay in addressing their issues. This has changed to some extent now that hard data are revealing the need for programs for girls. "Bad girls" are no longer anomalous, and it is clear that they are in need of violence prevention strategies.

Programs to Develop Nonviolent Nonvictims

Programs to address girls' violent behavior must address the larger context of the contemporary culture of violence, the persistence of violent female victimization in society and the media, the prevalence of low self-esteem in girls, and the increase in self-destructive behaviors among females, especially girls and young women (such as eating disorders, suicide, substance abuse, and self-mutilation). Girls are demonstrating numerous serious mental health and health problems, which now include violent behavior. This clearly indicates that girls are much more vulnerable than previously imagined.

However, new programs must be careful to take into consideration the unique needs of girls. Communities cannot merely replicate programs developed for boys and implement them with girls.

Chesney-Lind, for example, recommends that programs should emphasize health and wellness at a prevention and intervention level.[34] That is, programs should take into account the risk factors for young women and provide vocational training, stress management training, counseling geared toward substance abuse and sexual abuse, and support services for individuals with learning disabilities or academic difficulties. Girls' feelings about themselves and others are often framed in terms of their relationships with others. Almost half of the girls in the juvenile justice system have reported feeling little or no love or acceptance while growing up. We agree with Chesney-Lind on this issue.

Programs should address this gap, providing female mentors and peer counselors who can offer positive support and are sensitive to the issues with which the young women are coping. Young women are often very verbal but, lacking caring and supportive individuals in their lives, have begun to turn to violence as an expression of their frustration and hopelessness. Thus programs that provide both the skills to ensure employment and the support systems to validate and empower young women are crucial.

Integrated Approaches to Peer Violence and Dating Violence

Peer violence prevention and dating violence prevention are currently treated as separate areas with distinct approaches and strategies. In order to effectively address and integrate these issues for girls and young women, programs must acknowledge that girls are at risk for victimization and must defend themselves and at the same time acknowledge the powerful methods of conflict resolution and defense found in nonviolent strategies.

Currently, school-based curricula designed to prevent adolescent peer violence are typically either gender neutral or focused mainly on boys. They treat young women and men as if they existed in the same social context, assuming that they both need the same knowledge and skills in order to handle their anger and to resolve conflict nonviolently. These curricula do not address the differences between young women and men in risk of victimization, awareness of that risk, and motivation to commit violent acts; nor do they examine the relationship between being a victim and being a perpetrator. As primary prevention tools, these curricula tend to focus on making changes in an individual's behavior. The social context is also addressed from this perspective, looking at the ways individuals can refrain from creating the expectation of a fight and the context for a fight to occur.

At the other end of the spectrum, dating violence prevention curricula tend to define the roles of abuser and victim and typically assign these roles to males and females, respectively. These curricula also emphasize the effect that society's expectations have on relationships and the roles women and men have in these relationships. In addition, discussions of gender roles, stereotyping, cultural norms, and the influence of the media are integrated into most dating violence prevention curricula. Most also provide definitions of a healthy relationship and nonviolent conflict resolution skills. However, because the focus is on dating relationships, these curricula fail to address the larger context of violence in society. They fail to deal with the increasing role of girls as perpetrators of peer violence.

An alternative would be a curriculum that integrated peer violence prevention with dating violence prevention. This could create a curriculum for young women in which their past, current, and potential experiences in society as victims, witnesses, or perpetrators could be examined and discussed. It would provide a foundation for skill development and awareness in a social context, an area not currently addressed. Young women must be taught the skills they need to be both nonvictims and nonviolent.

Stemming the Tide

This nation is just beginning to recognize the potential of a third wave of the epidemic of youth violence. This third wave, likely to focus on a new level of violence among and involving girls, must be of as much concern to all of us as the waves that struck our inner cities and have now flooded into our nonurban communities. We need to apply what we have learned from these other waves, for we have a real opportunity to prevent or curtail this third wave before it evolves into something bigger or scarier. As with our approaches to violence among boys, we must take care to understand what is going on, step out of our stereotypical responses that have not worked in the past, and focus as extensively as possible on prevention. Girls have not yet fallen as deeply into this mess as boys. Let's keep it that way.

Chapter Nine

Violence at Home

So much has been made of the cliché "It takes a village to raise a child" that it has almost lost any real meaning. Children are most influenced by what they observe and experience very early in their lives. That means that what they see, hear, and experience in their homes during the first several years of their lives, before they have exposure to any other institutions in the community such as school or day care, has enormous impact on their behavior and perceptions of the world.

It would be more accurate, then, to say, "It takes a village to raise a family," because it is the environment in the family that is ultimately most important in shaping the future of the children in that family. Families that provide nurturing, healthy environments impart great resilience to their children that helps them withstand considerable insult and assault from the negative factors they may encounter once they venture outside their homes. Families that are dysfunctional and violent and that display unhealthy behaviors create significant vulnerability in their children. Although these children are not inevitably doomed to lives of failure and violence, they have tremendous odds to overcome. They are among the highest risk individuals and are much more susceptible to negative influences from the media and the outside world.

Children Face Many Kinds of Home Violence

Early childhood exposure to domestic violence is a potentially devastating experience with both short- and long-term consequences.

Families with a history of criminal violence, child abuse, adult violence in the home (most commonly battering), or regular and severe corporal punishment (spanking) expose children to a significantly higher risk of involvement with violence as adolescents and young adults. In the short run, children with such exposures often have difficulties with interpersonal relationships, have poor school performance and attendance, and display acute symptoms of isolation, withdrawal, and depression. They also tend to get into many altercations and fights. In the long run, these children have dramatically higher rates of involvement with the juvenile justice system and a greatly increased risk of being either the victim or assailant in violent altercations.

Abuse and Neglect

Of all of these home-based experiences with violence, only child abuse has a long history of being acknowledged as a medical problem with long-term consequences. Recognition of the *battered child syndrome* as a serious health problem first occurred in the American medical literature about fifty years ago. This in and of itself is a revealing observation. Prior to the middle of the twentieth century, child abuse was not formally acknowledged in the medical literature as a health problem. Although the medical profession as well as the criminal justice system most certainly had experience with battered children, child abuse was not recognized as a condition requiring serious intervention and was seen as a private matter.

Although children who are abused represent a relatively small percentage of the total population of children who experience violence in the home, they are not an insignificant number. In the mid-1990s, approximately 25 children per 100,000 were reported as being maltreated (abused or neglected). That number nearly doubles, to over 40 per 100,000, when those who are defined as at significant risk for harm are included. Equally important is the fact that both these numbers have doubled since the mid-1980s. These numbers represent about one million reports of child abuse a year and two thousand child deaths per year as a consequence of abuse or neglect.[1]

Abused children learn many of the wrong things that set them up for later dysfunction. They learn that the world is a mean and dangerous place. They learn that anger and violence are connected. They learn that the people who are supposed to protect them don't or can't. And they learn that the appropriate and "normal" way to relate to others is through violence, that violence is in fact the way to get what they want. This almost reflexive use of violence is right on the surface and often easily provoked. They feel alone, isolated, and afraid. Most important, the strategies they learn for coping with and accommodating the dysfunctional environment they live in are dysfunctional, dangerous, and counterproductive in and of themselves. These children can be set up for life in the cycle of violence.

These children also don't learn important skills essential to healthy interpersonal relationships. They don't learn how to develop loving relationships or how to positively connect and attach to others. They don't learn how to effectively get their needs met, a process from which they would eventually learn how to meet the needs of others. They don't learn how to resolve and work out conflict and frustration in nonviolent ways. They don't learn how to trust. They don't learn how to interpret situations and interpersonal interactions in a way that identifies nonthreatening motives and consequences. In essence they become particularly sensitive to negative social cues and insensitive to positive ones. Many situations are interpreted as threatening; nonthreatening or good intentions aren't considered.

Although infants and young children are particularly vulnerable in environments that involve abuse and neglect, children of all ages, including teenagers, suffer consequences from these experiences. In other words, it is important for the first years of a child's life to be nurturing and free from violence, but exposures to violence have consequences even when they occur later on.

Several research studies have observed the long-term consequences of child abuse. Researcher Cathy Widom has been most impressive in describing what has been labeled the *cycle of violence*. In long-term follow-up studies, adults who were abused as children had dramatically higher rates of arrest as teenagers and adults. Furthermore, their arrests were more frequently for violent crimes, their first offenses occurred at earlier ages, and they accumulated higher numbers of criminal arrests than a comparison group who were carefully matched for other descriptive factors.[2]

Domestic Violence

Being the victim of abuse is only one form of exposure to violence that creates risk for children. Equally traumatic is witnessing violence in the home. In such cases the child is not physically harmed by the violence but is very much affected emotionally. Actual physical injury is not necessary to establish a risk for violence in a child; just witnessing domestic violence such as the beating of one's mother provokes fear, rage, and the desire for revenge.

The number of families who experience domestic violence has not been reliably counted, and therefore it is difficult to determine the number of children affected.[3] Many professionals addressing domestic violence project that as many as a quarter to a third of families experience some degree of domestic violence. Surveys have reported that over 10 percent of adults remember witnessing physical violence between their parents at least once (which is most certainly an underestimate of the actual incidence because individuals often have poor recall of such events, especially ones that happened when they were very young). Surveys of parents have found physical violence rates of over 15 percent annually, with rates as high as 30 percent over the course of the marriage.[4]

Even if these numbers are on the high side, this implies that a huge number of children are growing up in homes where they are witnessing violence, whether they actually remember it later or not. Some researchers estimate that there are over ten million children in the country who have witnessed a physical assault between their parents. In a majority of these cases, the violence witnessed is repeated over and over.[5]

What we do know is that this exposure has major implications for the developmental, emotional, and behavioral health of children. Children growing up under these circumstances are disproportionately represented in the population of teenagers involved with the criminal justice system and dramatically overrepresented among those youth involved with violence. Furthermore, they make up a large portion of those involved with domestic violence as adults, both as victims (most commonly in the case of women) and assailants (most commonly in the case of men).

Witnessing violence between parents is deeply stressful for children. The later consequences of such exposures described in the scientific literature include mental and physical health problems; alcohol and substance abuse; involvement in violence and other criminal behavior outside the home; marital problems, including battering; and an increased likelihood of verbally and physically abusive behavior toward their own children. During the adolescent years, these children run away from home, make suicide attempts, and commit status offenses.

Overlapping Exposures to Abuse and Domestic Violence

It is difficult to isolate the consequences of witnessing violence between parents because parents who experience domestic violence are more likely than others to use physically abusive punishment with their children. Among those adults who recall witnessing violence between their parents, over half of men and almost half of women report having been hit by one of their parents during their adolescence. This is an important observation because hitting as a punishment is relatively rare in the teenage years, with hitting for disciplinary purposes being most likely during the preschool years, when children are three or four.[6]

Basically, however, it appears that children who witness domestic violence are similar to abused children in what they learn or don't learn. Primarily they learn that physical control of others is powerful and gets results. And the effects of this exposure may occur even before children are able to understand what they are witnessing. Some involved in the field of studying early brain development in early infancy have begun to suggest that even infants are influenced by the presence of violence around them. Exactly how this happens is unclear, but there are ongoing efforts to better understand and define how such environmental circumstances may affect the development of neural pathways.

Just as nurturing environments and appropriate identification of and responses to an infant's needs promote the development of certain neurological responses in an infant, so violent, unresponsive, and dysfunctional surroundings likely influence the biology and chemical activity of the developing brain. This may mean that permanent damage or at least long-standing vulnerability can result from exposures to violence even in the early months and years of a child's life.

Although it is obvious that the physical experiences of child abuse can do harm, there is an impressive body of science to support the view that exposure to violence without physical consequences can have similar or more damaging effects as well.[7] Certainly, children, especially young children, learn behavior from what they see. Given that young children's worlds are dominated by life at home, basic interpersonal skills are greatly influenced by the behavior of parents and other caretakers in the home.

When the process of dealing with anger, conflict, and frustration is modeled with violent solutions, that is what children learn. As a result of these childhood experiences, children are far more likely to learn to use coercion and violence to resolve conflict. They fail to learn how to use negotiation and other prosocial skills to get along with others. They often exhibit symptoms that have been used to describe posttraumatic stress disorder, including high anxiety levels, fearfulness, helplessness, low self-esteem, and depression. They fail to develop empathy for others and display decreased ability to nurture and care for others, particularly their own children. Trying to reprogram such learning later on and impart healthy social skills for interpersonal interactions is possible but very difficult and costly.

Spanking Doesn't Help

As noted earlier, raising the issue of spanking and corporal punishment as a risk factor for future violent behavior frequently provokes some of the strongest and most perplexing reactions we observe as we travel the country talking on the subject of violence prevention.

Spanking children as a disciplinary measure is deeply rooted in American culture. It is essentially a universal practice among parents in this country, with over 90 percent of parents reporting that they use hitting as a punishment during the preschool age years of three to four. Given the likelihood of underreporting for such questions, it is reasonable to suggest that the number actually approaches 100 percent.

Researcher Murray Straus has spent much of his career quantifying the use of corporal punishment and, more important, the consequences of this practice.[8] His work makes it clear that most parents equate discipline with physical punishment, especially for younger children. This is the case even though there is a major body of scientific work that has found hitting to be a relatively ineffective disciplinary practice for changing the behavior of children. In fact, numerous studies have found nonviolent disciplinary strategies to be far more successful at eliminating negative behaviors and promoting positive ones.

The numbers also reflect that this practice crosses boundaries of class, race, cultural background, educational status, geography, and any other descriptor one cares to use in classifying populations. It is truly universal. Even the American Academy of Pediatrics, which recently published a policy statement strongly recommending that pediatricians actively work to reduce the use of corporal punishment, took years for its members to come to agreement on promoting this agenda. Surveys of pediatricians showed that many of them used spanking as a disciplinary practice with their own children. Although the science provided strong evidence that corporal punishment is both harmful to children and less effective than other strategies in influencing child behavior, it took considerable time, energy, effort, and persistence to counter the deeply rooted belief that spanking was an acceptable and effective mechanism for discipline.

The fact that pediatricians, who are highly motivated and committed advocates for children, had such difficulty coming to closure on this issue helps to explain why the reaction we and others get to this subject is so complex.

Why Parents Spank Despite the Evidence. Cultural norms and legal statutes support and promote the use of corporal punishment. Nearly every state has statutes on its books allowing parents to hit their children (in contrast to Sweden, where national law prohibits hitting children). Numerous states still have laws that allow the use of corporal punishment in schools as well. The legal situation reflects the fact that spanking children is culturally expected and encouraged in many settings when a child misbehaves.

Hitting is by no means limited to the punishment of preschool age children. Over one-fifth of parents report hitting their children as infants, and this number may be as high as one-half. Although rates of spanking decline as children get older, the practice does not go away entirely with age. One-quarter of parents report hitting their teenage children, and for many adolescents this practice does not end until they leave home.

These numbers would not be important if there was not convincing evidence that hitting children is harmful in both the short and the long run. In the short run physical punishment always runs the risk of getting out of hand. As parents often resort to spanking when they are angry, there is certainly the risk that the hazy line between punishment and abuse will be crossed and that physical and emotional injury will occur. Parents themselves, particularly those that use corporal punishment frequently and regularly, often express fear that they will lose control and go too far. This, however, does not necessarily change their behavior and reduce or eliminate their use of hitting as a punishment.

Even more important are the long-term consequences. Children who experience regular use of corporal punishment have been observed to be at increased risk of a number of emotional problems. Again, the work of researcher Murray Straus has contributed invaluable information that increases our understanding of this. The more regular the experience of being hit or spanked, the more severe the consequences and the greater the risk. The more extensive the use of corporal punishment, the more likely children are to behave violently toward siblings and, when they get older, the more likely they are to use violence with spouses or partners.

Interestingly and importantly, Straus has also observed that this appears to be the case for both men and women. The implications for men are considerable and obvious. That fact that this experience also affects women may be one of the factors related to the increasing rate of violence being observed among girls and women. The studies that have looked at what happens when interventions reduce parents' use of hitting and coercive behavior are equally interesting. They show that subsequently the children often exhibit a reduction in aggressive behavior.

People in Jail Were Spanked. Spanking can ultimately affect behavior outside the home as well. Involvement with the juvenile justice system and violent crime is substantially increased among males in this population and possibly among females too. A parallel observation is that those states that permit use of corporal punishment in schools, and particularly those with a comparatively higher actual use of corporal punishment in that setting, have significantly higher rates of school vandalism and of school violence. This observation held even when the data were corrected for confounding factors such as rates of poverty, racial distribution, and geographical region.[9]

Breaking the Cycle

It is clear from the data and observations outlined previously in this chapter that the family environment, particularly but not solely for young children, has a crucial influence on individuals' risk for and potential resilience to violent behavior as teenagers and young adults. Experiences of physical and emotional abuse, of witnessing violence, particularly between parents, and of regularly receiving corporal punishment all appear to independently influence risk in a significant way. These experiences all too often occur concurrently, and this only exacerbates the potential risk, as there are likely to be cumulative effects with multiple exposures.

Exposure to violence in the home is among the strongest influences on risk for involvement in violence, and it may be that the earlier it occurs, the worse or more serious the effect. Even though ours is a society that emphasizes privacy and independent choice, we must respond assertively and definitively to this situation. Protecting children and minimizing what might be perceived as invasion of the privacy of the home should not be and must not be incompatible agendas. We must consider new ways of approaching these issues and challenge the status quo that permits these circumstances to persist.

The issue of child abuse has been out in the open for years, and at this point every state has laws that require reporting of suspected abuse. These efforts need to be enhanced and promoted to ensure as rapid and appropriate a response to child abuse as possible. But this is not enough. When child abuse is recognized and confirmed, the response needs to be more than just ensuring the safety of that child. The long-term effects of the experience must be addressed as well.

Most states have allocated enormous resources for the investigation of child abuse. The primary objective of these efforts is to ensure the safety of the child. However, all too often the long-term and potentially expensive services that can help a child recover and avoid or minimize the long-term consequences are not a part of the services. Even though it is important to ensure a child's safety, it is equally important to ensure or improve his or her probability of experiencing a healthy life. The cycle of violence is real and must be broken at the critical places.

Teaching Parenting Skills

Furthermore, there are things communities can do to reduce and prevent child abuse. Teaching parenting skills and child development to all high school students is one. Parenting does not come naturally, especially in today's high-tech, complicated, consumer-focused world. We would do well to make the teaching of parenting skills a basic component of the U.S. educational system. Driving is much less complicated than parenting. In order to drive, one must obtain a license by passing a written test on the relevant laws and a practical test of one's driving ability. Licensing people before they can become parents is unthinkable, yet we should at the very least commit to promoting the basic knowledge and skills. Parenting may be the most important job adults do for a society.

Similarly, we must greatly enhance our services to support families in their efforts to create healthy, secure environments for their children. Postnatal home visiting, a regular practice in many other countries, has shown great promise in reducing rates of child abuse, among other positive results. Parents need nurturing and support if they are to be optimal caretakers of their children. This is basic.

Unfortunately, too many families don't have the essential support systems available to them. Through public policy and professional practices, the broader community needs to ensure that this support is present for all families. At first glance this may seem costly, but the projected long-term savings from reduced child abuse and better outcomes for both parents and children that have been observed in existing home visitation programs more than justify the initial investment. Researcher David Olds, who has studied this strategy in upstate New York (where he runs and evaluates home visiting programs) and other places, has provided important and encouraging information on this approach.[10] Some in influential positions, such as former U.S. attorney general Janet Reno and Senator Hillary Rodham Clinton, are now aware of its effectiveness. It is to be hoped that this knowledge will spread and begin to directly inform policy.

Providing Good Child Care

Similarly, good-quality, affordable child care, family support centers, parenting help lines, and other services that provide options and opportunities for parents all contribute to a family's ability to maintain a nurturing, nonviolent environment for childrearing. It is important to make policies and set professional practices that recognize a collective responsibility to children and reflect an understanding that to raise healthy children we must have healthy families.

In the area of domestic violence we must first recognize and accept the extensive presence of this problem in our country. For far too long, we have ignored or denied the extent to which violence in families occurs, setting the stage for other types of violence. For many women, the violence perpetuated against them goes unrecognized. Women regularly show up in emergency rooms with injuries that can only be explained by a violent altercation, yet they are often never asked what happened, or if they are asked, they are not challenged when they give inadequate explanations. Given the high prevalence of domestic violence, professionals must be more alert to the signs, not only for the sake of the victimized woman but in order to respond to the serious implications for the children in the home as well.

Recognition of the extent of the problem must be followed by a variety of services. Universal screening in all health care facilities allows all women seeking services for any reason to be asked about the presence of violence in their homes. Screenings should not be limited to health care facilities but incorporated into almost every community institution. Women are not angry when asked, "Are you afraid? Has anyone hit you?" Such questions are understood as a sign of concern, not prying. Not asking is tacit acceptance of domestic violence as inevitable and unchangeable.

It Takes a Village to Raise a Family

In addition, services to help women and children respond to and remove themselves from violent situations need to be more available. These services include safe housing, financial resources, mental health counseling, legal support, and job training or career counseling. Although some of these services exist where they are needed, there aren't enough, and there are very few services for the children in these families. In fact women with sons over the age of twelve or so are not allowed in most battered women's shelters because of fear that the son will display violent behavior.

Services offered must recognize that the children have been victimized as well, whether or not they have been physically abused. These children require interventions to help them deal with the short- and long-term consequences they are at risk for. When women go unrecognized as victims of domestic violence, as is all too often the case, then their children are ignored or forgotten as the indirect victims.

We ourselves believe that prevention is the most important element when addressing domestic violence. Education (both individual and broad-based public education), legal strategies, and efforts to change the community values and media images that affect gender socialization norms and behaviors all are part of the solution. "No tolerance" policies for domestic violence would go a long way toward changing public attitudes and cultural norms. Establishing such policies requires active participation and education of the public, the police, and the court system, so that all can respond consistently and firmly when they are in a position to do so. There have been many public service campaigns about child abuse; this nation now needs to do the same for domestic violence. Increased awareness is part of the solution.

Reducing Corporal Punishment

When hitting children was made illegal in Sweden, over twenty years ago, over three-quarters of the population opposed the law. Ten years later a similar survey found that popular opinion had completely reversed itself and that a majority now supported the law.[11] The law did not provide a specific punishment for those parents who did hit their children. It did, however, authorize services to help parents who were unable to comply. The message was that hitting children was not a healthy thing to do. The law recognized that most parents were not trying to harm their children, just having difficulty handling or managing them. Support and education were provided to give parents other options and help them work out whatever else might have been going on.

It strikes us that such a strategy has a place in this country as well. Think about the message it would give to both parents and children because it is so respectful of children and also so nurturing of parents in its recognition that most parents need help, support, and education to be good parents.

Instead of spanking or hitting, parents can use many other and more effective ways of disciplining children and supporting their use of positive social behaviors. Time-outs for younger children and clear rules that have consistent nonviolent consequences, for example, have been shown to be very effective for most children. Rewards and recognition for good behaviors have also been shown to be quite effective in teaching children how to behave and succeed. And for those children that have more difficulty responding, other services such as counseling and special school and child-care programs need to be brought into play.

The alternatives to violent punishment are extensive but not commonly known by professionals or parents. The consequences of violent punishment are equally unknown by many, and the false assumptions about the effectiveness and appropriateness of corporal punishment are far too common.

Reducing the Risk by Changing the Environment

It really does take a village to raise a family. Recognizing this is key to addressing the environments that put so many children at risk for violence. Understanding how early experiences in the lives of children can dramatically influence their future is part of the necessary change.

Part Three

What Happened in Boston

Chapter Ten

Violence Is Preventable

"So, what happened in Boston? Tell us the model in detail." We are asked these questions everywhere we go. We have trouble answering because we don't know exactly what happened in Boston. We do know that there is no single explanation. Despite the credit some are willing to take, no single program or person is responsible. In fact we attribute the success Boston has had in reducing youth violence to an accumulation of many programs and efforts over many years. Through training, public awareness, community activism, multisector involvement, and lay leadership, an avalanche of programs cascaded through the city. The result was a dramatic decline in youth deaths from violence.

The Boston experience offers a model of how one city reduced youth violence. It illustrates many strategies that work as well as some that don't. The work here was not easy and is far from done. But we are proud of the success so far in Boston and hope that what happened here can help and motivate others.

The Boston story is really about thousands of people who stepped up to the challenge. It's fascinating to think back and consider how this all came to be. The early pioneers of this movement were heroes and risk takers from many places, people willing to question the status quo and see things in a different way. Some seasoned participants came from expected sites like the criminal justice system, people who were trained and paid to deal with the problems of violence. Pioneers came from the fields of health and mental health, having seen and dealt with those who suffered the consequences of violent injury. Risk takers came from public health, bringing the statistics on lost lives and disabilities. Unexpected heroes came from among people in the religious sector, the families of victims, survivors, teachers and other educators, coaches and frontline workers in youth programs, community residents from some of the poorest and most vulnerable neighborhoods, and the youth themselves.

These early heroes had several things in common. They saw violence as preventable, not inevitable. They were willing to take chances even when faced with rejection, ridicule, and an overwhelming problem. They were creative and flexible, not accepting of doing things the same old way with the same nonresults. They brought commitment and caring beyond their own immediate needs. They remained optimistic. They had faith in young people, even those that appeared lost and unreachable. And they were in it for the long haul.

We can never describe all of what happened in detail. There were too many people involved to keep track of it all. What we do in this part of the book is to give pieces of the story, examples that bring the process to life. Through these individual stories we hope to convey the breadth and energy of the Boston violence prevention movement, to convey a sense of what happened at the outset and as the movement grew.

What happened in Boston can and is happening in other places. It can happen anywhere committed people come together.

Victory Has Many Handmaidens

In 1996, President Clinton and Attorney General Reno came to Boston to celebrate the exciting development that was countering a trend occurring in most of the rest of the country. Although youth homicide rates were plateauing and in some areas rising across the nation, Boston had gone for over a year with no gun-related juvenile homicides. There was real cause for celebration, not only because of the dramatically declining loss of young lives in the city but also because this change grew out of definable and describable efforts. Clinton and Reno saw that similar efforts could be used in other places to help turn around the epidemic of youth violence facing the nation as a whole.

In the late 1980s and early 1990s, Boston had not been making the headlines on a regular basis with violent events, the way New York City, Washington, D.C., and Los Angeles were, yet homicide was a leading cause of death for teenagers in the city. At the peak of this epidemic, one juvenile or more was killed each month in Boston. The victims and assailants were getting younger and younger. Over the years, through the work and commitment of hundreds, eventually thousands, of individuals, Boston put a halt to this tragedy. In fact the moratorium on juvenile deaths that the president and the attorney general celebrated continued for over two and a half years in Boston. Today the incidence of youth violence remains extremely low, with only several firearm-related deaths of children younger than seventeen in the last three and a half years.

The Johnny Appleseed Approach

The components of the Boston violence prevention movement, which began in the early 1980s, were basic community organizing, public education, training of professionals and community workers, and creative trial and error at the local community level. At the time, none of us who were involved knew what would work. Adopting traditional youth service and public health strategies, we used a deliberate Johnny Appleseed approach, sowing seeds around the city and watching what happened.

A decade and a half later we still see the fruits of that early work. Model programs and partnerships exist all over Boston involving health care, mental health, the police and the courts, the religious community, schools, youth programs, community centers, community coalitions, and countless others. Through a good part of the 1980s, Boston City Hospital was training one hundred people every other month. These trained people often started programs or incorporated violence prevention into existing programs. Program participants started spin-off programs. Over the years the young people who were trained grew up, wrote books, became program directors, and are now carrying the movement forward.

Knowing and understanding the issues that contribute to the risk of violence was central to what happened in Boston. Those of us involved at the beginning used a fundamental premise: violence is learned behavior. Most youth violence grows out of conflicts and arguments between friends, acquaintances, and family members, not between strangers and not in the context of premeditated criminal activity. The easy availability of handguns and the frequency of weapon carrying greatly enhance the likelihood of severe injury when an argument occurs. The normal developmental processes that all adolescents experience as they mature into adulthood create vulnerabilities that put them at particularly high risk for violence. These basic facts provided the starting point for creatively and successfully addressing the problem.

Getting Started

Our own work together in youth violence prevention began in 1982 with a four-year grant from the Robert Wood Johnson Foundation that was part of a larger initiative to address a broad range of problems of high-risk youth that included violence as well as substance abuse, sexually transmitted diseases, depression, and teenage pregnancy.[1] At the time, we were both working as clinicians for Boston City Hospital, and the grant proposal was submitted under the umbrella of the Boston Health Department. Ours was one of twenty programs around the nation awarded funding to develop programs to provide services to teenagers identified with problems involving the issues listed above. A formidable task for sure but one that stemmed from the growing recognition that young people in this country were in serious trouble, with disproportionately high rates of death and disability when compared to the rates for youth in most of the rest of the world.

The task also grew out of the recognition that most teenagers experienced these problems in combinations rather than individually. Few teenagers had a single issue; most had multiple concerns that needed to be addressed together, not separately. At that time, many programs for youth were organized to deal with a single issue, such as substance abuse, and were not necessarily prepared to deal with all the other problems that teenagers brought with them, even though all the issues were interrelated and stemmed from the same underlying causes.

Making Mistakes

We made many mistakes right from the beginning. First, we named our program the Boston Program for High Risk Youth, printing up several thousand glossy brochures with the name of the program in large letters on the front cover and proudly distributing them all over the city. Immediately we discovered that few teenagers were drawn to a program that labeled them "high risk." The program was quickly renamed the Boston Youth Program, and new brochures were printed—the old ones used for scrap paper. This was our first lesson. Teenagers needed to be involved in the development of the program from its name to its content and design. They need to be as much a part of the solution as adults and professionals were.

Our second and bigger mistake took longer to recognize. As physicians, we had been taught to think in what is called the *medical model*. This model, or approach to services, involves the identification of a problem and the implementation of a treatment or intervention plan in a clinical setting. We were funded to set up adolescent clinical programs in a number of community health centers and at Boston City Hospital; teenagers identified with problems were to be referred to these programs for medical and mental health services. The referral system involved collaborations with the public schools and other community agencies, and considerable efforts were established to engage referred youth in ongoing long-term relationships with the doctors and mental health professionals in the program.

Moving from Reaction to Prevention

During the first several years of the program, we observed several important phenomena. Teenagers were extremely reluctant to come for services in health care facilities, particularly when they did not perceive they had a problem. And teenagers with such problems as we were addressing did not necessarily perceive that they actually had a problem. Therefore seeking help was not on their agenda. Even those that did come were difficult to engage in longer-term services and rarely kept follow-up appointments. For the most part they came when they had to, for a sports physical or when in pain. As a result, we realized that we were not helping very many kids and were not developing the professional practices and skills that would turn these children's problems around and reduce the incidence of violence.

This realization led us to dramatically shift our perspective and implement major, midcourse directional changes. The most basic of these changes was a reorientation to prevention. Our original grant proposal to the Robert Wood Johnson Foundation was written as both a prevention and service project. We had proposed the development of three prevention curricula (for violence, substance abuse, and sex education). This mixture of prevention education and treatment services, although ideal, was a bit too ambitious and too much based in the medical model.

Although we knew that we had to continue services for those teenagers who were already in trouble, we also knew we needed to more deliberately embrace the public health approach and expand those activities that stopped the flow of kids into destructive behaviors. Furthermore, we had to step out of the settings that were familiar and comfortable for us, the traditional health care facilities, and go to where the kids were. If they weren't coming to us, we had to go to them.

Building Essential Collaborations

To go to the youth we had to develop approaches and strategies that could be used for prevention activities, and we had to nurture the relationships and collaborations necessary to extend our activities beyond the health care setting to the places where we could reach young people, the schools and other community-based settings. We also realized that many of the underlying factors that contributed to putting young people at risk were rooted in the larger community environment. True prevention efforts required working to change attitudes toward youth and community values that promoted or encouraged risky behaviors. Our efforts needed to extend beyond the youth themselves to the community as a whole.

This change in perspective, along with one other factor, planted the seeds of our work focusing on youth violence and the strategies needed to build a violence prevention movement. The other factor was our realization that violence and violent injury were becoming prominent and serious health problems for young people in our community. Although violence was one of the six issues we were funded to address, there was almost no prevention experience from which we could learn.

Labeling Violence a Public Health Problem: A Critical Step

Violence was just beginning to be recognized as a serious public health problem. The then surgeon general of the United States, C. Everett Koop, was about to come out with his declaration that violence was one of the most serious public health problems facing this country. This statement was based on the observation that the United States had one of the highest homicide rates in the world, dramatically higher than the rate for every other Western nation. In addition, it was clear that the consequences of violence disproportionately affected youth and that violence was one of the leading causes of years of potential life lost in this country.

Homicide had become the second leading cause of death among U.S. teenagers and the leading cause of death among African American teenagers. Public health and mental health studies were beginning to identify some of the characteristics and associated risk factors of violent behavior, strongly supporting the possibility of prevention strategies. The nation was beginning to learn that the violence young people were experiencing was not inevitable but preventable if communities could alter the risk factors that set children and youth up for violence.

At that time, the experience of the health care community with respect to violent injury was generally limited to the treatment of the injuries themselves, a "stitch 'em up and send 'em out" approach. There was no consideration that other things could be done and that these violent injuries could be prevented before they happened. Later studies have shown that individuals who experience violent injury are at particularly high risk for future injury and death, and yet nothing was being done to intervene beyond immediate medical treatment.

As a result we were essentially starting from scratch. In fact one of the unexpected obstacles we faced in our early violence prevention work was the resistance and skepticism of our own colleagues in the field of medicine. There was great resistance to accepting the issue of violence prevention as a legitimate part of health care, even though the victims of violence were presenting at hospital doorsteps in ever growing numbers and health care settings were actually seeing more of the people involved in violence than were the police. In general, health care professionals, like many others, viewed violence as an issue for the criminal justice system and were very slow to come to the realization that they had a role to play in the prevention of and response to violence. More important, no profession focused on violence prevention. If anything was done in any profession, it was a response to violence that had already occurred, not prevention.

The importance of prevention as a response to violence became obvious to us very early on in our work. As part of the preparation for the Robert Wood Johnson Foundation funded program, we did an analysis of the causes of death of teenagers in the city of Boston. We looked at the mortality data for teenagers in the city for the decade prior to the start of our program. Over that decade (the early 1970s through the early 1980s), homicide had become the leading cause of death for teenagers, surpassing even deaths from automobile crashes (an observation that has been made in a number of other large metropolitan areas as well). This led us to prioritize violence in our program agenda. Doing this made us somewhat different from the other programs that the Robert Wood Johnson Foundation was sponsoring.

Few of the other programs had chosen to address violence in any major way, and none had prioritized violence prevention. We focused on violence because of the statistics and because we were willing to take career risks to break new ground. Others lacked experience with the issue, felt a sense of helplessness, and did not define violence as a health problem.

Our initial, limited experience came from the efforts of one of us (Deborah) in addressing violence using a health education approach. A growing body of scientific evidence demonstrated that the use of violence was a learned behavior. Children were actually learning that violence was an acceptable and potentially successful way to deal with anger and conflict and could solve their problems. They were learning this from exposures to violence in their families and communities as well as through the media, particularly television. In addition, most of the violence young people were experiencing occurred in the context of arguments with family members, friends, and acquaintances. It stood to reason that if children and teenagers were learning to use violence in these situations, educational interventions to help them understand and develop alternative strategies and responses might change the way they behaved when angry or in conflict.

Making Health Education the Cornerstone

Using Albert Bandura's social learning theory model and curricula developed for adolescents on other health issues, we expanded work done by Deborah several years earlier as a medical school project. This project had involved teaching health education classes on homicide and suicide prevention in tenth-grade health classes at Boston Technical School in 1978. Out of this work came the Violence Prevention Curriculum for Adolescents, which was then piloted in Cathedral High School and the Jeremiah Burke High School in Boston, both serving some of the highest-risk students in the city.

This curriculum takes students through a process of understanding anger and acquaints them with the situations and behaviors that provoke a lot of the violence in this society. It uses a simplified *cost-benefit* analysis of fighting to highlight the choices they make in situations that can lead to violence and the alternative options they could consider. It uses videotaped scenarios so that students can practice alternative behaviors in conflict situations. It is extremely participatory, allowing students to think through the issues and identify risks and protective behaviors on their own, with guidance from the instructor and each other. It was developed on the premise that teenagers would not simply accept that violence is a risky option but would need to explore scenarios and come to conclusions on their own.

An overriding theme is that all students, even those who do not fight, have a role. Passing rumors, egging on fights, and joining the crowd are all examples of instigating behaviors that lead to fights. Violence prevention is defined as everyone's responsibility. This is exposed and explored in the curriculum.

We found that students could become extremely engaged in the subject of violence and that given the opportunity they opened up like faucets on the issue. It was clear that this was an important and intimate issue for them. They were quite open to discussion of the elements that led violence to be such a central part of their lives and also open to strategies for dealing with violence. Attendance rose in the Burke High School (the site that was more extensively evaluated) during the time the curriculum was offered there, and suspension rates for violent behavior fell, even beyond the period in which the curriculum was offered. Offering the curriculum each year for three years in required tenth-grade health classes at the Burke had changed the environment of the school.

However, students also reported that although they were fighting less in school, the level of violence they were involved with outside school had not changed. This was not surprising, as it was unrealistic to expect that a ten-session curriculum occurring in isolation from everything else in their lives would create enough behavioral change so they could resist the pressure to resort to violence outside of school. However, this did let us know that this approach was able to create change in a piece of children's lives, and that realization became a glimmer of light in an otherwise dark picture. It was a catalyst, allowing us to move on to the larger community level.

Community Organizing

Armed with this curriculum and what we had learned in the first several years of our efforts—the necessity of youth involvement, the need to go to where teenagers normally spend their time, the prominence of violence as an issue for youth, the importance of casting a wider net across the whole community, and the value of using prevention as the cornerstone of our work—we set out to establish the first community-based, public health youth violence prevention initiative in the nation.

Of course we didn't recognize the significance of this at the time, nor do we believe that the dramatic reduction of juvenile homicides in Boston is due to anything less than the hard work of thousands of individuals and programs. But we do believe that this program significantly contributed to what happened in Boston and, among other things, greatly increased the visibility of the issue in the city and the level of attention given to this issue over the next decade. It certainly contributed to the climate change that occurred, and influenced how people thought about youth and the manner in which violence needed to be addressed. We sold the city, both its professionals and lay community, on the concept that violence is preventable, not inevitable. We then helped motivate them to be creative and to start actively addressing prevention.

The Boston Violence Prevention Project Is Born

With the funding remaining from our original project and additional support from a local philanthropy, the Boston Foundation, we began the Boston Violence Prevention Project. We approached this newer effort very differently from our first effort. Rather than setting up a clinical program (although the Boston Youth Program continued), we spent the first year of our efforts literally pounding the pavement to build a community of support for violence prevention.

During that first year we went out and met with people. We approached everyone around the city who we thought might have a role to play in a large violence prevention effort. Our efforts included the obvious people: school personnel (both central administrative staff as well as individual school leaders), the Boston police, the key leadership in City Hall, juvenile court judges, mental health program staff, youth program staff, and local human service agency directors. But we felt this wasn't enough. We also approached religious and church leaders, tenants associations in public housing projects, and youth groups. We attended community meetings of various sorts and spent more time in community meeting rooms and church basements than we had ever anticipated.

Having Belief, Knowledge, Experience, Energy, and Conviction

We brought several things into these meetings and discussions. First was our belief that we were dealing with a preventable problem. Second was our understanding of the issue, both its magnitude and what we knew of the science available on the risk factors related to violence. Third was our experience of the two previous years, in particular, the curriculum and its influence on the environment of Burke High School. Fourth was our energy, excitement, and hope that something could be done. Fifth was our conviction that to be effective any effort needed to be broadly based in the whole community and required the commitment of many individuals and agencies across the city.

What we didn't do was come with answers. We wanted and needed to hear what others thought about what we were saying as well as what they had learned from their own experiences. We had identified a problem, which was really the problem of the whole community, and we had some thoughts on what could be done and what was possible. We knew that the real solutions would come from a broader community buy-in to the problem and from the collective thinking and ideas of all the players.

We wanted to be catalysts for bringing the community together on this and for creating a sense of hopefulness and empowerment. We structured all our activities toward achieving a climate in which something positive could happen, and this we believe we accomplished by seeking the input of many community members, careful listening, and avoiding suggestions of quick fixes and simple solutions.

From this initial groundwork we began to plan and develop the program itself. We entered this phase with support and interest from many of the people and institutions we visited. We had buy-in from most every segment of the community, including public sector leadership, criminal justice professionals, educators, religious leaders, clinical and human service professionals, and most important, grassroots community groups and youth groups.

Taking a Neighborhood Focus

Our first decision at this point was to focus our efforts on several specific neighborhoods of Boston. We did this in part to start at a manageable level of activity. We also hoped to scientifically evaluate the effectiveness of the program, and to do so we would need control groups, areas of the city that remained "untouched" and therefore available for comparison. The latter agenda was impractical and misguided, however. We learned quickly that it was impossible to restrict the activities of the program to specific geographical areas. Service agencies were unwilling, not surprisingly, to differentiate their services according to where a person or family lived. We found this out from agency staff who made it crystal clear that they would offer any of their services to any and all who came to them. They had no interest in a scientific evaluation if it interfered with their delivery of services,(indeed, this is a common issue in program evaluation in general). Furthermore, there were activities such as a large-scale public education campaign through the media that reached well beyond the designated neighborhoods and had to do so if they were to be in any way effective.

The neighborhoods in which we chose to start were South Boston and Roxbury. Roxbury, which was and still is a predominantly African American neighborhood, had the highest youth homicide rate in the city. South Boston, a predominantly white, Irish American neighborhood, had the third-highest but most rapidly rising youth homicide rate. Interestingly, when we looked at the most recent census data available at the time, apart from race these two neighborhoods looked almost identical. They had similar rates of poverty (being the two poorest neighborhoods in the city), housing density, unemployment rates, and other indicators of general health risk. These were also neighborhoods that had long been at serious odds with each other. In the previous five or so years the specific focus of this antagonism had been a court-ordered school busing plan implemented during the mid-1970s. Boston is a city with a long-standing history of racial conflict, and these two neighborhoods represented the two ends of the conflict spectrum.

Even more interestingly, in spite of this long-standing neighborhood conflict, during the first several years of our project many collaborations evolved between agencies and community groups across neighborhood boundaries as people began to discover the common ground they had when dealing with this issue. This was an unexpected outcome that offers lessons in and of itself. We learned from this not to assume that historical conflicts between neighborhoods would play out as a factor in the violence prevention effort. We also learned that providing information to communities could change perceptions and attitudes about other communities and other people. Information is a powerful change agent when used effectively.

Using Outreach and Training as Major Tactics

The initial program effort involved working with and training a broad spectrum of community agency staff in violence prevention. To accomplish this we recruited and hired two wonderfully dynamic men. We chose to recruit individuals who reflected the race and ethnicity of the youth in each of the neighborhoods.

Paul Bracy is an African American from Boston who at the time had recently retired from military service. He had worked in the military on race relations issues, among other things, and brought with him considerable experience in conflict resolution and large-group dynamics. He approached us after reading an article in the local newspaper about our work. We hired him almost on the spot to lead the work in Roxbury. It was one of the easiest and quickest hires either of us has ever made. It just felt right.

Finding someone to work in South Boston was a more difficult task. Despite extensive recruiting efforts, we failed initially to find the right person to lead the work in that neighborhood. We were facing considerable pressure from our funders to get moving on this but chose to hold out until we found the right person. We felt it would be a mistake to acquiesce to time and funder pressures and risk compromising the quality of the effort. We have never regretted this decision and strongly recommend a similar attitude for others doing this work.

We eventually connected with Mark Bukaras, a young white man from Boston. At the time, he was working as a salesman for a local fish distributing company but had aspirations to return to graduate school to become a psychologist (which he eventually did). He was dynamic and enthusiastic and, most important, he was familiar with the history and neighborhood politics of South Boston. We were most drawn to his personal characteristics and his level of energy and open-mindedness. In addition, we considered his experience as a salesman a plus, as selling was a big part of what we needed him to do. We had to convince people that violence is preventable. In effect, we had to sell violence prevention.

Our recruiting experience points out the importance of choosing staff carefully and being open to finding appropriate people in unexpected ways and situations. People who present themselves in a sensitive manner and who have the skills to be cultural filters for the program message are important components of program success.

Both of these men were sent out, after a period of training, to follow up with the various individuals we had initially met with in their respective neighborhoods. They went out with a basic understanding of the issue and the process we had been through over the previous year. They also went out with the violence prevention curriculum that had been developed for high schools as a starting point for discussion with agency staff and community groups. We did not expect the curriculum to be used directly in most of these settings. But we felt it was important to have a concrete example of what might be done, and we hoped that the curriculum might be modified for use in other settings. In some settings (particularly the more institutional ones) that is just what happened; in many other settings the curriculum became a base upon which other ideas were considered and developed.

A Change of Plans: Working Across Neighborhoods

One of the first modifications we made with respect to this plan was to scrap the restriction that limited Paul Bracy and Mark Bukaras to working in their respective neighborhoods. One of their first observations was that the commonalities between the two neighborhoods far outweighed the differences. As a result, they felt they could be more effective if both of them worked in both communities. This was most insightful of them as it facilitated cross-neighborhood collaborations and emphasized neighborhood similarities rather than differences to the community people working on the project.

Funding a New Idea

While Bracy and Bukaras were out in the field, we were continuing our efforts to build community-wide buy-in and raise the agenda of violence prevention to a more visible level in the larger community. This activity took several forms.

First and foremost we needed to build a larger and longer-term funding base for our work. It was clear to us that it would take years (and it did) to get the city Health Department to begin to support this work with public funding. So we pounded the pavement to raise funds. We wrote innumerable grant proposals and successfully constructed a broad base of funding that included several local foundations, a number of national foundations, the federal government, and several service contracts relating to work relevant to violence prevention. This was extremely time consuming, and we would have benefited greatly from a full-time grant writer had we had the resources. Like most real-world programs, ours didn't have that luxury. We blindly submitted proposals to a variety of private foundations and responded to every request for proposals (RFP) that even by the merest thread had anything to do with violence or youth. Nights and weekends were spent churning out proposals until we began to see a payoff. Even then we couldn't afford to relax and ease up on this activity.

Some of our funders of particular note were the Burden Foundation (which was the first to fund the development of the violence prevention curriculum), the Kaiser Family Foundation (which agreed to fund a multiyear program evaluation), the Boston Foundation and the Hyams Trust (two local foundations), the Maternal and Child Health Bureau of the U.S. Department of Health and Human Services, and the U.S. Department of Justice (which funded the evaluation of the violence prevention curriculum).

As another way of building the program's funding base we also went after public sector service contracts that related to treatment or evaluation of troubled youth. Among the service contracts we were awarded was a counseling contract from the Boston Public Schools' alternative program for students found carrying weapons. This not only brought us needed funding but also created an important bridge for collaboration with the city's public school system.

Obtaining diverse funding is always a challenge, but it is essential to the long-term survival of similar efforts. Our success in this effort was beyond our expectations, probably reflecting our role as pioneers. (The downside of being pioneers was that potential funders frequently seemed quite puzzled by our approach.) We were able to raise enough funding to allow the program to continue well beyond our own tenure as program leaders and until the city of Boston saw the light and agreed to take on the program as an institutional commitment. This city decision took far too long, and we hope that other communities learn from our experience and take ownership of such projects sooner. This would conserve community members' energy for the real work needing to be done. Raising funds drains the energy of volunteer and staff and distracts these individuals from the important service agendas, as many agency directors know as well as we do.

Setting a Role for the Media

In addition to this fundraising work we recognized the importance of developing a more public presence for the program and its agenda. Somewhat fortuitously, at the same time that we were beginning our effort the Advertising Council of Greater Boston was holding a competition for its annual public service campaign. The winner of this competition was to receive a free and full-blown advertising campaign donated by a council member. Traditionally, the council looked for worthy agencies to promote and support, and therefore the selection committee was somewhat taken aback but also intrigued by the concept we proposed, that this campaign be issue based rather than agency driven.

We suggested that the council consider a campaign to highlight the seriousness of the issue of violence, market the concept of violence as preventable, and promote alternatives to violence in dealing with conflict. We did not want to promote ourselves or our program as much as we wanted to sell an idea and build awareness. Not only was our proposal selected by the council, but Hill Holiday

Advertising Agency, one of the more prestigious agencies in the city and the country, offered to take us on as clients. Since then a number of groups have developed similar efforts (most notably the Squash It! campaign done for NCAA basketball), but at the time this was a breakthrough effort and daring commitment on the part of the advertising council and Hill Holiday. With this mid-1980s effort, we believe we were the first in the country to develop an interpersonal violence prevention (rather than crime prevention) media campaign.

The campaign's slogan was "Friends for Life, Don't Let Friends Fight." The advertising agency produced two thirty-second public service announcements (PSAs) that were both dramatic and engaging. The PSAs emphasized how some kids set up their friends to fight by passing on rumors and then encouraging a fight to resolve the conflict. This not only illustrated a common scenario that leads to violent injury and death but provided an important insight for young people, revealing how their behavior and choices can have unconsidered consequences.

This experience taught us that the skills developed to sell products can also be used to sell values, and it reemphasized for us the power of the media and marketing. As we discussed earlier, the media have been highly successful in marketing violence as an acceptable and valued behavior. They can be equally successful at marketing the opposite.

Enlisting More Support

Another of our tasks was to continue to build support and commitment from the larger institutional levels of the city. In this endeavor we had mixed success.

The Police Chief: An Ally

An outstanding result of this activity to acquire institutional backing was the collaboration we were able to develop with the Boston

Police Department and particularly with its then commissioner, Francis "Mickey" Roache. Roache was first involved with our activities while still a police officer heading the Civil Disorders Unit of the Police Department. From the beginning he showed a sensitive understanding of the issue of youth violence and was one of our first public supporters.

After becoming commissioner he was quoted as saying publicly, "You can give me all the police you want and build all the prison cells you can afford but until you stop the flow of kids into violence I cannot fix the problem." This was a courageous statement for him to make and one for which he was ridiculed by his peers. It ran counter to the thinking and attitudes of the time. The public pressure to be macho about crime and violence, promoting the traditional responses to violence even though they weren't working, was considerable. For a person in the public eye as much as he was to say what he did was remarkable and way ahead of the times. It was also an important boost for us, both personally and publicly.

Continuing in this vein he incorporated violence prevention into the DARE program (a curriculum addressing substance abuse and taught by police officers) and laid the groundwork for the development of community policing in Boston. In 1987, he cochaired a Massachusetts Public Health Department task force on youth violence. This early effort on his part led to a number of high-profile collaborations between the police and a number of other groups, including the juvenile probation unit of the Boston courts and the Ten Point Coalition (an ecumenical group of Boston ministers dedicated to reducing violence in the city).

It is these collaborations that have received considerable national attention, and although many take credit for these efforts, Commissioner Roache did the early work that allowed such projects to come to be.

At the same time, the magnitude of the public pressure to do things the same old way was considerable. So even though Mickey Roache clearly understood the problems underlying youth violence and understood that traditional police practices were unlikely to make a difference, at times he too gave in to public pressure. At a time when youth violence rates were soaring, he was quoted as saying that if he could just find and arrest the one hundred worst kids in the city, things would get better. He knew better than this, but this example points out how vulnerable public figures are to the pressure to promote muscle tactics as a cure for violence.

The Public Schools: Difficult to Reach

On the other hand we had mixed success with the Boston Public Schools. What we discovered over time in this process was that dealing with the bureaucracy of the central system required a considerable effort for even limited results. Getting central approval for the implementation of the violence prevention curriculum systemwide was essentially impossible because of the long, unwieldy approval process, even though the curriculum had originally been developed in one of the Boston schools. We did better, although it also required an extensive effort, in getting access to school suspension data, which was a key component in our larger program evaluation.

The better strategy for getting the curriculum in place, although it was very labor intensive, was to approach each school principal or headmaster individually, giving him or her the concrete examples of the successful implementation of the curriculum at the Burke and Cathedral High Schools. We learned that leaders at the individual school level had a fair amount of authority over what was implemented in each school and were generally more approachable than the downtown bureaucrats.

Unfortunately, this meant that the curriculum piece of the project was implemented in a spotty fashion, and it is hard to quantify the extent to which it was actually put in place. This was a significant disappointment for us, as the curriculum was being implemented in other school systems around the country at the same time as we were unable to fully accomplish this in our own community. In time we were invited to conduct systemwide in-service trainings, and through teacher and principal initiatives the curriculum was implemented throughout one of the public school zones (as the clusters into which the Boston Public Schools were then organized were called).

City Hall: Even More Difficult

City Hall (in which we include the Boston Health Department) was yet another story. It was not so much that there was resistance to our work or our agenda at this level of city government as that there were many complex dynamics that resulted in the low level of interest, attention, and support we received. At the Health Department itself, there just wasn't much interest at all. We were pretty much allowed to do what we wanted as long as there was outside funding to support it. Fortunately and luckily that was not a problem for our project, but it did create ongoing concern about the project's long-term future. It was not until several years after we had both left the Health Department that movement toward the institutionalization of the program occurred. By this time both of us had received considerable national attention for our efforts, and the success of the program and of Boston in reducing violent deaths had begun to attract the interest of many beyond the city.

The factors that made support from City Hall hazy at best were multifaceted. As noted earlier the public pressure on politicians forced tough-minded, knee-jerk responses to violence, reactions that generally failed to recognize many of the realities. Traditional police responses were most often called into play, as they were in promoting the perception that if enough "bad kids" were locked up everything would be all right. It is, however, important to restate that in this climate the early seeds of community policing and some other of the newer criminal justice strategies were also beginning to take hold.

One of the best examples of an inappropriate response to violence was the highly publicized 1990 case involving the murder of a pregnant woman after she and her husband had attended a prenatal class in a downtown Boston teaching hospital. The woman's husband, Charles Stuart, who was wounded as well, claimed that both of them had been shot by a young African American man after they had gotten lost in the neighborhood around the hospital.

The political response from City Hall was dramatic and extensive. Random searches were instituted in inner-city neighborhoods, and all the misguided stereotypes relating to race and youth were evoked. Within days of the event, however, it was determined that the husband had done the shooting, a possibility that anyone who knew the data on violence should have suspected from the start. In most homicides the victim and the assailant do know each other. This is particularly true for an overwhelming majority of the women who are murdered.

This single event and its aftermath (including the suicide of the husband) not only set back the violence prevention movement in the city but also greatly strained important relationships needed to build the collaborations crucial to turning the tide on violent injury rates.

There were additional dynamics that made working with City Hall difficult and that might be issues for other communities as well. Collaboration appears to be generally difficult in local government circles. Interpersonal rivalries; jockeying for position, influence, and credit; and other such behaviors greatly affect how people operate in this context. Furthermore elected officials often seem to have a great reluctance to take risks and to try to explain or address complex issues that cannot be boiled down to simple sound bites. A further complication is the difficulty of getting elected officials to consider programs, activities, or agendas that extend beyond the next election or whose results may not appear for a number of years, again, beyond the next election period.

Focusing on the Grass Roots

It is our experience that new ideas and activities are far more likely to occur at the neighborhood level and slowly work their way up to the leadership of the larger community than they are to occur the other way around. This is an important consideration for those trying to generate changes similar to the ones we were working toward. It is very helpful to have political leadership on board, but it is not essential at the outset. Elected officials will eventually join in a movement when it is safe to do so. Often this will happen after much of the hard work is done and the risks have lessened.

Chapter Eleven

The Movement Grows

Our efforts were paying off. We were invited to the 1985 Surgeon General's Conference on Violence as a Public Health Problem to discuss the violence prevention curriculum and our community-based efforts. The *New York Times* wrote a story about us, and the *McNeil/Lehrer NewsHour* did a feature story. We were connecting with like-minded colleagues, and the heroes kept coming.

Meanwhile much was happening at the community level through the work of Paul Bracy, Mark Bukaras, and others. Many local agencies eagerly joined in on the efforts, and although they were unsure about how to proceed, they were most willing to try. Bracy and Bukaras became catalysts, technical assistants, sounding boards, trainers, and cheerleaders. Of particular note is that these two men trained approximately one hundred people every other month in violence prevention strategies, possibly one of the biggest contributions our program made to the movement. Although the task at hand was large, many people began to feel that they could do something and discarded their feelings of helplessness.

More People Join the Movement

Over the next several years and in many venues, numerous programs began to appear in the two target communities, reflecting the partnerships that Bukaras and Bracy were developing with the staff of various agencies serving children and youth.

Youth Programs Start Up

Youth programs focused on violence prevention were among the first to be developed. One such effort involved the South Boston Boys and Girls Club. It developed youth groups called Friends for Life Clubs, named after one of the tag lines in the advertising campaign developed by the Hill Holiday Advertising Agency (described in Chapter Ten). These groups not only taught members conflict resolution but also showed them how they could use their influence with friends to devalue violence as an acceptable behavior. Among other things the groups sponsored contests in which community kids designed posters with antiviolence messages that were then distributed around the community.

Similarly, youth groups in the city's Community School Program (which was separate from the Boston Public School Department) were taught violence prevention and conflict resolution, adapting the Violence Prevention Curriculum for Adolescents to after-school settings. Teenagers involved with the Community School Program were taught peer counseling and peer education skills and worked with the program's outreach worker staff to reach out to other kids in the community. In addition, the Youth Congress, an annual event involving teenagers from around the city and sponsored by the community schools, dedicated itself to addressing the issue of violence and provided a very public mechanism through which youth could give input to city officials about the issue.

Coaches and recreation directors in a number of youth facilities around the city started to identify opportunities to incorporate violence prevention into their work with kids. Using pieces of the violence prevention curriculum and applying them when conflicts or arguments developed during practices or games, they took advantage of real-life opportunities to teach players about conflict resolution strategies. Although these were not settings where a formal curriculum could be applied, they were ideal for teaching and modeling practical and pragmatic skills for social interactions, with immediate and visible outcomes.

Black Clergy Make Early Efforts

Bruce Wall, a young minister with the Twelfth Baptist Church in Boston and a court officer for the Boston Juvenile Court, laid the earliest groundwork for the involvement of churches in the violence prevention movement. Reverend Wall began his work with youth in the early 1970s, as youth pastor for Twelfth Baptist. In the early 1980s, around the time that we were getting started on our own efforts, he began to focus his attention on the violence issue.

His interest developed out of experiences and conversations he was having as youth pastor as well as in the context of his work as an assistant court magistrate in the Boston Juvenile Court. From his parishioners (both adults and youth) he was hearing a growing concern about the level of violence in the community. In the court he was hearing from judges and youth that the violence in his community was escalating, as was drug use. Furthermore, he was told by police officer friends that they were under instructions to contain the violence within the black neighborhoods. This policy of containment of violence within specific neighborhoods did nothing to improve the situation and reduce violence. Bruce Wall was angry and frustrated.

In conjunction with a friend in the community, Georgette Watson (who later chaired the Massachusetts Governor's Council Against Drugs), Wall started to organize a march against crime. This project met with considerable opposition and even threats to Wall's and Watson's lives. However, they persisted, and the march took place, starting in one of the central squares of the Roxbury community with fifty people and ending in a second neighborhood, Dorchester, with over five hundred people. This was quite a turnout for a community that was generally difficult to organize and where fear of retribution was considerable. Out of this effort grew a number of programs, including the Drop a Dime Program, which encouraged local residents to report drug dealing and other criminally related activity. With this program the community responded for the first time to the violence and crime that had been allowed to fester and grow there.

Wall also began to work with youth from his church to promote community involvement and responsibility. This effort included demonstrations and marches with the youth to increase awareness of the issues of violence and drugs on the part of youth and adults alike. Some of these marches were organized specifically to bring attention to the drug dens in the neighborhood, with media invited and the marches ending at drug house sites. As best as we can tell, these activities were among the first of their kind in the city (possibly the nation), not only addressing community violence and crime but also bringing young people into the process.

Bruce Wall eventually left Twelfth Baptist in the late 1980s to start his own youth ministry. He felt the kids he had been working with were reachable because they and their families were members of the church. He wanted to get to those kids who were harder to reach. Those who weren't church members, who weren't in school—the street kids. He has since set up shop in the community (in a skating rink—the ultimate example of going to where the kids are and not waiting for them to come to you) and continues to build programs that reach and engage many kids who would otherwise go ignored until they got into trouble.

He has been not only an early pioneer in the movement but also a hero who practiced what he preached and broke new ground for the rest of us and for the involvement of churches in the movement. He laid the groundwork for an expanded collaboration between the clergy and the police and improved community relationships.

Law Enforcement Engages Further

In the criminal justice arena a variety of activities were developed. Several youth detention centers run by the Massachusetts Division of Youth Services incorporated the violence prevention curriculum as a standard component of their program, which focused on youth already in trouble, many of whom were soon to be released back into their communities. This was an important group to reach as some, if not many, would be seen by the other kids in their old neighborhoods as heroes and role models. Of note here is that a juvenile justice–funded evaluation of the violence prevention curriculum showed that kids with the highest scores on violence risk assessment scales were also the ones who showed the greatest change in their attitudes about violence after going through the curriculum.

The juvenile courts, through our outreach to several juvenile court judges, incorporated violence prevention activities into the programs they had in place for juvenile offenders. One such effort was implemented under the direction of Julian Houston, the juvenile justice at the Roxbury district court. Judge Houston was one of our early allies, and his experience with and insights about youth involved with the court system were invaluable. Like Police Commissioner Francis "Mickey" Roache, Houston was one of the people who early on gave us much needed support at a public level and helped to legitimize our efforts.

Roxbury Youthworks, a program for young offenders developed under the Roxbury court, took on some of the components of the violence prevention curriculum. In addition, the court clinic associated with the Roxbury court, which provided mental health assessments and services for youth appearing in the court, began to assess youth for risk of violence and to recommend interventions to mediate these risk factors. Many of these recommendations were then passed on to the youth probation officers, who in turn were responsible for implementing the suggestions and linking kids with services.

Community Policing Begins

Concurrent with these efforts were a number of activities implemented by the police. Many of these efforts occurred independently of our program, initially with the leadership of Police Commissioner Roache and then carried on by his various successors. The first step of these activities was implementing community policing strategies that took a number of police out of their patrol cars and put them on the streets and into public housing projects.

Community policing reestablished police as real people who were part of the community and not faceless authority figures who appeared only when there was trouble. It allowed police to get to know members of the community, including youth, and vice versa. It also established more lines of communication between the police and other community agencies and leaders. This in turn helped in the development of a number of important collaborations between the police and others, several of which have received considerable national attention.

One such collaboration, called the Youth Strike Force, which was started in 1995, involves the police working with youth probation officers from the court system. Together they make regular visits to youth who are on probation to ensure that they are where they are supposed to be and are staying out of trouble. This program promotes a firmer sense of responsibility and accountability on the part of youth under probation and makes their probationary status far more significant than it had been in the past. Prior to this there was a joke among the youth of the city that "the first five are free," meaning that they wouldn't get into serious trouble until they had gotten caught more than five times. Clearly, many kids did not take the juvenile probation system seriously.

One important result of this new program is that more kids stay out of trouble and comply with the probationary plans that have been set up. It also gives a visible sense to young people in general that the consequences of their behavior have serious implications and that getting into trouble does have consequences. Maybe more important is that this partnership demonstrates enough caring and concern for young people that it is clear to adults and children alike that something is being done. Children and youth aren't just being ignored.

Police and Clergy Work Together

A second collaboration that developed involved the police and the religious leadership in the African American Community. An ecumenical group of Boston ministers felt strongly that they had to become aggressively proactive in reducing violence in their community and reducing the extensive loss of life among young black men. The immediate catalyst that brought the group together was several episodes of violence that had occurred in churches. One such incident involved a shooting during the funeral service for a young man who had been murdered in the context of a gang rivalry.

After the group's initial meeting (which was attended by, among others, the cardinal of Boston's Catholic Archdiocese), Reverend Eugene Rivers (who has since made the cover of *Newsweek* magazine), Reverend Ray Hammond, and Urban League director Joan Wallace Benjamin started an initiative called the Ten Point Coalition.

Among other things, the Ten Point Coalition began to work directly with the police to identify kids who were getting into trouble and to recognize situations that were developing into conflicts as early as possible in order to respond proactively rather than reactively. The intent was to identify problems and respond before situations escalated into violent altercations. Mediation and other intervention tactics were applied to resolve conflicts and the individuals who were feeding into the conflicts were brought into services or made aware of potential consequences of their continued disruptive behavior. This effort helped to defuse situations of concern before they got out of hand, and it also gave out yet another message at the community level that there were caring and concerned adults in the community who were both watching out for trouble and willing to step in and intervene. Such messages not only have implications for community pride and empowerment but also support the important notion that the raising of children is a community responsibility.

It is extremely important to the well-being of children and youth that they feel cared about and valued by their communities and in turn feel accountable and responsible to their communities. The efforts of the Ten Point Coalition and its members' collaboration with the police is a significant example of a way to accomplish this. The work of this group deserves all the recognition it has received around the nation and is certainly replicable in most communities.

In addition to its collaboration with the police, the Ten Point Coalition has contributed considerably to the public's awareness of the problem of youth violence. Through their messages to their congregations and to the media, these clergy have given the issue of violence prevention an enhanced sense of immediacy and have spread the word that violence is not inevitable, that we are all responsible for dealing with it, and that youth need to be considered a valuable resource requiring commitment from all.

This was not the only involvement from religious groups. Early on in our program, several other ministers bought into a similar message. We worked with these clergy ourselves to assist them in incorporating violence prevention messages into their sermons and in working with their congregations to establish youth programs that would provide both safe activities for youth and opportunities for learning prosocial values and behaviors.

Engaging the Health Care System

Getting the health care community to accept ownership of a violence prevention agenda and join the movement did not come easily at first. The basic attitude was that the criminal justice system was responsible for responding to violence and that prevention wasn't really possible. All health care providers could do was treat the violent injuries once they occurred. Despite the fact that more people with violent injuries are seen in health care settings than are dealt with by the police, these attitudes prevailed. Through considerable effort the message was conveyed that health institutions were not only seeing more of the consequences of violence but also had an important opportunity to do something about preventing violence.

Creating Buy-In

Through deliberate training and outreach efforts, health care institutions began to establish important components of the violence prevention movement. There were several general efforts that laid the groundwork for specific programs in individual sites. One of the most important of these was the national recognition of domestic violence as a serious problem not only for the battered women but for their children as well. A growing acceptance of the need for universal screening for domestic violence grew out of the recognition that many women who were presenting to health care facilities were battered but that this fact was going unrecognized.

Furthermore, there was a growing recognition that children living in homes with adult violence were at particularly high risk for involvement with violence later in their lives as a result of this exposure. In addition, the overlap between domestic violence and child abuse was becoming clearer. Some studies have found that domestic violence is present in many families where child abuse is found, pointing out that when one form of violence is discovered in a family, other forms of violence need to be explored as well. This made it important to look for abuse once domestic violence had been found, and vice versa.

Establishing New Hospital Protocols

One initial area of concern in health care emerged directly from our emergency room experiences. We recognized early on that we had to change the manner in which people with injuries from violence were addressed when they showed up at the ER door. At Boston City Hospital we implemented a program to ensure that all children and youth admitted to the hospital with violent injuries received a prevention assessment and follow-up to try to reduce their risk for further injury. We used a model similar to one used for patients with asthma. The asthma model made a multidisciplinary team responsible for long-term care in order to reduce future exacerbation of the disease. For patients with injuries from violence, the multidisciplinary team included a violence prevention counselor whom we had trained. The presence of this counselor was important for many reasons but particularly because it appears there is a very high risk of these individuals' experiencing further violent injuries in the future and as much as a 20 percent chance that they will die from a future violent injury.

Each injured child was visited in the hospital by an outreach worker, who continued to follow up and work with the child after he or she was discharged from the hospital. Eventually this service was extended to injured youth seen in the emergency room but not admitted to the hospital. We also worked with the ER staff to improve their evaluation of patients with violent injuries. We developed a standard practice of not only treating the injury but also assessing the patient for risk of future injury. Availability of weapons, intent of revenge, past history of fighting and weapon carrying, presence of violence in the home, and the circumstances of the episode that led to the injury, among other things, became standard information contributing to the formulation of a treatment plan above and beyond the injury treatment itself.

Such a prevention-focused evaluation and treatment plan is important and should be required in all health care settings to reduce further risk of injury. Our work in this area was also built on the traditional emergency room response to suicide prevention. A patient who shows up in an emergency room as the result of a suicide attempt is fully evaluated for the risk that he or she will repeat the attempt once discharged. If the patient states that he or she will go out and try again, that person is not sent home but hospitalized until there are clear indications that the risk of future attempts is no longer present. No patient having made a suicide attempt or gesture is ever sent out without clearly defined follow-up for longer-term services.

Why should it be different for a person with a violent injury who states he (or she) is planning to go out and get the person that did it to him? There is a great likelihood that either that person or someone else will be back with an injury or worse. Similar risk exists when a person continues to carry a weapon and expresses other factors that make a repeat injury or an injury to another likely. Follow-up with appropriate services, and possibly hospitalization if there is an immediate risk of further injury, should be standard practice for these individuals, as it is for those with a self-inflicted injury.

More Services Develop

These efforts have produced a number of important spin-offs. One is a program for children who have witnessed violence. A study in the Boston City Hospital emergency room found that 10 percent of the children seen there had witnessed a stabbing or shooting before their sixth birthday. Linking that information with the observation that children who witness violence early in their lives are at high risk for involvement later as adolescents or young adults (as described in Chapters Four and Nine) led social worker Betsy McAllister Groves to start the Child Witness to Violence Program.

This program provides assessment and counseling to children referred because of an exposure to a violent event of any sort. The program recognizes that such children have short-term consequences, often with symptoms of stress and dysfunction. It further recognizes that these children generally have longer-term consequences, sometimes similar to those seen in posttraumatic stress disorder. They can experience problems with anger and conflict, display regressive behaviors, have sleep disturbance, decline in school performance or other areas of function, become very fearful or anxious, and display other such symptoms.

A relatively immediate response that helps children understand their experience and develop coping mechanisms gives them considerable help in dealing with their immediate symptoms and may help them avoid longer-term consequences.

Given the number of children exposed to violence in this country (again, those working in the field of domestic violence estimate that as many as a third or more families experience some form of violence in the course of each family's life), many more such programs appear to be needed. Parents and caretakers also need to know what to do and how to respond, as well as needing help for themselves in dealing with their own reactions to the experience.

Today most of the hospital emergency rooms in Boston routinely screen for domestic violence, and increasingly, other units in hospital and outpatient facilities are doing the same. One program of note, Project AWAKE at the Children's Hospital Medical Center in Boston, specifically screens for domestic violence in all families where child abuse has been found and provides extensive social, legal, and mental health services to address both issues concurrently.

Pediatric Care Joins In

One of the first doctors to discuss violence prevention with his child patients and their parents in the course of clinical practice was family medicine physician Peter Stringham.[1] In the early 1980s, on his own and independently of our work, he noted the major effect violence was having on his patients. At the time, he was a pediatric clinician at the East Boston Health Center, serving a predominantly white, ethnically Italian, working-class neighborhood. He began two activities. The first was to collect information on the toll violence was having on the youth of this community. The second, and more important, was to counsel the families and youth under his care on the risks of violence and the things they could do to reduce risk.

He started this counseling at the first infant visit for each child and continued it throughout the time that that child came to him for care. At the first visit he let parents know that violence was one of the most serious threats facing the health of their child and that their child was more likely to be killed by violence than by almost any other health threat. Over the period of early childhood, at each visit he addressed a variety of issues, including handguns in the home; disciplinary practices, particularly spanking and corporal punishment; the importance of healthy, nonviolent conflict resolution modeling by the parents; the value of praising children and actively participating in their activities; the serious effects of television violence; the importance of a supportive, nurturing home, and so on.

As the child grew up, he began working directly with the child, discussing issues such as bullying and victimization, fighting, alternatives to fighting to deal with anger and conflict, strategies for getting along with others, and television violence, among other things. For adolescents, he continued with these issues and added topics such as dating relationships, dating violence, and the concept of manliness as it relates to getting along with others. He brought a sensitive and respectful approach to these discussions, guiding patients by means of discussion rather than by lecturing or preaching. Furthermore, all the factors he discussed were rooted in good science that clearly identified them as contributing to children's risk of becoming involved with violence.

His development and refinement of these efforts is impressive. It is particularly impressive that he did this on his own at the beginning. Later he heard about our work and approached us, and he and we were able to offer mutual support. He has since extended his collaboration with us to others and serves as a model for the incorporation of violence prevention in primary care health care. Others are now developing formal materials for clinicians working with children to use in these activities, and the American Academy of Pediatrics has issued a formal policy statement calling on pediatricians and others to incorporate violence prevention as well as screening for risk factors into general health care practice.

Peter Stringham's work is an important example of something we have observed and learned throughout our experience with the building of the violence prevention movement. It demonstrates the value of the Johnny Appleseed approach. With each seed that is planted, a tree (that is, a program or effort) grows. The fruit of that program provides new seeds, which in turn sprout their own new efforts. The size of the initial effort may be less important than the seedlings that develop around it.

Peter Stringham's initial project was quite small, involving one person working in one health center in one neighborhood. But the fact that out of this has grown a number of similar efforts involving groups as large as the American Academy of Pediatrics with fifty thousand members is not only significant but amazing. In this same vein, each initiative we developed or observed others doing seemed to generate spin-offs, more than we could ever keep track of. All the while we were hosting conferences and trainings as part of our broader effort, we were recruiting and preparing people for the movement. We were watering and nurturing the seeds, at least some of which sprouted into much more.

Community Health Centers Establish Programs

Another important groundbreaking program was developed at a community health center in Boston (the Roxbury Comprehensive Community Health Center) by a psychologist who had worked with us early in the development of the Boston Youth Program. Jeanne Taylor, who later went on to become the executive director of the health center, found that many families using the health center had lost a family member to violence. This is an unfortunate reality for many families living in inner-city communities and a growing number of families in other communities as well. In her work with these families Jeanne came across family members displaying symptoms of stress, unresolved grief and anger, and strong feelings of frustration around wanting to do something constructive that would give meaning to their loss.

Out of this experience came the Living After Murder Program, started in the early 1990s. Initially Jeanne and then others began to work with these families not only to help them through their grief and to deal with other symptoms they were having but also to help them identify ways of contributing to the community from their experiences. This program was one of the first among our experiences that led us to an understanding of the powerful contributions that "survivors" could bring to the violence prevention movement. Some became community activists; others worked with children and youth in prevention efforts; still others identified specific activities with which they could contribute to the broader violence prevention agenda and, in some cases, preserve the name of the person they had lost.

Survivors Step to the Forefront

One very moving example of the work of survivors, although it did not come out of the program at the health center, is the story of the Chery family. Their son, Louis Brown, was shot and killed at the age of fifteen in the crossfire that resulted from an altercation between two rival gangs. He was walking to a Christmas party given by a youth group to which he belonged. Ironically, the youth group was called Teens Against Gang Violence; Louis was part of the growing army of youth in the city dedicated to violence prevention.

His parents, as part of their coming to grips with the tragedy, became community activists in the violence prevention movement. One of their contributions was the development of the Louis D. Brown Peace Curriculum, which was both a violence prevention and a conflict resolution curriculum, designed for use in the Boston Public Schools. Through their activism and persistence as well as the power of their personal experience, they successfully accomplished what we could not. They were able to get the school department to agree to implement the curriculum fully across the system, and this became the first systemwide violence prevention curriculum in Boston. They further expanded the effort by founding the Louis D. Brown Peace Institute to broaden their activities to community-wide efforts.[2]

Survivors are very powerful players who bring a level of passion and commitment as well as persistence that no one else can bring to the process. They are an important resource and can be the cornerstone of any community violence prevention effort. Find them and support them. In fact, at our most recent conference in a series of conferences built around the experiences and perspectives of survivors, the theme "we are all survivors" was developed for the next conference. This recognizes the growing number of people who realize the effect violence has on everyone in this country. Think of all the seeds such a perspective can bring to the movement.

Gang Prevention Takes Its Place

The Chery family's experience raises yet another component of the violence prevention activities that developed in Boston, that of gang prevention activities. Although only a small percentage of homicides in this country occur in the context of gang-related activity, gangs are certainly major components in the presence of violence, particularly in but not limited to inner cities. They are certainly one avenue through which young people get involved with violence, and they greatly contribute to the sense of fear in some communities. Gang prevention work did not originate in Boston; however, a number of efforts along these lines became integral parts of the larger violence prevention process in Boston.

Teens Against Gang Violence (the group to which Louis Brown belonged),[3] led by Ulrich Johnson, is a fine example of a gang prevention program. Teenagers are herd animals. They are naturally drawn to groups of their peers, partly as a component of their developmentally normal separation from their family, partly to meet their need to feel accepted at a social level, and partly for the opportunity of being in an accepting environment where they can grow and mature. Teenagers need to feel they belong someplace, are safe, and are accepted by others. Gangs, in the negative sense that term is now usually used, have become one venue for meeting this need. Loosely speaking, almost any group of teenagers is a "gang" of sorts, but most of these groups don't incorporate violence or territorial protection as a central component of their culture. It is the ones that do use violence and territoriality that we are concerned with here.

Kids need alternative options to gangs involved in violence. When they lack other options, their risk of gang involvement greatly increases. Programs like Teens Against Gang Violence provide such an alternative. When kids are growing up in communities with a great deal of violence, making violence prevention part of the agenda of a group creates an opportunity for group members to deal with this issue of concern in their own lives. Violence prevention is very much a part of the agenda of Ulrich Johnson's program.

Other gang prevention programs that have developed around the country and in Boston deal directly with violent gangs, creating avenues for members to leave and opportunities for gangs to resolve their differences and meet their needs without resorting to violence. All of these are significant elements of a broad-based violence prevention effort, as gangs cannot be ignored. Gang members are often heroes to younger kids in their neighborhoods as they are seen as powerful and successful. If they can be engaged in prevention activities, their heroic image means they can serve as powerful agents of change as they promote the values that kids need to stay safe and healthy.

The Importance of a Range of Programs

The programs and efforts we have been describing are just a few of those developed in Boston over the decade before the city experienced its dramatic decline in juvenile homicides. There were and are numerous others that are equally powerful and interesting. In total, these programs reflect the work and commitment of thousands of people, all dedicated to making the city safer for everyone and for children and youth in particular. We helped set the stage for this. We didn't train everybody, but many times over we trained somebody who trained somebody else who recruited and trained yet somebody else.

What is also interesting is the range and diversity of these programs. The programs in Boston reflect not only many professional and community perspectives but also many different methods of program development. Some were large-scale, citywide efforts developing out of public sector institutions, but many were developed at the local neighborhood level out of small community agencies, out of community coalitions, or even out of the commitment of an individual or a small group of people with vision and commitment. Each of these was a small tree sprouting from a seed, and it in turn produced new seeds for new efforts. Soon a forest had grown. It was the total accumulation of these efforts that made the difference. This was and is a movement.

Letting Go

As we got further and further into the work of catalyzing a violence prevention movement, we both became increasingly invested and committed to the work. Our passion grew with each small success, our optimism with our growing recognition that many people were buying into the issue and the agenda. We were increasingly sought after to speak around the country and work with other communities. We felt ownership of the issue, the curriculum, and the strategies and had to constantly balance that with the realization that we owned neither the issue nor the solutions.

Although we take great pride in Boston's violence prevention landscape, we also know that it was the work of others who made the real difference. We were catalysts more than anything else. And as in a chemical process, catalysts speed up and move along the reaction, but the final outcome is ultimately due to the other components in the process.

We never sought a cookie-cutter franchise. We always believed that those we were training were capable of developing authentic, effective strategies once they believed in violence prevention, had the information to act, and had the tools to begin. Even those programs that we were directly responsible for getting started or that we catalogue as spin-offs developed a life of their own as they matured and grew. We had little or no part in many other programs that were developed except that they were likely spin-offs or spin-offs of spin-offs. We did push the issue of violence to the forefront before many others had recognized its seriousness or the possibilities for prevention. Even though we understood why we had to lack control and intentionally designed our work that way, occasionally we had to keep each other from becoming possessive and turf oriented so as to not lose sight of the vision and stifle any work that others were taking on.

Ultimately, two things happened that helped us to maintain the balance. The first was that we moved on in our careers. By the late 1980s, we both had left the Boston Health Department and Boston City Hospital. One of us (Deborah) became the public health commissioner for the Commonwealth of Massachusetts; shortly after, the other (Howard) became deputy public health commissioner. With these job changes came new responsibilities that were, if nothing else, a major distraction from our day-to-day violence prevention work and a major platform for taking the violence prevention movement outside our city. For the Boston Youth Program and the Boston Violence Prevention Project, these changes meant hiring a new director and passing the baton.

Our new venue brought with it fertile ground for planting new seeds. We were at the Johnny Appleseed stage again. Together we created the first state-level Office of Violence Prevention. Under the umbrella of the Massachusetts Health Department, we were able to move out to a larger base of activities. These activities included starting up violence prevention programs in other cities in the commonwealth, the establishment of the first statewide emergency room weapon-related intentional injury surveillance system in the nation, and use of our bigger public platform to increase awareness of the importance of resource commitments to violence prevention. All of this didn't remove our attention from the activities in Boston, but it did broaden our attention, introducing us to a larger field of possibilities. There were more places that needed forests.

The second thing that happened was that we received constant reaffirmation that our success with and contribution to the work in Boston was in fact rooted in many others' developing as much of a sense of ownership, passion, and commitment as we had. It would have served little purpose if the movement had rested in the hands of just a few. It wouldn't have been a movement. Success lay not in seeking to control but in letting go and watching the movement grow. This was our last and maybe most important lesson from the Boston experience. There were now many others doing exceptionally fine and valuable work. It was time to stay involved but also make more room by moving on.

Part Four

Lessons Learned

Chapter Twelve

There Is No One Model

Having the attention of the nation on the success in Boston has been most exciting but has also brought us and others great concern. In 1996, when then president Clinton and then attorney general Reno came to our city to highlight the accomplishments, they brought with them three messages: two of these messages were right on target but one reflected a common misperception of what happened here.

The first message was that violence is preventable and that with investment of resources and commitment, the perception that violence is inevitable can be changed. The second was that the tide of youth violence that was sweeping the nation could be reversed and that the activities and results in Boston clearly illustrated this. Both of these were important messages for others around the country to hear. This recognition of the work of violence prevention and the necessary investment of resources and commitment brought attention and hope to others grappling with the problem in their own communities. Unfortunately, the third message pushed people in the wrong direction.

The Simple Solution Fallacy

The third message was that the success in Boston was specifically the direct result of an improved community-police relationship and programs involving the police and criminal justice system. Bill Clinton and Janet Reno highlighted three programs: the Youth Strike Force, a collaboration between the police and the juvenile probation officers of the court system; the police collaboration with the Ten Point Coalition, a local community organization that grew out of the work of several black ministers; and the Cease Fire Program, which focused on carrying out federal prosecution of minors with guns along with making direct contact with gang members to inform them about the federal prosecution.

Although these three important programs contributed to the reduced juvenile homicide rate in the city, they were not by any means the only or even the major contributing factors to this success. In fact the pattern of decline of juvenile homicides and violent injuries in the city had begun several years before these programs were started. The federal prosecution for gun possession is given singular or substantial credit by some, but the rate of stab wound injuries declined as well, indicating the successful efforts of a broader and more complex constellation of programs.

This emphasis on the police role in the success of the Boston experience reflected and reinforced the political climate that is pushing this country's political leadership into knee-jerk criminal justice responses that are short on prevention, such as "three strikes and you're out." The U.S. default strategy is spending more money on prison cells rather than investing in prevention. However, mandatory sentences, severity of threatened punishment, and filling the nation's prisons have done little to stem the tide of violence. It was during the height of the growth of the youth violence epidemic that this country tripled the number of people in its jails and prisons with little effect on the rising rates of violence and homicide. What America needs is a new and fresh perspective on violence that is weighted more toward prevention and less toward reactive responses.

Complex Problems Demand Multifaceted Solutions

An understanding and examination of the underlying causes of and contributing factors to youth violence strongly supports the idea that a single approach to the issue of youth violence will not be effective. A singular focus on either traditional or creative criminal justice solutions, even with community support, just will not work. Threatening punishment, hiring more police, or building more prison cells simply does not curtail the waves of the epidemic. A change in social norms and cultural attitudes and behaviors is essential, and this requires involvement from a much broader group of responders than criminal justice alone. A collective effort involving every discipline, every family, and especially the entertainment media is necessary.

The complex issue of youth violence requires multifaceted and creative approaches that ultimately engage every sector of the community. The police, the courts, and the juvenile justice system are important players, but they cannot do it alone and should not be burdened with the unrealistic expectation that they can. Even those working in the criminal justice system acknowledge this, as evidenced by the early support given to our work by Boston police commissioner Mickey Roache and the acknowledgment that the current police commissioner, Paul Evans, gives to prevention efforts.

Many in Boston, from the community level to City Hall, reacted to the president's third message with concern because in emphasizing the work of a single sector it undervalued the work of all others. It also set the wrong direction for the rest of the cities in America seeking to tackle their own youth violence problem. Also, it failed to recognize the importance of the process of generating a movement and the length of time that process takes. Synergy requires a foundation; spin-off efforts are generated when programs accumulate over time. The chart in Figure 12.1 illustrates this program accumulation as it occurred in Boston and superimposes it on a graph of the decline in child homicides. No one program—no simple solution—caused this change.

The programming in the popular media is not designed to deliver complicated messages, and as a result, politicians and program staff seeking media exposure portray singular solutions—the one best practice. But when it comes to preventing youth violence there is no one answer. There is no one model.

Figure 12.1. Violence Prevention Programs.

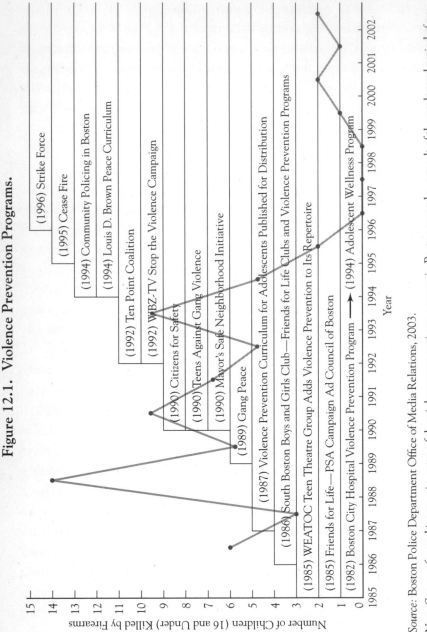

Source: Boston Police Department Office of Media Relations, 2003.

Note: Support for and interest in many of the violence prevention programs in Boston waned as a result of the prolonged period of no juvenile homicides. We are unable to quantify to what extent this decline in support resulted in fewer programs and services or how it may have contributed to the reemergence of juvenile violent deaths in the city.

Our travels around the country have made us aware of the growing number of communities that have begun to take on youth violence in a serious and meaningful way. Many more communities will have to join in if the nation as a whole is to turn this epidemic around. The experiences in Boston as well as in other communities have helped us to formulate a set of principles that can guide others in this work.

Building a Base

We strongly recommend that communities begin their violence prevention work by building a broad-based coalition of support and participation at the same time as they dive into solutions. This building process is crucial to establishing the critical mass of involvement and buy-in necessary for the long-term sustained effort required to tackle the problem successfully. This coalition needs to include the leadership of the community and the ordinary people who live in the community. Neither can do it alone.

Our experience is that it is easier to get the support and participation of community residents and local community agencies than the support and participation of higher-level leadership, particularly the political leadership. Political leaders are generally short-sighted (with a field of vision that goes only up to the next election) and reticent to take risks. They are more comfortable doing things the same old way and repeating the old rhetoric about the problem than they are trying new things or talking up new ideas. Community residents, local agency staff, and community institutions like churches, local schools, and recreation programs live with problems like youth violence every day and face them when they wake up every morning. The issues are more immediate and personal for them, and their motivation is high. Often they are more open to thinking outside the box than elected leaders or professionals are. Once the grassroots are convinced, then the people who hold the purse strings and control public policy have to be convinced, because some of the changes require resources and government involvement. Community residents can organize to influence and motivate political leadership and with committed persistence can be quite effective in pushing leaders toward a violence prevention agenda. Groups of survivors and of other young people who bring knowledge, experience, and passion are especially effective if connected to the professional community who bring science and power to the table.

Lining Up New Windows

A risk factor by risk factor approach to reducing violence (focusing, for example, on the windows of risk described in Chapter Four) helps to organize the work.

Poverty is an overriding factor in youth violence, but approaching this window of risk is a bit daunting and requires a long-term perspective. Many extremely bright people have thought about this factor, many strategies have been proposed, and a number of these strategies have been tried. Economic development in poor communities has to be a part of violence prevention. The benefits of improving the economic conditions in poor inner-city and rural areas are considerable and affect all of us whether we live in these communities or not.

It would serve this nation well to deal with poverty more aggressively and not from the perspective of a welfare model. Reducing poverty should be approached from the perspective that it would benefit this nation as a whole in innumerable social and economic ways, reduced violence and violent injury rates being one of them. It should be rooted in real economic opportunity and development that leads to the establishment of strong economic bases in these poor communities, not handouts. These communities are rich in human resources but lack the financial resources to get started.

The violence-as-a-learned-behavior window is also one that deserves a great deal of attention and for which many things can and should be done. There is a role for literally everyone in addressing this aspect of the problem. Children learn violence in every venue of their lives, and reducing this message or countering it is the responsibility of all. Every aspect of the community has something to do.

The exposure of children to violence in the home, schools, and the community can be addressed by all community institutions. There are obvious things that can be done that enhance learning of prosocial behaviors (for example, conflict resolution curricula in schools and other community settings), family supports (for example, home visiting programs, crisis hot lines, family centers, parenting and nurturing programs), adult role modeling (for example, mentoring programs, teacher training), screening (for example, universal screening for domestic violence), mental health services, health services (for example, response to violent injuries, screening for risk), reduced access to handguns (for example, gun buybacks), youth programs (for example, youth centers, after-school programs, organized recreational activities), and so on.

Involving Anyone and Everyone

As you can see, there is no single place or professional arena where such activities should reside. Police, community groups, neighborhood associations, local schools, churches, health and human service agencies, mental health agencies, social groups and clubs, youth programs, and others must participate. Moreover, many of these activities do not take much in the way of money. What they do take is commitment and time. Many of the programs in Boston did not require grants or fundraising but started with the energy of one person or several people with a good idea and the willingness to give of themselves. Others will join in and resources can follow.

Children need to feel part of a community. This is not an abstract concept. Caring adults who provide enjoyable activities can consistently engage kids and make them feel valued. For young children, home visiting programs and early childhood centers and activities are among the best practices. Evaluations of such programs are extremely encouraging, showing that they promote healthy child development, result in stronger families, reduce child abuse, and generate better long-term outcomes in school performance and success beyond childhood. A particularly interesting model for these programs features both professional staff and community resident participation. This practice provides valuable opportunities for health, mental health, and social and human service professionals to collaborate with community residents on service program development. Similarly, community residents can be introduced to professional skills and use entry-level jobs in the human service system as a career development strategy.

Turning Schools into Community Centers

For older children and teenagers, schools become at least as important as community and often more important than family as places for activities and services. This realization means rethinking schools as community and service centers for children and families and staffing accordingly. Service programs that have been located in schools include health centers; mental health services; a range of after-school programs, often organized and supported by parents; evening family events, such as potluck dinners; talent shows; book clubs that include parents; mentorship programs; school trips with parents as chaperones; and many more. What these programs often have in common are the involvement of parents, a view of schools as multiservice centers, and a philosophy that schools need to be places that promote success, not failure.

School buildings are often underused, yet they can be places where many activities happen that can bring together all aspects of a community. It makes children feel important, good, and respected when there are opportunities for their parents to see what the children do and to interact with them. Think about the messages given to children when schools are places where a multitude of their needs can be met. Think about what these buildings can be when they are places that promote the success of children. Joy Dryfoos, a leading expert on adolescents, has been promoting the view of schools as full family and community centers for a number of years.[1] She is right!

Now, think about what the message is when these things are absent. What does it mean when art, sports, music, shop, home economics, and other nontraditional and nonacademic areas disappear? When school buildings are locked up after 2:30 or 3:00 P.M. and on weekends? When parents are uninvolved and uninvited? When failure rather than success is the experience of a significant number of students? What a lost opportunity! It makes us sad to imagine the impact this absence of programs and this experience of failure have on children's feelings about themselves and others. A whole community—the people who live there, the people who provide services, the people who govern—can determine the outcome for their children. It takes money, but it also takes many other things that cost little and pay off in a big way. It is through changing public policy and professional practices that society can ensure the success of children.

Taking Action to Change Community Values

These are just a few examples of how communities can be changed into environments where children and their families can feel nurtured and supported. A big component of violence prevention is accomplishing just that. Activities that help make communities visually pleasing and that make people feel included rather than isolated result in communities that are far less likely to experience or promote violence. Communities where the institutions that serve children reflect the commitment and investment of everyone are communities that promote the healthy development of children and where children are far less likely to become involved in violence.

When children have positive things to do, they watch less television and are exposed to less media violence. This is particularly true when parents, including working parents, have options for their children other than using television as a cheap and convenient baby-sitter. Children also do better and are less violent when they have prosocial adult role models. As noted earlier, a number of studies have shown that the presence of a nurturing adult in the life of a child greatly enhances his or her chances for success, whether that adult is a family member, a neighbor, a teacher, or someone else in the community. This type of effort in and of itself creates many opportunities for people to participate in a very personal way in violence prevention.

Valuing and Supporting Families

Families that are involved in the community rather than isolated and that have access to support services also experience less violence. That is true in the area of child abuse, and it may also be the case with respect to domestic violence. If nothing else, women who have access to social or service networks have more options for seeking help when battering does exist. When they have this access, it means that their children are less likely to experience chronic exposure to the witnessing of violence. Although this advice may sound clichéd, it is nevertheless true that isolation and lack of support lead to problems, particularly violence. Children in isolated families are far more likely than other children to experience or witness violence, which then puts them at much greater risk for involvement in violence as teenagers and young adults.

The opposite is true as well. Nurturing and being a part of a larger community promotes physical, social, and emotional health, and children reap the benefits of such environments. Being at lower risk for future violent behavior is one of those benefits. Establishing this supportive environment is a community-wide endeavor. Police programs won't do this. A school curriculum won't either. Nor will a recreation league or an outreach program or a child-care center. But combined they will because together they can create a community that supports its members and they can influence the community's defining values.

Other Community Agendas

In addition to implementing the basic strategies discussed in the previous sections, communities need to consider some specific elements of violence prevention and integrate them into the larger violence prevention effort.

Tackling the Media

Dealing with media violence is one of these elements. Activities for children that compete with television viewing make up one part of the answer. Helping kids to better understand what they are seeing is another part, and media literacy (the new catchphrase for the skills children need to handle what they see on TV and videos), taught through programs such as the Flash Point II media literacy curriculum, may be useful here. Media literacy can be taught in school or in a variety of settings where children spend their time. Helping parents understand the possible effects on their children of watching violent television is important as well, and they should be encouraged to either watch with their children and talk about it or more carefully monitor what is being watched.

Large-scale efforts that might help to control the content of television programming or make the people who produce such programming more responsible and accountable are beyond the scope of any individual community, but any community group or agency can register its concerns by supporting such larger efforts. National organizations (some of which were discussed in Chapter Six), which multiply the effect of individual adults and communities, are beginning to have some impact.

Addressing Access to Handguns

Dealing with children's access to handguns also requires collaboration among many groups. Community education on the serious risks of handgun ownership is a good place to start. The widespread misconceptions about handgun ownership need to be addressed through public education and individual communication. Too many people believe that owning a handgun is protective when it is actually quite dangerous. Efforts to promote the community value that handgun ownership is bad for children can be incorporated into everyone's activities. Programs like gun buybacks, even though taking few guns out of circulation, have important symbolic value and can publicize the risks of gun ownership. Such programs work best when they result from collaborations between the police and a wide variety of community groups and agencies.

Anything that gets the word out on the risks of guns in the home is good and should be seriously considered. The larger issue of gun regulation is a state and national issue. As with media violence, individual communities need to participate in the larger debate and actively work for reduced handgun access.

Establishing Safe Havens

Providing adolescents with safe places to be where they can enjoy themselves and fill their free time with healthy, positive activities is also central to violence prevention. Unstructured time can lead to situations that increase kids' risk of getting into trouble. Furthermore, creating activities that increase the exposure of teenagers to good adult role models is extremely beneficial. Mentoring programs, athletics, youth clubs, organized social events in schools and other community settings are all examples of safe havens.

Helping Children in Trouble Early On

An important part of the community involvement in preventing violence is the effort to identify kids who are isolated or having difficulties with peer interactions, and the younger these kids are identified the better. It is easier to help them early on than later when they are more difficult to engage. Teachers, even in the very early grades, can be particularly helpful in this endeavor, as they often know which children are having such difficulties. Excessive school absence, poor social interactions, bullying, chronic victimization, isolation, acting out behaviors, and poor development of basic academic skills, among other things, are red flags signaling a child is doing badly. These children need a big brother or big sister or mentor or some other adult who will invest time in their development and well-being.

Early identification, good evaluation, and supportive services are all appropriate elements of helping these kids. Older children may also display signs of alcohol or drug abuse or carry weapons, serious signs that help is needed. They need to be evaluated and given services, not expelled or rejected. In addition, families of these children and youth should be involved as much as possible in the effort, as a child having such problems is often reflecting difficult situations in his or her home.

Children cannot be served in isolation and must be considered in the context of their families. Although this area is not prevention in the classical sense in that these children are already having problems, their early identification, assessment, and engagement in services can help to prevent further problems and avoid more serious consequences such as violent injury to themselves or others. To this end the federal Department of Education has published and distributed an early warning manual to help teachers and others enhance their skills in identifying at-risk children and responding to their needs.[2]

Teaching Skills to Children

As part of the activities with children and youth, the skills for dealing with anger and conflict need to be taught. All children will become angry at times and all will face conflicts throughout their lives. The strategies for dealing with anger and conflict that they witness around them must go beyond those they generally see in the media—treating the option of walking away as unrealistic, resorting to violence, acting like a superhero, and "chicken whining." Educational curricula and good role modeling are two strategies for teaching effective conflict resolution strategies. In Boston these interventions were delivered in schools and in various ways in many other settings. All those who work with children can identify opportunities to address conflict resolution. In the classroom, on the basketball court, during social gatherings—these are all times and places to teach and reinforce nonviolent strategies.

Adults working with kids need to be acutely aware that the behaviors they display are learning experiences for the children around them. It is imperative that parents, teachers, coaches, and other adults in the lives of children be trained in these skills and then model healthy behaviors as much as possible. Training for this can and should be included in the professional training of all people involved with children.

The programs and approaches we have been discussing in this chapter are just a handful of the components that can be used in the development of a violence prevention movement in any community. Many more pieces and more examples were provided in earlier chapters addressing specific elements of the issue of violence. What readers should take away from this broad overview are several messages.

Basic Messages

No one is in this violence prevention effort alone nor can anyone do this by himself or herself. It takes a community-wide effort that must involve all levels and sectors of a community. No one part of the community is responsible for this problem; no one part can fix it. We are all in this together. It is a serious mistake to delegate the effort to one sector, such as the police or the schools or a psychologist, which is the current tendency.

Nurturing communities are healthy communities. One of the primary principles of violence prevention is to accept and promote the value of communities that take responsibility for all of their children and that support the families and individuals in the community. Isolation is bad and unhealthy. It results in many difficulties, including violence. There are many things that can be done in communities to provide support and inclusion, and these things can involve the whole community and do not need to cost a lot of money.

Organize and Create Buy-In

Building a violence prevention movement needs to start with basic community organizing. As many players as possible need to be involved, including community residents and the youth themselves. Community-wide buy-in is essential, but it is less likely to happen if people are left out of the process. In fact the quality of the process is as important as the outcome because the process will shape the outcome.

Take Bottom-Up Approaches

Bottom-up approaches may work best and are more likely to experience successes early on, which will help people to sustain the effort long term. Grassroots work will pay off in the end. The political leadership will eventually follow, when it is less risky to do so and when public pressure forces it to. Do not be dismayed at this dynamic; it is the reality that many have experienced and dealt with.

Understand That Prevention Is Best

Prevention is better than early intervention. Early intervention is better than treatment. Treatment is better than nothing. It is cheapest and healthiest to develop programs that teach children that violence is unacceptable, that it is not a problem solver but a problem creator. Early identification of those who develop or are exposed to risk, followed by intervention before more serious problems develop, is more likely to have a benefit than allowing the situation to persist and become more resistant to change. Even those who are involved with violence, fighting, weapon carrying, drug or alcohol abuse, or other serious conditions can still be helped. The worst thing that communities can do is to reject these youth or write them off. They don't go away, and their isolation only exacerbates the risks of more serious consequences. Doing nothing is not an option. Writing children off is not practical, acceptable, or smart.

Step Out of the Box

We all need to begin to think outside our boxes. Doing things the same old way with the same nonresults isn't the answer. We have to identify ways of working together, collaborating, and considering activities and opportunities that aren't in our job description. This is true whether we are professionally trained or just live in the community. We all have something to contribute to the larger effort. We all have to take chances. We are all responsible, and we will all benefit from working for a better outcome just as we all suffer from the consequences of doing nothing and ensuring a bad outcome.

Make Schools Multiservice Centers

Schools are particularly important places in our communities for violence prevention. Schools need to be restructured as multiservice centers for children and families. In addition to being academic centers, schools need to become community sites for a multitude of activities that address the needs of children and promote the active participation of families and other community members. They cannot be isolated fortresses, standing apart from the community in order to give the illusion of safety, not if children are the central focus. They must be places of nurturing that promote success and not failure.

Our Children Are Shaped by What We Do for Them

Each community's children and youth are extremely valuable resources. We need to treat them all with respect, nurture their development, protect them from harm, teach them good values, and look out for their well-being. This is basic. They will eventually reflect what we have invested in them.

Chapter Thirteen

The System Is Part of the Problem

A number of years ago, a mother brought her fourteen-year-old son into one of the local health centers in Boston to see one of us (Deborah) for an annual physical exam. During the routine discussion about how things were going for her son, she mentioned that she was concerned about her son's safety. He was not having any significant problems with fighting, peer relationships, or school performance, nor was he exposed to any other risk factors related to violence. However, as she was working, she was concerned about her son coming home after school to an empty house in a neighborhood that had experienced more than its share of violence, and she was afraid he might get hurt or into trouble. She had looked into after-school programs and could find only programs that cost about $4,000 per year, money she did not have. An outreach worker from the health center was brought in to help find a placement for the teenager but was unsuccessful in identifying an affordable program. There was nothing for this young man.

Had this teenage boy been shot, he would have required, assuming he survived, medical services in an emergency room and a hospital that would have cost anywhere from $50,000 to $100,000 or more just in short-term costs. Had this young man been involved in violence leading to arrest or incarceration, he would have incurred costs in the tens of thousands of dollars or more. The stress and anxiety resulting from the mother's and the son's fears most likely resulted in less than fully productive work performance or attendance for the mother and may well have interfered with her son's ability to do his best in school. Both of

these effects have clear financial and human costs even if it is difficult to assign an exact value to them. Yet there was nothing that
could be done. An upfront investment of $4,000 was unavailable,
even though it would reduce the risk that the community would
end up paying the dramatically higher cost of medical care for the
young man if he became the victim of violence. Something is very
wrong with this picture.

Challenging the Status Quo

When we think about this situation, which is far too common, it
makes us intensely uncomfortable. And when we raise it with
groups of other professionals in the health and human service system, the discomfort level of those we are talking with is palpable.
The reality is that most of the service systems in most communities,
be they health or mental health or social service or criminal justice
or any other system, are set up to address problems and pathology,
not prevention or health. And the example we gave earlier is just
one of the numerous examples that illustrate the problem. People
in the service systems are not encouraged to attend to preventing
problems and promoting health. All of their attention and all system resources are directed to responding to problems. Under these
circumstances, investing $4,000 rather than risking costs of tens of
thousands of dollars or more is just not a consideration.

All of us need to face this issue head on and own up to the fact
that all of us are responsible for the current situation in the service
system and that it is also we who have the responsibility to promote
change. For if we continue to do the same things the same old way,
nothing will change and problems such as youth violence will
never be properly addressed.

Professionals Are Taught Only to React

This situation is a direct result of the training given to those in the
professional sector. Doctors are taught to gather information to

identify what is wrong with their patients and treat what they find. Psychologists and psychiatrists are trained to diagnose mental illness and treat it. Social workers are taught how to respond to people who are in trouble or are hurting or can't get the treatment services they need. Police learn how to respond to criminal situations. Lawyers are taught how to litigate. And so on. Little if any training in any of these professions is directed toward understanding how to prevent illness, suffering, or serious problems either for individual people or for communities.

Programs Treat, Not Prevent

And the problem goes well beyond training. Most programs are designed and funded to treat problems after they occur, not before. About ten years ago the Massachusetts legislature approved funding for teen pregnancy prevention, which was then distributed among a number of agencies around the state that worked with teenagers. Although all involved were well-intentioned and well-meaning people, almost all of the funds ultimately went into services for teenage parents, not into the intended agenda of preventing teen pregnancies in the first place. The money was well spent and helped many teenage parents, but the prevention agenda was lost. The system wasn't equipped to do anything else.

Health Care Survives on Illness

In health care the same situation exists. Enormous amounts of money are invested in intensive care units, little in the prevention of the problems that might reduce the need for such services. Neonatal intensive care units are a superb example of this. Although such units, which do a fine job of saving very sick premature infants, are clearly needed, it is remarkable how little, relative to the cost of caring for these sick newborns, is invested in the prevention of prematurity. This is partly the responsibility of the medical profession, but it is also a consequence of how the reimbursement system works. Insurance companies are willing to pay out millions of dollars for the care of babies born too early but invest little and reimburse poorly for interventions that prevent premature labor and birth. This practice should be compared to the practice in other countries, such as France, that have created financial incentives for pregnant women to seek prenatal care early and stay in that care throughout their pregnancy. In this country we try instead to save money by pushing women out of the hospital as fast as possible after they have their babies, and in some cases too fast.

The reality is that neonatal intensive care units are big money-makers for hospitals, in part because of the reimbursement system. A reduction in the number of premature infants requiring such expensive services would cut into the income of these hospitals, a factor that lessens even more any incentive there might be for reducing the flow of patients needing these services. It is perhaps not surprising then that this country has prematurity rates and infant mortality rates way above those in most other developed nations and rivaling rates in far less developed nations.

Criminal Justice Invests in Prisons

Similarly, we have invested enormous amounts of dollars in the development of trauma centers to treat severe injuries like gunshot wounds. Comparatively little resource investment or thought has been put into preventing the injuries. The parallel in the criminal justice system is obvious. Almost all of our investment has been put into identifying, catching, prosecuting, and incarcerating criminals. Very little has been put into stopping the flow of young people into criminal and violent behaviors. We spend billions for reacting to violence, barely millions for preventing it. We train and pay millions of people to respond to crime, few to prevent it. And the multibillion-dollar corporate industry that has evolved to warehouse criminals is literally making out like bandits. As we have in the health care system, we have put our money, our creativity, and our human resources at the wrong end of the equation.

Taking a Different Approach

We can choose to perpetuate this situation and drown in it, as we currently are, or we can put our creative energy into doing things in a different way. And it bears repeating that doing things in the same old way will produce the same old results. Doing things differently, stepping out of our boxes and looking at issues like youth violence in a different way, will create change and will bring us different and potentially better results.

Stepping out of our boxes requires courage and some risk taking. It is not easy to do, and as we ourselves learned in our early efforts in Boston, it sets the risk takers up for ridicule and rejection, at least in the short run. The two of us know that even presenting our concerns in this book is a risk. Challenging our own profession and the professions of many others to look critically at what they are doing is likely to result in negative reactions and consequences. That is a risk we are willing to take. We are asking others to do the same. Little or nothing will change if we and others don't or won't.

Taking Risks

There are clergy in Boston who took big risks. They chose to go out at 3 A.M. in the morning to stand on street corners and interact and work with the kids who were already out there. However, many of the risks involved in violence prevention are not really so big. This effort requires committing the time and the energy to go into school classrooms and develop and deliver curricula addressing violence and conflict resolution. It requires those working in the fields of youth violence, violence against women, gang violence, child abuse, and suicide to take the necessary steps to work together, rather than competitively, to identify commonalties and differences and to figure out how the pieces fit together. After all, these areas are all linked and represent the broad spectrum of violence in this country.

All of us have more to gain from collaboration than from competition. We need to seek out resources that promote such collaboration, rather than maintaining the present circumstances in which programs that address violence are often pitted against each other to compete for inadequate funds. We need to speak out against the suspension or expulsion of kids who get into trouble in school, and urge the use of alternatives that work to lift these kids out of violence rather than trying to cast them aside.

Taking Responsibility for Public Policy

Affecting public policy must be as much a part of our professional agenda as being the best clinician or educator or police officer or judge. Saving one patient, teaching one child, locking up one criminal is not enough. As an old African proverb puts it, we can exhaust ourselves pulling people out of the river or we can go upstream and find out why people are falling in. It would even begin to make a difference if we just found out how far upstream we need to go.

We must step out of our boxes and take some professional and personal risks. There are some big risks, like those the clergy in Boston took, but there are also a great many small risks. If we professionals take those small risks, we can significantly improve the outcome of our efforts to save children. Professionals have long been more likely to hold onto the status quo, outdated training, and ineffective protocols than to take work-related risks. This pattern of behavior must change in light of the preventable and horrendous tragedy of youth violence.

Taking Responsibility for Children

A rap artist serving as a guest speaker on a town hall–style television show on the entertainment media and violence was approached by the mother of another guest during intermission. She asked the rap artist whether, if he saw her fourteen-year-old daughter doing something wrong, he would ask her to stop. The rap artist responded,

"I don't have any children; that's not my responsibility. I'm just 'kicking-it,' having fun, and making money. When I have children, I'll take that responsibility." The mother rephrased her question, "I'm not asking would you stop her, really. I just mean would you say something to her—let her know this isn't something she should be doing?" The rap artist repeated his first response.

The mother was flustered, and one of us (Deborah) jumped into the conversation and asked the rap artist if he would go out into the street to help a three-year-old crossing by himself. After thinking a minute, the rap artist asked an interesting question. He said, "Am I going to get hit?" Deborah said no, and he then stated, "In that case, I would probably help." The truth is that a person might get hit going out into the street to help a three-year-old. Most adults would be inclined to help, after looking both ways to minimize the risk. Yet as children get older we become increasingly less inclined to take risks, even small ones, to help them.

Professionals often sound a lot like the rap artist: "I am just a few years from retirement and I'm not rocking the boat now." "I've done all I'm supposed to do—I'm not required to do any more." "That's not in my job description." "I've got two children in college; all I'm going to do is follow the protocols—and that's it." The ability to refrain from doing more—from doing the things we would want done for us or our children—is remarkable. The justifications and explanations are similar to those of the rap artist.

There are many examples of the small risks professionals can take that would make a difference: change the protocols so that they are more effective; reach out across disciplines and work with those who have a different approach; define children as assets and involve them in the solutions rather than defining them as the problem. The challenge is not to go out on the street corner at three in the morning, a risk that we suggest be taken only by those close to God. The challenge is to take all the small risks so as to literally change the nature of our professions. We have to focus on outcomes and not be satisfied just with process.

The Risk Takers

The two of us have many examples of people who have taken professional risks and have had successes, making important contributions to the violence prevention movement. Although big changes need to happen, small steps do make a difference, but they require a bit of courage and a new vision. What follows are examples of people who have demonstrated the courage, vision, and tenacity to take risks and make changes in professional practice. We have discussed some of them in earlier chapters as well. Here we focus on the risks they took and the significance of this risk taking. Their actions give insight into what each professional can and should do.

Jeanne Taylor: A Psychologist

Jeanne Taylor, a psychologist and director of the Roxbury Community Health Center, located in one of the Boston neighborhoods with high rates of violence, was involved in the care of many people who had lost family members to violence. Her training had prepared her to help people deal with grieving and address the emotional consequences of their loss. But something was missing. Applying the traditional clinical strategies to the care of these patients was not bringing them to the outcomes they desired and was certainly not doing much for the level of violence in the community.

Parents would slowly learn to cope with the loss of a child but were nevertheless developing chronic symptoms that affected their ability to function as parents to their other children and to support their families. Siblings of murder victims were going back to school and going through the motions of their lives but were beset with lower levels of functioning than they had had before. And the rates of violent injury in the neighborhood were going up, not down.

From these patients, Jeanne Taylor learned that she needed to approach this differently. She began to develop the Living After Murder Program, which provided the individual counseling that was needed but also added a new component. This new element involved bringing people with similar losses together to begin to address the issue of violence at a broader community level. She found that efforts to empower people to do something about the bigger problem both allowed them to come to some closure on their loss and provided them with an opportunity to contribute proactively to addressing violence. It gave their loss meaning, addressed their sense of hopelessness and helplessness, and brought some sense to their senseless experience.

Out of this has come a long-standing program at the health center and numerous efforts to bring the community together with candlelight vigils, community forums, and other activities. Although this program is by no means solely responsible for the reduction of violence that has occurred in the neighborhood, it brought some important players to the table and was therapeutic at the community as well as the individual level. In terms of resources it was not a big deal to start this program, but it did require a different vision of the role of a mental health professional in the care of her patients. It was a risk for this professional because she was stepping out of her traditional role and taking on a new responsibility.

Michael McDonald: A Kid from the Projects

Michael McDonald grew up in the South Boston neighborhood experiencing shameful amounts of violence in his community and in his family. He lost three brothers to homicide and suicide and his sister had been severely brain damaged by violent injury. He also grew up in a neighborhood that was predominantly white and Irish, with a long history of prejudice toward people of color, exemplified by the increase in violence in the community that occurred from the late 1970s well into the 1980s around court-ordered busing of minority children to the community's schools.

He took these experiences and did a number of remarkable things. He helped to organize gun buyback programs in several neighborhoods of Boston. In and of itself this was important but not necessarily remarkable. What was remarkable was that he went into minority neighborhoods and worked with local residents and community leaders. Overcoming his preconceptions about how he would be received in these neighborhoods and having the courage to proceed required a new vision on his part. After all, this ran counter to everything he had been taught.

When asked what he learned from this experience, he responds by saying that he was surprised by how easy it was and how sad he was that it took such tragedy for him to discover how much poor communities had in common in spite of racial differences. Courage, a bit of risk taking, and a vision to create change are what it took.

Michael McDonald has since written a book to share his experiences of growing up and taking control of his life.[1] He realized that others could learn from his experience and better understand the plight of poor people irrespective of ethnic background. In doing this he exposed personal information about himself and others from his neighborhood. This not only made him personally vulnerable but resulted in a number of death threats from others in the community. He knew this might happen but felt the value of sharing his life with others was worth it. We believe he was right to do this, right to take the chance. But we also acknowledge his courage in doing so and believe that part of advancing the violence prevention movement involves people like Michael McDonald coming forward to share their pain and their growth.

Peter Stringham: A Doctor

Peter Stringham is a family medicine physician working at the East Boston Health Center, which serves a predominantly white ethnic community. Early on in his work there, he noted the extensive toll that violence was taking on his patients and their families. On his own initiative he began to counsel families on the risks of violence and the factors that created risk for their children. His counseling evolved into a full protocol that involved discussions at every patient visit about subjects ranging from guns in the home to disciplinary practices, bullying and fighting, and how to treat girls on dates.

At the time, no one else was doing anything like this, so he had no one to seek advice from or model himself after. Nor was this standard care in the medical community. But even though his approach was unconventional, he continued it and also created opportunities to talk with other professionals about what he was doing. Not surprisingly, his descriptions of his methods were met with odd reactions and skepticism by his colleagues. Yet he was developing groundbreaking work. This undertaking was not a big risk nor was it likely to change a whole community. But it was a piece of the violence prevention puzzle, and it required him to apply a different way of looking at his responsibilities as a physician. Peter Stringham began a new paradigm for treating and working with high-risk children.

Francis "Mickey" Roache: A Police Commissioner

Mickey Roache, currently a city councilman in Boston, was commissioner of the Boston police during part of the period when Boston experienced extremely high violence rates. He was under considerable pressure to put a lid on this violence, arrest as many people as possible, and take as strong a punitive and traditional criminal justice approach as possible to make the city safe. Although he did some of this, he also recognized that there were limits to what a police department could do. He became an advocate for violence prevention strategies. Standing up in very public settings, both in the city and at national police leadership conferences, he would state that even with all the police he wanted and all the prison cells that could be built, the problem would not change. Until the community made an investment in resources, programs, and policies that intervened earlier in children's lives, changes in the attitudes and behaviors that led young people to become involved in violence would not occur and violence would not be reduced.

Needless to say, this was not a popular stand with the public or with the politicians. It certainly ran counter to the mainstream thinking of the criminal justice community. It posed a risk to his career. But it was the right thing to do. Again, courage and vision were important elements in Mickey Roache's stand. His beliefs are now no longer as out of line with majority sentiment as they were then, although still not quite in the mainstream. His willingness to publicize his views was a small step in the bigger process that created a climate for change in police activities, allowing the introduction of community policing and of collaboration with others in the community to initiate programs that eventually contributed to the dramatic decline in youth homicides in the city.

Paul Bracy and Mark Bukaras: Outreach Workers

Paul Bracy and Mark Bukaras were the first two community outreach staff that we hired in our Boston Violence Prevention Project, which we ran from the Boston Health Department. We hired Paul Bracy, who is African American, to work in the Roxbury neighborhood with a predominantly African American population. Mark Bukaras, who is white, was hired to work in the white Irish neighbor of South Boston. We chose each of them because we thought they knew and would fit in well in their respective communities.

Shortly after starting, the two of them came to us and stated that they wanted to revise the plan. They wanted to go out together and coordinate work in the two neighborhoods. They felt there was much to be gained by emphasizing the similarities of the communities rather than the differences. They chose to challenge the thinking of us so-called experts, who had so carefully thought this through. Although we responded to their thoughts on this openly and supportively, quickly recognizing the wisdom of their approach, it took courage on their part to challenge their bosses after so short a time on the job. They were of course right in their thinking and in what they proposed.

Working across racially different neighborhoods ran counter to how things were done at that time in Boston. But promoting and highlighting the similarities rather than the differences between neighborhoods brought a new perspective to violence prevention efforts and challenged the ways things had typically been done.

Mayor Kurt L. Schmoke and Congresswoman Carolyn McCarthy: Politicians

We have been focusing on the Boston experience, but others in other parts of the country have also been taking chances and promoting new ways of taking on the violence epidemic, often challenging the status quo as they do so. Some courageous politicians around the country have begun to take stands on controversial issues as part of the violence prevention movement. One such issue involves the way drug addiction is addressed and viewed in this country. Although much of the world sees drug addiction as a health problem requiring medical and mental health interventions, this country has staunchly held to the belief that drug abuse is a criminal behavior requiring criminal justice interventions. Former Baltimore mayor Kurt L. Schmoke was one who stood up and said this was the wrong way to go about it. He became an advocate for legalizing drugs in a way that would allow a health and medical approach to the problem. Given the important role that substance abuse plays in the level of violence experienced in this country, this is one of the important issues that must be addressed and resolved in the effort to reduce violence.

Similarly, Congresswoman Carolyn McCarthy, from Long Island, New York, has become a major advocate for regulation of handguns. She ran for office after her husband was murdered by a gunman on the Long Island Railroad. In fact her campaign centered around her stand on guns. Few people are elected to office with such an agenda, which not only runs counter to popular opinion but also takes on the powerful and extremely well financed gun lobby. But she did it and won. She took a personal tragedy and turned it into activism, working against all odds. Her success points out that at least at a local level, people have been able to accept a perspective on violence and guns that is different from the traditional U.S. set of beliefs.

For an elected public official to take such a stand is enormously risky as its potential for unpopularity creates opportunities for political opponents. However, such courage is essential if this society is to make changes at the policy level in order to address drug abuse, handgun regulation, and media violence, among other things. We all need courageous politicians who are willing to take chances as Mayor Schmoke and Congresswoman McCarthy did.

Clementine Barfield: Mother Survivor

The important role of survivors in the violence prevention movement has grown entirely out of personal courage and risk taking. Coming forward publicly with such personal tragedy is not easy. Victims of violence and the families of those who have been murdered not only have to overcome their own pain and guilt but have historically not been treated kindly in this country. We seem to have a value system that often blames victims for their experience and isolates them from the rest of us. And we seem to have an it-will-never-happen-to-me complex. Survivors are scary reminders of our own vulnerability, and we protect ourselves from believing that it could happen to us. This is how we have treated victims of domestic violence, rape, murder, and many other such painful events.

Yet some survivors have overcome these obstacles and made a difference. Clementine Barfield is one. After the homicide death of her son, Derrick, she began to organize other parents in the city of Detroit who had lost children to murder. Starting the organization SOSAD (Save Our Sons and Daughters),[2] she brought together parents with similar experiences to promote change in their city. Much like Jeanne Taylor in Roxbury, she saw the need and value of doing something proactive for personal healing and for change.

This took great courage because sharing personal pain is hard and putting yourself up publicly as the parent of a murdered teenager does not necessarily bring with it a great deal of sympathy or empathy. After all, don't inner-city teenagers do things that put themselves at risk? Isn't it their fault it happened? And aren't the parents somehow responsible?

Clementine Barfield chose a different way of looking at it. As a result, she created a valuable resource in her city and was one of the first to recognize the power that survivors could bring to the movement. She was right to take the chance. She was right to bring a new vision to her own circumstances and to the effort to bring change.

Stepping out of our boxes, our preconceived notions of how things should be done, involves taking risks. Letting go of some of the usual assumptions about how people will react or respond makes the risks seem manageable, and often, when things are done differently, people respond differently.

Azim Khamisa: Father Survivor

The actions of Azim Khamisa, father of a murdered son, make an amazing story. He overcame his fear of rejection and his fear of being consumed by anger and reached out to the grandfather of the fifteen-year-old boy who shot and killed his son. In his book he tells the story of the power of forgiveness.[3] He and the boy's grandfather are now working together to present violence prevention assemblies and forgiveness seminars to children all over California.

The grandfather took a risk as well, the risk of ridicule and rejection, when he accepted Azim Khamisa's overtures and began working with him.

Making a Difference

All of these people have some things in common. They looked at the problem of violence in a new and different way. They saw violence as preventable and, rather than feeling helpless and hopeless about it, took action. These actions brought with them some risk and took some courage but these individuals were willing to take that chance. They saw their roles as professionals, community residents, survivors, and leaders as something more than the traditional definitions. They took responsibility and they took leadership even when tradition and popular opinion were not on their side. They made a difference, often with small, pragmatic steps that contributed to the larger endeavor.

Everyone can learn from these individuals; those of us who are health care professionals have a particular responsibility to learn from them. We can make a difference. But we have to shed some of what we have been taught and have learned. As professionals, we are taught to put some distance between ourselves and our patients or clients. "Professionalism" allows us to treat patients and clients and students as "others." We are protected by that distance, which is artificial at best. It keeps us from truly connecting with them and prevents us from having to acknowledge that what has happened to them can happen to us or our children. This isn't necessarily good. It is only by identifying with and learning from them that we will develop the insights that will help us figure out what to do.

All of the people described in this chapter applied what they experienced themselves and what they learned from listening to their patients or constituents in ways that allowed them to identify new and creative ways of taking on a seemingly overwhelming problem. They crossed the artificial boundaries of their training, of tradition, and of professionalism to do something different. And look what they have been able to accomplish and the public aware-ness they have brought about.

The two of us have learned so much from the work of these and other people. We entered the field of violence prevention knowing very little and learning on the job. The energy we have garnered from the work of Jeanne Taylor, Michael McDonald, Mickey Roache, Mark Bukaras, Paul Bracy, Clementine Barfield, and others is enormously motivating and provides a powerful lesson for us all. Their contributions are special. But not so special that everyone reading about them cannot do the same. We all need to step back and take a fresh look at what is going on and what we can do about it. There is so much that can be done, and there is so much work to do. We just have to start at our own bases and critically question and challenge the way things are done. The system is part of the problem, and even more important, it is a crucial part of the solution.

Chapter Fourteen

Going Into the Future

Our major concern, as Boston celebrates its success in reducing youth homicide, is that the city will become complacent and not continue the creative efforts that to date have characterized its violence prevention movement. Despite the decline in violent deaths, the pain and tragedy of the episodes of violence that still do occur are intensely real, and homicide is not the only area of concern. During 1998 and 1999, the city experienced a significant cluster of youth suicides in South Boston that kept many aware of the pain of some of Boston's children. We hope this book will not only add fuel to the national movement but also help Boston and other cities to stay the course.

Avoiding Quick Fixes

Occasionally, we are disturbed by some activities offered in the name of violence prevention. Even schools that are constantly struggling to offer effective violence prevention strategies occasionally make misguided choices. This happens particularly when there is an impulsive effort to provide a rapid response or quick fix in response to an episode of violence that hits close to home.

Because schools are extremely important in violence prevention work, it is essential that their involvement be built on good practice and not knee-jerk reactions. With the growing number of highly visible violent events that have occurred at schools over the past several years, more and more schools are looking for ways to prevent violence. The tendency, however, seems to be to make schools fortresses, with armed guards, metal detectors, and locked doors.

One horrific example for us of a possibly well-intentioned but misdirected effort was a report that the Los Angeles County Morgue was selling personalized toe tags, with the proceeds going to prevent violence.[1] This is an extreme example, but it is easy for such efforts to go wrong. There is also a school focus on efforts to identify the bad kids through "profiling," with subsequent efforts to isolate or label children identified in this way, and on rigid zero tolerance policies that result in excessive suspensions or expulsions. As we have argued previously, this is a reactive rather than a proactive approach, which is generally the less desirable way of addressing a problem. It is certainly less likely to bring long-term results, if any results at all.

Most of these efforts are misguided and involve strategies that are ineffective. They create a false sense of security but little real safety. Armed guards and metal detectors do not prevent violence, tend to be provocative, and create an oppressive and uncomfortable environment. Locked doors are a serious danger should fires or other emergencies occur. Kicking out so-called bad kids and those who are caught carrying weapons results in the loss of an important opportunity to actually help them and doesn't result in a safer environment. These kids don't disappear but remain in the community and often hang out around the school where their friends are. Most episodes of youth violence occur outside the school building. In-school shootings are still a relatively uncommon occurrence.

Choosing Carefully

We are impressed when school systems choose the more preventive and tested strategies, making schools more nurturing places that support success rather than failure. Even though it is often politically difficult, a principal or school board must take the risk of raising the long-term issues and not focus solely or even primarily on the crisis response. We join many others who propose making schools multiservice centers for children and families. These are schools that provide health centers, mental health services and other human services, and after-school activities; that encourage increased parental involvement in school activities and services; and that reinstitute nonacademic curricula such as art, music, sports, and shop, all of which allow a greater number of students the chance to be successful.

Furthermore, teaching prosocial skills and behaviors such as conflict resolution and mediation is as important as teaching reading and arithmetic. The development of alternative programs for kids who aren't doing well or are having trouble fitting in is a necessary option in place of suspension and expulsion. Smaller schools and smaller classrooms, where kids can get more attention and are better known by teachers and staff, reduce the chances that some kids will fall through the cracks. All of these approaches promote success among children and provide opportunities for kids to feel good about themselves and others. Such successful kids are far less likely to commit or participate in violence. Adopting these strategies does not mean losing discipline or surrendering high expectations. On the contrary, it creates an environment within which such expectations make sense and are valued because the kids themselves feel valued.

During a panel discussion, we once heard a superintendent of schools relate a scenario that illustrates the power of the knee-jerk reaction political forces. One of the schools in his district experienced a shooting. The usually locked doors had been opened at the end of the school day for students to exit, and a man ran in followed by another man with a gun. The first man was shot, but fortunately no children were hurt, as they had not yet emerged from their classrooms. Needless to say, the community was in an uproar, and the school committee hearing on the episode was packed.

The response was to place metal detectors in the schools, a $2 million proposition. The superintendent knew that this $2 million was poorly spent, given his multiple ungranted requests for student support services and violence prevention activities and the con-current decreases in the physical education and art and music budgets. Yet the political demands prevailed, even though the rare episode precipitating the concern would not have been stopped by the presence of metal detectors. The only difference would have that the alarms on the metal detectors would have been going off as gunman ran through the open doors into the building and fired his gun.

It is critical for professionals to take the risk of saying what they know is true and advocating for the comprehensive approach, even in the midst of a crisis. Not only should cooler and wiser heads speak the truth but they should also use the crisis moments to move the prevention agenda forward. They must do this even though it's sometimes lonely for those who take such risks because the masses are demanding the knee-jerk, often very expensive but not necessarily well thought out, solutions.

Displaying Patience and Persistence

Starting and nurturing a movement is often lonely for any number of reasons, including the reason that it is hard work. Both of us have found ourselves speaking at events where there were fewer in the audience than expected. In these circumstances we try to convince those who have come that though small in number they can do something. It takes only a few people to get things started. The Bible (Matthew 18:20) says that even when only two or three people are gathered in the Lord's name, the Lord will come. Well, maybe when only two or three are gathered to care about children, community will happen as well.

We are finding it helpful to continue with the Johnny Appleseed approach as we move around the country. We are trying to help build a national movement to prevent violence by energizing a critical mass of activists and leaders across the country who understand the complex causes of violence and effective prevention strategies. To that end, we have also engaged in a satellite broadcast training series, *Partnerships for Preventing Violence,* collaboratively funded by a number of federal agencies.[2] This six-part series has reached over 10,000 people. We have trained ninety facilitators who host local downlink sites and serve as local leaders in the movement. Each one of these 10,000 people is a seed. Some will germinate and eventually create more seeds. We have come a long way and, for the sake of our children and ourselves, we will continue the long way yet to go to bring an end to this American tragedy.

Deborah's Closing

When I sign my book *Deadly Consequences,*[3] I write, "This book offers my prayers for a world without violence." That pretty much sums it up for me. Not only do I believe that each of us has to work hard to improve personal skills, professional practices, and public policy to save children, but I also believe that we need prayers. Prayers for courage to take risks, prayers for a humane spirit, and prayers for the healing of all of us affected by violence.

Survivors Bring Insight and Passion

At our first conference of parents who had had a child murdered, held in Chicago in June of 1996, I had an epiphany. I watched people of different races, from different economic classes, with different levels of education, dressed in clothes from K-Mart and Neiman Marcus, speaking with different accents, and from all over the country come together and bond tightly within a few hours. The junk that usually gets in the way of human connections dissolved steadily as people shared their stories. The group was amazing, and I learned many things. I learned that it is offensive to say that a parent "lost" his or her child when the child was murdered. "I didn't lose my son; he was killed. And you need to call it what it was."

I learned that those of us who have been fortunate enough not to have experienced such an unthinkable tragedy often look for a euphemism to protect us. We don't want to hear the stories. And when we do hear them, we are looking for all the things that distinguish us from those parents or families. We think, "my son would never be outside at three in the morning," or, "if my daughter had a boyfriend like that, I would have done something about it." These thoughts give us a false protection from the reality—we are all vulnerable.

At the conference, involving sibling survivors, in Boston in July of 1999, I continued to learn. I learned that we were all following the lead of survivors. This comment by a student at Columbine High School captures the lesson.

> It's like it hit me with a ton of bricks, sitting here. I saw the correlation of a language; it's like a language of grief through violence that I knew existed. I knew this language existed but until you go to live in that country, maybe you understand some of the phrases and some of the words—bits and pieces, here and there—you don't understand because you're not fluent in that language until you actually live in that country. And unfortunately you can move to that country, in a heart—I started to say in a heartbeat—in a lack of a heartbeat, you can become fluent in that language.[4]

We ended the meeting with the realization that we were all survivors in some way, though we find ways to forget our experiences where possible.

Sharing Personal Experiences

Even though Howard and I have worked together for about twenty years, I never knew that he had experienced violent abuse as a child until the last year or so. We all hide our victimization because of the stigma and the shame. I learned from the survivors that to become a survivor—that is to move from victim status—you have to talk about what has happened.

At the survivors meeting I began to acknowledge the ways I had been victimized. When my husband was a fourteen-year-old boy growing up in St. Louis, long before I met him, he was shot in the chest. The bullet went in and out, passing an eighth of an inch from his heart. I had never thought of myself as a survivor until that meeting, even though I have been robbed at gunpoint and my mother-in-law was stabbed in front of her home. But I too am a survivor and know the stigma of the victim because I haven't talked about any of this as connected to my work until now. I wouldn't ever compare my experiences to those of parents who have had a beloved child murdered. I have come close enough to their daily struggles to know that they are bearing the unbearable. When they turn pain into power and anger into action, they inspire me.

I do this work for my children and unborn grandchildren. I do this work because I know we can live differently and have a different kind of society. I saw it in the bonding of the survivors. That was an epiphany for me—humankind can bond across and in spite of the junk that separates us. I pray that America has had enough tragedy to cause us all to see beyond the junk to what's really important, and bond. I pray we don't wait until the worst violence we can imagine happens to us to make the change. As Clementine Barfield, the Detroit mother who started SOSAD after her son was killed, often says in her speeches, "I lived a middle-class life and never imagined this would happen to me—don't wait until it happens to you."

Forgiveness

From the survivors I have learned to struggle more with forgiveness—to consider it a strategy.

Trevor, a young man of twenty-five, lives his life from wheelchair to bed and is dependent on a respirator. He spoke at the Chicago conference about the healing power of forgiveness: "I had to forgive the young man who shot me, because my anger and hate were eating away at my mother and keeping me from healing." What power is in that story—in his life.

Frank Johnson, a survivor-counselor with the Living After Murder Program, told a deeply powerful story of forgiveness. His efforts to forgive were based in religious beliefs. Some years after his son was killed, the murderer was released from prison. Frank saw the newly freed man crossing at a red light in front of his car. He said that he knew he had forgiven the man because he had no impulse to run the man over.

I learned that forgiveness is not for every survivor all the time, but that it is powerful and often underestimated. I know that it is also unpopular and un-American. Reginald Denny, the truck driver beaten during the Los Angeles revolt following the Rodney King verdict, appeared on the *Phil Donahue Show* some years ago. Henry Watson, accused and acquitted of the crime, was also on the show. Reginald Denny evoked hostility from the audience because of his stance of forgiveness. He had hugged Henry Watson's mother during the trial, and many in the audience were hostile toward him. "Why didn't you just let the courts put him in jail," shouted one woman. "Why were you hugging that man's mother and talking about forgiveness?" asked another. Reginald Denny responded that it was in his religion to forgive. "What kind of religion do you have?" asked the woman. Reginald Denny responded, "I am a Christian." "Well, what kind of Christian are you?" the woman retorted.

This episode let me know just how unpopular forgiveness is. Most people don't remember Reginald Denny's act of forgiveness the way they remember Jeffrey Dahmer's horrific acts or those of the Menendez brothers. There is no national Reginald Denny prize for forgiveness.

I am struggling with forgiveness as a strategy for healing and helping because I don't completely understand its power and place. I know that it's unpopular and often demeaned. But I also think that some of the hurt children need to be forgiven and embraced rather than punished.

I have learned so much. I am a better, more skillful person because of my work in violence prevention. I am a more humble and forgiving person because of my contact with survivors. My prayers for a world without violence are constant. I pray for courage to take risks, for a humane spirit, and for the healing of all of us affected by violence.

Howard's Closing

One morning, in the spring of 1998, I was running late and happened to still be home when my son, just turned twelve, was ready to leave for school. He said good-bye, walked down the hall to the front door, threw his fifty-pound bookbag over his shoulder, and opened the door. Just as he was walking out, he looked back over his shoulder and said, "You know, Dad, I risk my life every day when I go to school." A moment later, he was out the door and on his way. Although this seems like a small thing, what he said rolled off his tongue in such a nonchalant way that it was clear he had thought about this and maybe even said it before. My wife and I, who were sitting at the kitchen table, just stared at each other. It was a clear example of the way what was happening around the country was affecting children all over.

Jonesboro, Arkansas: Community as Survivor

I had in fact just returned from Jonesboro, Arkansas. I was invited down there a month or so after the tragic shooting deaths of four students and a teacher by two young boys. I was not there to respond to the acute crisis but to talk and meet with numerous people (physicians, community leaders, elected officials, human service and mental health professionals, parents, community residents) after the acute shock and mourning period to discuss long-term solutions and agendas.

I must say, I was a bit nervous about going there. Although I had traveled around the country for many years by then, I had spent very little time in what I am told is the "Deep South." After being invited, my first comment to my wife was, "How should I look and act; I don't want to come across as a know-it-all northerner with all the answers." Her advice was, as usual, simple and direct, "Just be yourself." She had heard me say in many forums that no one has all the answers for this, that we all have to work together to find them.

What I found in Jonesboro was a community devastated by tragedy and loss, struggling not only with the deaths of the victims but trying to understand why this had happened. What drove those young boys to do what they did? What was going on in their safe, protected, insulated, far away from high-risk inner-cities community that had allowed this to happen? Their loss of the children and the teacher was bad enough. But they had lost more than that. They had lost their sense of taken-for-granted safety and security. And some of the basic values of their culture and community had been seriously shaken.

What I also found was a palpable energy and commitment to take action. They were not going to be immobilized by grief and anger; they were going to do whatever it took to make sure that this wouldn't happen again. They were even willing to discuss, in a serious and open manner, such difficult subjects as guns, family violence, and some of the other cultural norms and hidden, never-to-be-talked-about issues that might have played a part in what had happened. They were not victims. They were survivors.

I left Jonesboro sad but also encouraged and energized by the people I had met there. I also returned home feeling exhausted, needing to be someplace that felt familiar, safe, and comfortable. I needed to feel grounded after such an intense and emotional experience. My son's casual, off-the-cuff comment that reflected his own take on the Jonesboro tragedy jolted me back to reality. Everyone everyplace was deeply affected by what was happening in communities like Jonesboro. Everyone everyplace needed to recognize that and deal with it.

It was at that point that I began to reflect on how far I had personally come, how far my work with Deborah had progressed, and how much had happened with the violence prevention movement.

Visible Changes

Over ten years earlier, in 1986, I had presented our first scientific evaluation of violent deaths among the youth in Boston. We had analyzed the causes of death of teenagers in our city over a ten-year period and had found that homicide had become the leading cause of death for that age group. Although there was nothing elaborate about this analysis, we decided to submit it for presentation at annual conference of the American Public Health Association (APHA), which was in Las Vegas that year. It was accepted, and I went to the meeting expecting to hear about the work others were doing in this area.

To both Deborah's and my surprise, our work turned out to be the only paper on the subject of youth violence in this entire huge conference featuring hundreds of, maybe even more than a thousand, papers and presentations. In fact it turned out that our paper was assigned to a session on teenage pregnancy, I guess the closest subject matter that could be identified. So there I was talking about youth violence, sandwiched between three papers on teenage pregnancy before me and three on the same subject after me.

It is an indicator of how far the violence prevention movement has come that the annual meetings of the APHA for the past several years have offered whole sessions on youth violence. These sessions have addressed everything from understanding the causes and risk factors of violence to evaluations of violence prevention programs from places all over the country. There have even been keynote addresses, centerpieces for the conference, on the subject. What a change!

The Pediatric Community

The other professional association that I work with, the American Academy of Pediatrics (AAP), has also made enormous progress. In the early 1990s, I met with the board of the AAP at the time that the AAP first raised the prevention of violent injuries to its highest priority agenda list. Prior to this, the focus on injury prevention had primarily addressed unintentional (accidental) injury and death, with only modest attention to violence. Even gun-related injury prevention was focused more on unintentional events even though the number of injuries and deaths from intentional events was much higher.

Since that time much has happened. The AAP has set up a task force on violence and published a number of policy statements on the role of pediatricians in the violence prevention movement as well as statements on guns, corporal punishment, the adolescent assault victim's needs, media violence, and more. The organization's public policy work has also focused more aggressively on issues related to violence prevention. The violence prevention agenda has been incorporated into the fabric of the organization. I must add that I am proud of my colleagues and professional peers for this action they have taken. They have been out there on this issue in ways that many other professional groups need to be.

The Power of Marketing

I also find it worthwhile to reflect on our experience with our first public media campaign for violence prevention in the mid-1980s. As described earlier, we had been selected to receive the annual Advertising Council of Greater Boston's public service campaign development prize. As a result we had the good fortune to work with the Hill Holiday Advertising Agency, which offered to develop and promote several television and radio spots for us.

We wanted to use this media exposure to promote the idea of violence prevention, not specifically our program of services. This was a new area for the creative staff of Hill Holiday to explore. They were used to selling products and services, not beliefs or behaviors. Initially we found ourselves in discussions with these staff members that reflected all the misconceptions and misunderstandings that many people have about the issue. How do communities separate the bad kids from the good ones? Aren't people innately programmed to be violent and enjoy violence? Isn't the risk of serious punishment the best way to get the message across?

It took time and patience, on their part as well as ours, to move the discussion to the point where their creative talents could develop messages that were accurate and potentially effective. But they got there, which showed that the time invested was worth it for all of us. It just took time, patience, and commitment from everyone involved. In many different ways this process has been repeated over and over again in our work of the past twenty years.

Survivors

Possibly the most gratifying collaborations that we have experienced have been with survivors. Deborah has already discussed what this experience has been like for her. I can only reiterate that these individuals bring so much to the movement. They have helped me to understand and come to even greater peace with my own past. They bring energy that moves me and fills me up as powerfully gasoline does for cars.

It was painful and shocking to hear my own son announce his fears that were generated by the violence he was seeing around the country. Like so many parents, my wife and I had tried hard to protect him from these scary images. This violence was clearly affecting him, possibly because it was happening in places that were much like his own environment. It was "too close to home." As we said at the start of this book, maybe violence needed to get "too close" before people could see what was going on and start to take some responsibility for dealing with it. This is sad and unfortunate, but it has also created a real opportunity for change.

Personal Growth

Like Deborah, I do this work for personal as well as professional reasons and very much want to make a contribution to creating a safe and peaceful world. At the personal level I want my own children and their future children to be safe, unafraid, and confident that the future is bright. But I don't want, nor do I expect, my children to be special, to be different from any other child. What I want for my children, I want for every child. I want this to happen not by low-ering my expectations and hopes for my children, but by elevating my hopes for all children.

Professionally, I want it to be both safe and expected for people to take risks, the risks essential for change. I want be people to be acknowledged and rewarded for looking at things differently, and I want them to value real movement, not illusions of change or the status quo. And I want to continue to grow myself, as a professional and as a person, and to help others to grow.

For this country and the world, I pray with Deborah for noth-ing less than a world without violence.

The Last Word

We would like to share, as a parting word, some basic principles about preventing violence among youth that we have learned in our work. We have listed them here for you to use as you wish. We find ourselves referring to these ideas regularly to help our thinking and keep us on track.

1. Violence *is* preventable.
2. Survivors and youth themselves are central to the violence prevention movement and to the solutions.
3. In an avalanche no one snowflake feels responsible. In fact, all of them are.
4. The system is part of the problem, but it can be and needs to be part of the solution.
5. "Bad kids" can sometimes be the most responsive.
6. Hurt children become hurtful children.
7. Kids aren't the problem; adults are. Recognizing this is an essential first step.
8. The process is as important as the product.
9. Work from the bottom up; that's the way change happens.

10. There is no one person, solution, or program that will fix violence. Everyone has a role.

11. Forgiveness for our children and ourselves is crucial.

12. Small steps add up to big change.

As we closed individually, we close together, with our prayers for a world without violence.

Notes

Chapter One

1. J. Garbarino, *Lost Boys: Why Our Sons Turn Violent and How We Can Save Them* (New York: Free Press, 1999).
2. S. Bok, *Mayhem: Violence as Public Entertainment* (Reading, Mass.: Addison-Wesley, 1998).

Chapter Two

1. Many adolescents at risk for violence are in school. For this reason schools are instrumental in disseminating information about violence prevention. The Violence Prevention Curriculum for Adolescents was designed to fit a tenth-grade health course. It was not seen as a magic bullet that would, on its own, save children. Rather, it was developed as a beginning, a first step that would be joined with other steps, other interventions. The curriculum's purpose was to teach young people two important lessons:

   1. They are at risk of becoming perpetrators and victims of violence.
   2. Violence is not inevitable; they have choices.

   The curriculum combines didactic presentations, interactive exercises, role playing, and problem solving. It is designed to create opportunities for young people to better understand the things that put them at risk and how they, both as individuals and as members of peer groups, can make other choices. The curriculum is built on the assumption that with appropriate information and guidance, students have the capacity to understand their own circumstances and identify their own options. It also assumes that students will learn better through an interactive process and that they need the opportunity to play out and practice the various choices they can make.

Chapter Three

1. Centers for Disease Control and Prevention, "Rates of Homicide, Suicide, and Firearm-Related Death Among Children: 26 Industrialized Countries," *Morbidity and Mortality Weekly Report*, 46, no. 5 (7 February 1997): 101–105.

2. Centers for Disease Control and Prevention, "Rates of Homicide, Suicide, and Firearm-Related Death Among Children: 26 Industrialized Countries."

3. Centers for Disease Control and Prevention, "Deaths Resulting from Firearm- and Motor-Vehicle-Related Injuries: United States, 1968–1991," *Morbidity and Mortality Weekly Report*, 43, no. 3 (28 January 1994): 37–42.

4. L. A. Fingerhut and J. C. Kleinman, "International and Interstate Comparison of Homicide Among Young Males," *Journal of the American Medical Association*, 263, no. 24 (1990): 3292–3295.

5. Centers for Disease Control and Prevention, "Deaths Resulting from Firearm- and Motor-Vehicle-Related Injuries: United States, 1968–1991."

6. J. I. Barancik, B. F. Chatterjee, Y. C. Greene, and others, "Northeastern Ohio Trauma Study," *American Journal of Public Health*, 73 (1983): 746–751.

7. See, for example, U.S. Department of Justice, Federal Bureau of Investigation, *Crime in the United States, 1998*, Uniform Crime Reports (Washington, D.C.: U.S. Department of Justice, 2000).

8. Uniform Crime Reports (Washington, D.C.: U.S. Department of Justice, 2000).

9. F. Butterfield, *All God's Children: The Bosket Family and the American Tradition of Violence* (New York: Knopf, 1995). Butterfield became interested in the issue of violence while covering Willie Bosket's trial for murder.

10. Butterfield, *All God's Children*.

11. Butterfield, *All God's Children*.

12. B. Centerwall, "Race, Socioeconomic Status and Domestic Homicide, Atlanta, 1971–72," *American Journal of Public Health*, 74, no. 8 (1984): 813–815.

13. V. Mark and F. Irvin, *Violence and the Brain* (New York: HarperCollins, 1970).

14. J. P. Lecanuet and B. Schaal, "Fetal Sensory Competencies," *European Journal of Obstetrics, Gynecology, and Reproductive Biology*, 68, no. 1–2 (1996): 1–23.

15. C. C. Bell, *Psychiatric Aspects of Violence: Issues in Prevention and Treatment* (New York: John Wiley & Sons, 2000).

16. E. Balaban, J. S. Alper, and Y. L. Kasamon, "Mean Genes and the Biology of Aggression: A Critical Review of Recent Animal and Human Research," *Journal of Neurogenetics*, 11, no. 12 (1996): 1–43.

17. D. Olweus, *Bullying at School: What We Know and What We Can Do* (Oxford, U.K.: Blackwell, 1994).

18. F. Earls, *The Project on Human Development in Chicago Neighborhoods* (Cambridge: Harvard School of Public Health).

19. U.S. Department of Justice, Federal Bureau of Investigation, *Crime in the United States, 1982*, Uniform Crime Reports (Washington, D.C.: U.S. Department of Justice, 1984).

20. Barancik, Chatterjee, Greene, and others, "Northeastern Ohio Trauma Study."

21. WRISS (Weapon Related Injury Surveillance System) was begun in 1989, as a project funded by the Centers for Disease Control, with Howard Spivak, then deputy commissioner of the Massachusetts Department of Public Health, as principal investigator and Deborah Prothrow-Stith, then commissioner of public health, as coprincipal investigator. WRISS was the first system for surveillance of nonfatal weapon-related injuries in the United States.

22. H. Spivak, D. Prothrow-Stith, and A. J. Hausman, "Dying Is No Accident: Adolescents, Violence and Intentional Injury," *Pediatric Clinics of North America*, 35, no. 6 (1988): 1339–1347.

23. The Sentencing Project. *State and Federal Prisoners (1925–2002), Incarceration Trends Chart*. Retrieved June 2003 from www.sentencingproject.org.

24. C. S. Widom, "Cycle of Violence," *Science*, 244 (1989): 160–165. Exposure—increased risk of violence—exposure of others—increased risk—and so forth.

25. For more information about violence as a cycle, see National Institutes of Justice, *Breaking the Cycle: Predicting and Preventing Crime* (Washington, D.C.: National Institutes of Justice, 1994).
26. H. Spivak, D. Prothrow-Stith, and M. Moore, "A Comprehensive Approach to Violence Prevention: Public Health and Criminal Justice in Partnership," in *Crime and Community Safety: Chicago Assembly Background Papers* (Chicago: Center for Urban Research and Policy Studies, 1992).

Chapter Four

1. *The Youth Gang Problem: Perceptions of Former Youth Gang Influentials, Transcripts of Two Symposia*, National Youth Gang Suppression and Intervention Program, School of Social Service Administration, University of Chicago, January 1990 (Rockville, Md.: Juvenile Justice Clearinghouse).
2. W. J. Wilson, *The Truly Disadvantaged: The Inner City, the Underclass, and Public Policy* (Chicago: University of Chicago, 1987).
3. Wilson, *The Truly Disadvantaged*.
4. B. Centerwall, "Race, Socioeconomic Status and Domestic Homicide, Atlanta, 1971–72," *American Journal of Public Health*, 74, no. 8 (1984): 813–815.
5. R. Oakley, *Drugs, Society and Human Behavior* (St. Louis, Mo.: Mosby, 1983).
6. University of California and the Centers for Disease Control, *The Epidemiology of Homicide in the City of Los Angeles, 1970–9* (Washington, D.C.: U.S. Department of Health and Human Services, 1985).
7. J. H. Sloane, A. L. Kellerman, D. T. Reay, and others, "Handgun Regulations, Crime, Assault, and Homicide: A Tale of Two Cities," *New England Journal of Medicine*, 319, no. 19 (1988): 1256–1262.
8. R. Sege and W. Dietz, "Television Viewing and Violence in Children," *Pediatrics*, 94, no. 4 (1994): 600–608.
9. M. A. Straus and R. J. Gelles (eds.), *Physical Violence in American Families: Risk Factors and Adaptations to Violence in 8,145 Families* (New Brunswick, N.J.: Transaction Press, 1990).
10. The Boston Commission on Safe Public Schools, *Making Our Schools Safe for Learning*, Boston Commission Survey of Weapons Carrying (Boston: Boston Commission on Safe Public Schools, November 1983).
11. K. Zinsmeister, "Growing Up Scared," *Atlantic Monthly* (June 1990).
12. J. Garbarino, *Lost Boys: Why Our Sons Turn Violent and How We Can Save Them* (New York: Free Press, 1999); *Children in Danger: Coping with the Consequences of Community Violence* (San Francisco: Jossey-Bass, 1992).
13. A. Poussaint, in a speech made at the Harvard Street Neighborhood Health Center, 1985.
14. D. S. Elliot (ed.), *Blueprints for Violence Prevention: Big Brothers Big Sisters of America* (Boulder, Colo.: Institute of Behavioral Science, University of Colorado, 1997).

Chapter Five

1. Data from B. Sipchen, "Putting a Price Tag on Violence," *Los Angeles Times*, 5 June 1994, A22.
2. U.S. Department of Justice, Federal Bureau of Investigation, *Crime in the United States, 1998*, Uniform Crime Reports (Washington, D.C.: U.S. Department of Justice, 2000).

3. Centers for Disease Control and Prevention, "Rates of Homicide, Suicide, and Firearm-Related Death Among Children: 26 Industrialized Countries," *Morbidity and Mortality Weekly Report*, 46, no. 5 (February 7, 1997): 101–105.

4. M. A. Schuster, T. M. Franke, A. M. Bastian, S. Sor, and N. Halfon, "Firearm Storage Patterns in U.S. Homes with Children," *American Journal of Public Health*, 90, no. 4 (2000): 588–594.

5. G. J. Wintemute, C. A. Parham, J. J. Beaumont, M. Wright, and C. Drake, "Mortality Among Recent Purchasers of Handguns," *New England Journal of Medicine*, 341, no. 21 (1999): 1583–1589.

6. Centers for Disease Control and Prevention, 1997.

7. See, for example, J. H. Sloan, A. L. Kellerman, D. T. Reary, et al., "Handgun Regulations, Crime Assaults, and Homicide: A Tale of Two Cities," *New England Journal of Medicine*, 319 (1988): 1256–1262.

8. This material is taken from two articles that appeared in *Legal Action Alert*, the newsletter of the Center to Prevent Handgun Violence: "CPHV Seeks Reversal of Lone Federal Court Ruling on Second Amendment," *Legal Action Alert*, 19 (January 2000): 3; "Federal Courts Unanimously Reject Emerson Court's Flawed View of Second Amendment," *Legal Action Alert*, 19 (January 2000): 6–7.

9. See, for example, A. L. Kellerman, F. P. Rivara, N. B. Rushforth, and others, "Gun Ownership as a Risk Factor for Homicide in the Home," *New England Journal of Medicine*, 329 (1993): 1084–1091.

10. CNN.com, "Michigan First-Grader Fatally Shot by Classmate," 1 March 2000, retrieved April 2003 from www.cnn.com.

11. More information about the Center to Prevent Handgun Violence may be found at the organization's Web site: www.cphv.org.

12. "Illinois Court Permits Public Nuisance Suit Against Gun Makers to Proceed," *Legal Action Alert*, 19 (January 2000): 6.

13. M. McDonald, *All Souls: A Family Story from Southie* (Boston: Beacon Press Workshop, 1999).

14. For information about this program see the National Rifle Association's Web site, www.nra.org.

15. American Broadcasting Corporation, "Kids and Guns," *20/20*, 21 May 1999.

Chapter Six

1. Associated Press, "Star Wrestler Subpoenaed by Attorney for Boy Charged in Playmate's Death," 4 March 2000.

2. In September 2000, the Federal Trade Commission released its report on the marketing of violent entertainment to children. Among other things it discussed memos written by members of the entertainment industry regarding a concerted effort to focus marketing of adult programming to children. These marketing memos detail methods used to lure underage viewers to adult movies. Studios hired teens to pitch R-rated films to peers. Other tactics included targeting kids' hangouts.

3. M. St. Peters and others, "Media Use Among Preschool Children as a Function of Income and Media Options" (paper presented at the biennial meeting of the Society for Research in Child Development, 1991).

4. A. Bandura, D. Ross, and S. A. Ross, "Imitation of Film: Mediated Aggressive Models," *Journal of Abnormal Social Psychology*, 66 (1963): 3–11.

5. D. V. Levin, *Remote Control Childhood? Combating the Hazards of Media Culture* (Washington, D.C.: National Association for the Education of Young Children, 1998).

6. A. N. Meltzoff, "Imitation of Televised Models by Infants," *Child Development*, 59 (1988): 1221–1229.

7. L. Eron, et al., "Does Television Violence Cause Aggression?" *American Psychologist*, 27 (1972): 253–263.

8. L. R. Huesmann, "The Effects of Childhood Aggression and Exposure to Media Violence on Adult Behaviors, Attitudes, and Moods: Evidence from a Fifteen-Year Cross-National Study," *Aggressive Behavior*, 25 (1999): 18–29.

9. B. J. Wilson, et al., "Violence in Television Programming Overall." In M. Seawall (ed.), *National Television Violence Study* (Thousand Oaks, Calif.: Sage, 1998).

10. C. W. Turner, B. W. Hesse, and S. Peterson-Lewis, "Naturalistic Studies of the Long-Term Effects of Television Violence," *Journal of Social Issues* (1986): 51–73; W. Wood, F. Y. Wong, and J. G. Chachere, "Effects of Media Violence on Viewer's Aggression in Unconstrained Social Interaction," *Psychological Bulletin*, 109 (1991): 371–383.

11. C. O. Cosby, *Television's Imageable Influences: The Self-Perceptions of Young African-Americans* (Lanham, Md.: University Press of America, 1994).

12. K. Ross, "Viewing Pleasure, Viewer Pain: Black Audiences and British Television," *Leisure Studies*, 16, no. 4 (1997): 233–248.

13. G. Gerbner, et al., *Television's Mean World* (Philadelphia: The Annenberg School of Communications, 1986).

14. "Warning Shots at TV," *U.S. News and World Report*, 12 July 1993.

15. Mediascope, *National Television Violence Study, Vol. 1* (Thousand Oaks, Calif.: Sage, 1996) and *National Television Violence Study, Vol. 2* (Thousand Oaks, Calif.: Sage, 1997). For more information about Mediascope, Inc., see the organization's Web site: www.mediascope.org.

16. For more information about the Rocky Mountain Media Watch, see the organization's Web site: www.bigmedia.org.

Chapter Seven

1. See, for example, the home page of the organization's Web site: www.childrensdefense.org. The Children's Defense Fund has a mission to "leave no child behind." It was founded in 1973 as a private, nonprofit organization to provide a strong, effective, voice for all the children of America who cannot vote, lobby, or speak for themselves.

2. "Superpredators," *Newsweek*, 22 January 1996.

3. D. Z. Jackson, "New York State Is Starving Schools to Build Prisons," *Boston Globe*, 2 December 1998, http://nl.newsbank.com/nl=search/we/Archives?p_action/list&p_topdoc/51.

4. T. Litthcut, personal communication, n.d.

5. S. Buel, personal communication, n.d.

6. P. Mones, *When a Child Kills: Abused Children Who Kill Their Parents* (New York: Pocket Books, 1991).

7. "America Under the Gun," *Newsweek*, 23 August 1999, 20–49. This special report includes ten articles.

8. T. Egan, "Where Rampages Begin: A Special Report: From Adolescent Angst to Shooting Up Schools," *New York Times*, 14 June 1998.

9. R. Ferguson, *The Case for Community-Based Programs That Inform and Mentor Black Male Youth* (Washington, D.C.: Urban Institute, 1989).

10. D. D. Lewis, et al., "Racial Bias in the Diagnosis and Disposition of Violent Adolescents," *American Journal of Psychiatry*, 137, no. 8 (1980): 1211–1216.

Chapter Eight

1. *The Youth Gang Problem: Perceptions of Former Youth Gang Influentials, Transcripts of Two Symposia*, National Youth Gang Suppression and Intervention Program, School of Social Service Administration, University of Chicago, January 1990 (Rockville, Md.: Juvenile Justice Clearinghouse).

2. S. S. Stone, "Changing Nature of Juvenile Offenders" (presentation at U.S. Department of Justice, Office of Juvenile Justice and Delinquency Prevention Conference), audiocassette, track 1.

3. U.S. Department of Justice, Office of Juvenile Justice and Delinquency Prevention, *Guiding Principles for Promising Female Programming: An Inventory of Best Practices* (Washington, D.C.: U.S. Department of Justice, October 1998).

4. U.S. Department of Justice, Office of Juvenile Justice and Delinquency Prevention, "Training and Technical Assistance Programs: Juvenile Offenders and At Risk Girls," Request for Proposals (Washington, D.C.: U.S. Department of Justice, July 1996).

5. M. Chesney-Lind, quoted in P. Boyle, "Are Girls Getting Worse, or Are Adults Getting Scared?" *Youth Today*, 1 February 1999, 1116–1118.

6. Girls Inc., *Prevention and Parity: Girls in Juvenile Justice* (Washington, D.C.: U.S. Department of Justice, Office of Juvenile Justice and Delinquency Prevention, 1996).

7. M. Chesney-Lind, J. Koo, D. Kata, and K. Fujiwara, *Girls at Risk: An Overview of Gender-Specific Programming Issues and Initiatives*, Report No. 394 (Honolulu: University of Hawaii, Social Science Research Institute, Center for Youth Research, 1998).

8. L. Prescott, *Improving Policy and Practice for Adolescent Girls with Co-Occurring Disorders in the Juvenile Justice System* (Delmar, N.Y.: Gains Center, 1998).

9. E. A. Sirles, S. Lipchik, and K. Kowalski, "A Consumer's Perspective on Domestic Violence Interventions," *Journal of Family Violence*, 8, no. 3 (September 1993): 267–276.

10. D. B. Sugarman and G. T. Hotaling, "Dating Violence: A Review of Contextual and Risk Factors," in B. Levy (ed.), *Dating Violence: Young Women in Danger* (Seattle: Seal Press, 1991).

11. U.S. Department of Justice, Federal Bureau of Investigation, *Crime in the United States, 1994*, Uniform Crime Reports (Washington, D.C.: U.S. Department of Justice).

12. Sugarman and Hotaling, "Dating Violence."

13. Sugarman and Hotaling, "Dating Violence."

14. L. Bergman, "Dating Violence Among High School Students," *Social Work*, 37 (1991): 21–27.

15. J. Makepeace, "Courtship Violence Among College Students," *Family Relations*, 30 (1981): 97–102.

16. C. P. Ewing, *When Children Kill: The Dynamics of Juvenile Homicide* (San Francisco: New Lexington Press, 1990).

17. U.S. Department of Justice, Office of Juvenile Justice and Delinquency Prevention, *Guiding Principles for Promising Female Programming*.

18. Chesney-Lind, Koo, Kato, and Clark, *Girls at Risk*.

19. Chesney-Lind, Koo, Kato, and Clark, *Girls at Risk*.

20. Chesney-Lind, Koo, Kato, and Clark, *Girls at Risk*.

21. Chesney-Lind, Koo, Kato, and Clark, *Girls at Risk*.

22. U.S. Department of Justice, Office of Juvenile Justice and Delinquency Prevention, *Guiding Principles for Promising Female Programming*.

23. U.S. Department of Justice, Office of Juvenile Justice and Delinquency Prevention, *Guiding Principles for Promising Female Programming*.

24. K. H. Federle and M. Chesney-Lind, "Special Issues in Juvenile Justice: Gender, Race, and Ethnicity," in I. M. Schwartz (ed.), *Juvenile Justice and Public Policy: Toward a National Agenda* (New York: Maxwell-Macmillan International, 1992).

25. American Correctional Association, *The Female Offenders: What Does the Future Hold?* (Lanham, Md.: American Correctional Association, 1990).

26. C. M. Renzetti and D. L. Curran, *Women, Men, and Society* (Needham Heights, Mass.: Allyn and Bacon, 1992).

27. C. S. Widom, "Cycle of Violence," *Science*, 244 (1989): 160–165.

28. R. Reece, *Child Abuse: Medical Diagnosis and Management* (Philadelphia: Lea and Febinger, 1994).

29. Center for Women Policy Studies, *Teen Women Ask Their Peers About Violence, Hate, and Discrimination: The Report of the Teen Women Leadership Development Initiative Survey* (Washington, D.C.: Center for Women Policy Studies, 2001).

30. Center for the Study of Youth Policy, *Mediation Involving Juveniles* (Philadelphia: Center for the Study of Youth Policy, 1991).

31. W. J. Bailey, "Three Critical Hours—Three Critical Years: Toward Precision Targeting in Prevention," Prevention Newsline 11, no. 3 (1998), http://www.drugs.indiana.edu/publications/iprc/newsline/three_critical.html.

32. Department of Justice, Office of Juvenile Justice and Delinquency Prevention, http://ojjdp.ncjrs.org/pubs/principles/contents.html.

33. Department of Justice, Office of Juvenile Justice and Delinquency Prevention, http://ojjdp.ncjrs.org/pubs/principles/contents.html.

34. Chesney-Lind, Koo, Kato, and Clark, *Girls at Risk*.

Chapter Nine

1. R. J. Gelles and M. A. Straus, *Intimate Violence* (New York: Simon and Schuster, 1988); M. A. Straus and R. J. Gelles (eds.), *Physical Violence in American Families: Risk Factors and Adaptations to Violence in 8,145 Families* (New Brunswick, N.J.: Transaction Press, 1990); M. A. Straus, R. J. Gelles, and S. K. Steinmetz, *Behind Closed Doors: Violence in the American Family* (Thousand Oaks, Calif.: Sage, 1980).

2. C. S. Widom, "Cycle of Violence," *Science*, 244 (1989): 160–165.

3. B. M. Goves, B. Zuckerman, and S. Marans, "Silent Victims: Children Who Witness Violence," *Journal of the American Medical Association*, 269, no. 2 (1993): 262–265.

4. Gelles and Straus, *Intimate Violence*; Straus, Gelles, and Steinmetz, *Behind Closed Doors*.

5. Gelles and Straus, *Intimate Violence*; Straus, Gelles, and Steinmetz, *Behind Closed Doors*.

6. Gelles and Straus, *Intimate Violence*; Straus, Gelles, and Steinmetz, *Behind Closed Doors*.

7. Gelles and Straus, *Intimate Violence*; Straus, Gelles, and Steinmetz, *Behind Closed Doors*.

8. M. A. Straus, "The Conflict Tactics Scale and Its Critics: An Evaluation and New Data on Validity and Reliability," in Straus and Gelles, *Physical Violence in American Families*.

9. Straus, Gelles, and Steinmetz, *Behind Closed Doors*; M. A. Straus, "Children as Witnesses to Violence," in *Report of the Twenty-Third Ross Roundtable: Children and Violence* (Ross Laboratories, 1992): 98–109.

10. D. Olds, et al., "Long-Term Effects of Home Visitation on Maternal Life Course and Child Abuse and Neglect, Fifteen-Year Follow-Up," *Journal of the American Medical Association*, 278 (1997): 637–643.

11. H. Spivak, "Community Approach to Violence Prevention," in *Children and Violence* (Columbus, Ohio: Ross Laboratories, 1992).

Chapter Ten

1. H. Spivak and D. Prothrow-Stith, "An Analysis of Mortality Among Fifteen- to Nineteen-Year-Olds in Boston" (paper presented at the annual meeting of the American Public Health Association, Las Vegas, Nev., 1986).

Chapter Eleven

1. P. Stringham and H. Spivak, "What Primary Care Clinicians Can Do When Confronting Violent Youth," *Bulletin of New York Academy of Medicine*, 71, no. 2 (1994): 1–18.
2. Louis D. Brown Institute, 5 Louis D. Brown Way, Dorchester, MA, 02124–1011, 617-825-1917.
3. Teens Against Gang Violence, 2 Moody Street, Boston, MA, 02124, 617-282-9659.

Chapter Twelve

1. J. Dryfoos and S. Maguire, *Inside Full Community Service Schools* (Thousand Oaks, Calif.: Sage, 2002).
2. Office of Special Education Programs, U.S. Department of Education, *A Guide to Safe Schools*. Available at http://www.ncela.gwv.edu/pathways/safeschools.

Chapter Thirteen

1. M. McDonald, *All Souls: A Family Story from Southie* (Boston: Beacon Press Workshop, 1999).
2. SOSAD (Save Our Sons and Daughters), 2441 West Grand Blvd., Detroit, MI 48208, 313-361-5200.
3. A. Khamisa with C. Goldman, *Azim's Bardo: A Father's Journey from Murder to Forgiveness*. Los Altos, Calif.: Rising Star Press, 1998.

Chapter Fourteen

1. From APBNews.com: http://www.randydotinga.com/giftshop.html.
2. Harvard School of Public Health, Prevention Institute, Inc., and Education Development Center, Inc., *Partnerships for Preventing Violence: The Six-Part Satellite Training Forum* (Boston: Harvard School of Public Health, 2000).
3. D. Prothrow-Stith with M. Weissman, *Deadly Consequences: How Violence Is Destroying Our Teenage Population and a Plan to Begin Solving the Problem* (New York: HarperCollins, 1991).
4. D. Anna, statement made at Sibling Survivors Conference, Boston, 18 September 1999.

Further Reading

Bok, S. *Mayhem: Violence as Public Entertainment*. Reading, Mass.: Addison-Wesley, 1998.

Butterfield, F. *All God's Children: The Bosket family and the American Tradition of Violence*. New York: Knopf, 1995.

Canada, G. *Reaching Up for Manhood: Transforming the Lives of Boys in America*. Boston: Beacon Press, 1998.

Commission for the Prevention of Youth Violence. *Youth and Violence: Medicine, Nursing, and Public Health—Connecting the Dots to Prevent Violence*. Chicago: American Medical Association, 2000.

Coordinating Council on Juvenile Justice and Delinquency Prevention. *Combating Violence and Delinquency*. Washington, D.C.: U.S. Department of Justice, 1996.

Garbarino, J. *Lost Boys: Why Our Sons Turn Violent and How We Can Save Them*. New York: Free Press, 1999.

Gilligan, J. *Preventing Violence*. New York: Thames and Hudson, 2001.

Horn, D. *Bruised Inside: What Our Children Say About Youth Violence, What Causes It, and What Do We Need to Do About It*. Washington, D.C.: National Association of Attorneys General, 2000.

Katzmann, G. (ed.). *Securing Our Children's Future: New Approaches to Juvenile Justice and Youth Violence*. Washington, D.C.: Brookings Institution, 2002.

Khamisa, A., with Goldman, C. *Azim's Bardo: A Father's Journey from Murder to Forgiveness*. Los Altos, Calif.: Rising Star Press, 1998.

Krug, E. *World Report on Violence and Health*. Geneva: World Health Organization, 2002.

Prothrow-Stith, D., with M. Weissman. *Deadly Consequences: How Violence Is Destroying Our Teenage Population and a Plan to Begin Solving the Problem*. New York: HarperCollins, 1991.

Snyder, H., and Sickmund, M. *Juvenile Offenders and Victims: 1999 National Report*. Washington, D.C.: U.S. Department of Justice, 1999.

Thornton, T. N., Craft, C. A., Dahlberg, L. L., Lynch, B. S., and Baer, K. *Best Practices of Youth Violence Prevention: A Sourcebook for Community Action.* Atlanta, Ga.: Centers for Disease Control and Prevention, National Center for Injury Prevention and Control, 2000.

U.S. Department of Health and Human Services. *Youth Violence: A Report of the Surgeon General.* Rockville, Md.: U.S. Department of Health and Human Services, 2001.

About the Authors

Deborah Prothrow-Stith is a nationally recognized public health leader. As a physician working in inner-city hospitals and neighborhood clinics, she recognized violence as a societal "disease" that could be prevented through implementing effective public health strategies. Appointed commissioner of public health for the Commonwealth of Massachusetts in 1987, she expanded treatment programs for AIDS and drug rehabilitation. During her tenure she also established the first Office of Violence Prevention in a department of public health.

As a chief spokesperson for a national movement to prevent violence, Prothrow-Stith developed and wrote the first violence prevention curriculum for schools and communities (titled Violence Prevention Curriculum for Adolescents) and coauthored *Deadly Consequences* (with M. Weissman, 1991), the first book to present the public health perspective on violence to a mass audience. She is also the author or coauthor of over eighty publications on medical and public health issues, and she served as a member of President Clinton's National Campaign Against Youth Violence. Innovative in her approach to violence prevention, she continues to develop programs and nurture partnerships with community-based programs locally and nationally, including the Community Violence Prevention Project and *Partnerships for Preventing Violence*, a satellite broadcast training forum.

Prothrow-Stith currently serves as associate dean for faculty development as well as professor of public health practice and director of the Division of Public Health Practice at the Harvard

School of Public Health. She is also the principal investigator for the Harvard Center for Public Health Preparedness, whose mission is to train the public health workforce to respond to bioterrorism. She received her B.A. degree from Spelman College and her M.D. degree from Harvard Medical School, and has been awarded ten honorary doctorates.

Howard Spivak is chief of the Division of General Pediatrics and Adolescent Medicine and vice president for community health programs at the New England Medical Center in Boston, Massachusetts. He is professor of pediatrics and community health at Tufts University School of Medicine and director of the Tufts University Center for Children. He has served as deputy commissioner of public health for the Commonwealth of Massachusetts and, prior to that, as director of adolescent health services for the city of Boston.

Spivak has been involved with activities in youth violence prevention for over twenty years, including cofounding the Boston Violence Prevention Program (the first community-based public health violence prevention program in the nation); the development of the Office of Violence Prevention for the Commonwealth of Massachusetts (the first such initiative at the state-level in the nation); the writing of numerous articles, book chapters, and editorials on the issue of violence prevention among youth; participation in numerous studies and evaluations of youth violence prevention efforts; and the development of the first emergency room surveillance initiative for weapon-related injuries. He speaks regularly around the nation on youth violence prevention strategies and engages in ongoing work with many communities in the development of violence prevention programs. He holds a B.A. degree from the University of Rochester and an M.D. degree from the University of Rochester School of Medicine.

He is married, with two children, and lives in the Boston area.

Index